Simply Philosophy: Guided Readings

Edited by Brendan Wilson

Edinburgh University Press

Edinburgh University Press Ltd
22 George Square, Edinburgh

Typeset in Minion and Gill Sans Light
by Pioneer Associates, Perthshire, and
printed and bound in Great Britain by
Scotprint, Haddington

A CIP record for this book is available from the British Library

ISBN 0 7486 1823 6 (paperback)

For Makiyo

Contents

Introduction

Compilers of anthologies are guilty men – and if they're women, guilty women too. Even those who deal in whole texts, perfect and unabridged, feel bad about the things they put aside. And those (like the present author) who not only abridge but interpolate and comment too, feel guiltiest of all. It's understandable, therefore, that introductions to anthologies should brim with good advice about going back to the original text, reading it whole and in its context – all that sort of thing.

But I take it that my reader already knows all that. I prefer to think that readers of a good anthology will genuinely *want* to go back to the originals. This is the pious hope which permits the anthologist to hack his ancestors to pieces and dance on the remains.

And this is not my worst offence. I have also made efforts to modernise some of the English. Locke, for example, regularly talks about physical objects existing 'without the mind'. What he means is *outside* the mind, and where appropriate, I'm afraid I've substituted the word 'outside' (in square brackets) for the word 'without'. I know what purists will make of this, and I'm very much afraid they're right.

Most of all, there is the danger that selective editing will make philosophical progress seem easier and more linear than it really is. Longer omissions are marked by the symbol [. . .], but the difference between this and . . . is easy to overlook. It bears saying, therefore, that this book contains only a tiny part of what there is – though I hope not entirely unrepresentative.

How to Use this Book

Simply Philosophy: Guided Readings is a source book focussing on the central problems of Western philosophy, as those problems occur in a selection of primary texts. It differs from thicker anthologies, first, by editing the primary texts more stringently, so that the central ideas appear more clearly, and second, by guiding the reader, not to a text's historical significance or setting, but towards the underlying issues and problems.

The readings are divided into seven 'Areas' – a term intended to suggest both spread within, and overlap between, the different Areas. Philosophy is an unruly discipline, which constantly oversteps the boundaries we set for it. The companion volume to this one – *Simply Philosophy* (Wilson, 2002) – reveals one pattern in this unsettling behaviour, and the readings in the present book follow the same general framework. But it would be silly to pretend that any organisation which respects the nature of the subject is going to be *neat*.

Each of the sixty readings is preceded by a short introduction, and followed by a 'Comments and Questions' section. The aim has been to let the reader get into the original text as quickly as possible, but to provide an opportunity, after reading, to think over its main ideas. At the end of each group of readings there is an 'Overview', which relates the readings to each other, and characterises the 'Area' as a whole.

The book presents some of the best work in the main areas of Western philosophy, and provides – either in combination with *Simply Philosophy* or without it – a text-based way into the heartland of Western philosophy.

To the Teacher

Philosophy's canonical texts are, for many beginning readers, bewildering and difficult. Yet even an introductory course has to present philosophy's Great Books (and Articles). In my opinion, the best way into this wonderful material is problem-based. The crucial thing for a beginner – it seems to me – is to understand what problems the texts are trying to solve. The readings in this anthology have been selected and edited to display these problems clearly.

The 'text-first' approach of the anthology complements the 'theme-first' approach of *Simply Philosophy*. Let me illustrate.

- *SP* Chapter 1 sets up the basic problems of the philosophy of science: is scientific method data-led or theory-driven? And if it's data-led, what kind of process is it by which we move from data to theory?
- *GR* Readings 1, 2 and 3 (from Aristotle, Bacon, and Hume) set out three seminal answers to these questions.
- *SP* Chapters 2 and 3 take up Hume and the problem of induction, then Popper and scientific progress in more detail.

- *GR* Readings 4, 5 and 6 deal with contemporary theories of scientific method, including Popper and Kuhn.
- *SP* Chapter 4 shows how decisions in the philosophy of science affect wider questions of what is real and what isn't.
- *GR* Readings 7, 8 and 9 set out different attempts (by Skinner, Peirce, and Russell) to relate science to the reality of the mind.
- *SP* Chapters 5 and 6 explain some of the problems which arise (dualism and the other minds problem).
- *GR* Readings 10–15 provide a range of responses to these problems (Carnap, Ayer and Malcolm on other minds; McGinn, James and Churchland on dualism).

In general, the readings of *GR* and the discussion of *SP* track each other, I hope, to their mutual advantage.

The use of short chapters in *SP* and short readings in *GR*, should make both books flexible and 'teacher-friendly' in classroom use. Most of all, I hope both books reconcile a fundamentally problem-based approach with good first exposure to the original texts.

Acknowledgements

I am grateful to the following friends and colleagues who have read earlier drafts of the book: Angus Collins, J. Patrick Barron, Richard Francks, Brian Harrison, Colin Lyas, Paul Rossiter, George Weir, Martin Wilson.

I am also very much indebted to my colleagues at the University of Tokyo, for making possible the period of sabbatical leave during which this book was put together, and to my receiving institution, the University of Strathclyde, for being the perfect hosts.

Finally, I am happy to have this chance to thank Jackie and the team at Edinburgh University Press, who have put so much enthusiasm and hard work into both books.

AREA 1

Science

The reading selections in this Area deal with our ongoing attempts to understand what makes good science.

They focus on the question: is there a distinctive *method* followed by good or successful science, and if there is, what is it?

Aristotle (384–22 BC) on scientific knowledge – from *Posterior Analytics*

Logic, which Aristotle more or less invented, is a way of representing our thought processes more clearly. It aims particularly to represent those processes which lead from existing knowledge to new knowledge, and to represent them in a form which is as explicit as possible. The point is to make it easy to see whether the attempted derivation of new knowledge really works. For Aristotle, this meant setting out a chunk of thinking in the form of a syllogism, a three-line argument leading from two premises to a conclusion.

For example, suppose you're trying to persuade someone not to take drugs. 'Only losers take drugs!' you say. Set out in

syllogism form, this might be represented as:

1. All those who take drugs are (or become) losers.
2. You are not (or do not want to become) a loser.
3. Therefore you should not take drugs.

This is certainly cumbersome – its role is not to be snappy but to make the underlying thought processes clear. For example, it brings out an ambiguity (between being a loser before taking drugs and becoming a loser as a result of taking them), and it reveals unstated assumptions.

Aristotle made a list of the syllogism structures which lead reliably from premises to conclusion and noted some of the structures which don't. If we use a syllogism structure which is reliable or 'valid', and if our premises are true, we can be sure that the new assertion made in the conclusion is also true.

Logic can be applied to clarify many different types of thinking. In the following extracts, Aristotle tries to explain what is distinctive about scientific thinking by saying what is special about a scientific syllogism.

Stylistically, Aristotle tends to be a bit closely-reasoned (which explains the larger-than-usual number of explanatory comments). The reading which follows this one, by Francis Bacon, rejects not only the Aristotelian concept of science, but also the densely-packed style, in favour of something more relaxed.

'We suppose ourselves to possess unqualified scientific knowledge of a thing, as opposed to knowing it in [an] accidental way ... when we think that we know the cause on which the fact depends, as the cause specifically of that fact, and, further, that the fact could not be other than it is [given the cause] ...

...What I now assert is that at all events we do know by demonstration. By demonstration I mean a syllogism productive of scientific knowledge, a syllogism grasp of which constitutes such knowledge. If my thesis about the nature of scientific knowledge is correct, the premisses of demonstrated knowledge must be true, primary, immediate, better known than and prior to the conclusion, which is further related to them as effect to cause ... It's possible to have a syllogism without these conditions, but such a syllogism will not be productive of scientific knowledge ...

Now since the ground of our knowledge ... of a fact is the possession of such a syllogism ... [and] since the primary premisses are the cause of our knowledge ... it follows that we know them better – that is, are more convinced of them – than their consequences, precisely because our knowledge of the latter is the effect of our knowlege of the premisses ...

Some hold that, owing to the necessity of knowing the primary premisses, there is no scientific knowledge. Others think there is, but that all truths are demonstrable. Neither doctrine is either true or necessary [...]

Our own doctrine is that not all knowledge is demonstrative: on the contrary, knowledge of the immediate premisses is independent of demonstration. (The necessity of this is obvious; for since we must know the prior premisses from which the demonstration is drawn, and since the

regress [of demonstrations] must end in immediate truths, those truths cannot be demonstrated) [...]

Our knowledge of any attribute's connection with a subject is accidental unless we know [the reason the thing has that property] [...]

It is hard to be sure whether one knows or not; for it is hard to be sure whether one's knowledge is based on the basic truths appropriate to each attribute ... We think we have scientific knowledge if we have reasoned from true and primary premisses. But that is not so: the conclusion must be homogeneous with the basic facts of the science [...]'

Here, Aristotle seems to allow that the 'fit' of a particular conclusion with the rest of theory might influence our judgement about whether we really have found the basic truths from which to draw that conclusion.

'...We clearly cannot obtain scientific knowledge by the act of perception ... for perception must be of a particular, whereas scientific knowledge involves recognition of the appropriate universal. So if we were on the moon, and saw the earth shutting out the sun's light, we should not know the cause of the eclipse: we should perceive the present fact of the eclipse but not the reasoned fact at all, since the act of perception is not of the appropriate universal. I do not, of course, deny that by watching the frequent recurrence of this event we might, after tracking the appropriate universal, possess a demonstration, for the universal is elicited from the several groups of singulars.'

What does Aristotle mean by the 'appropriate universal'? His point is that in any particular case, we perceive only one particular fact. For scientific knowledge, we need a more general concept which covers many particular cases.

'The universal is precious because it makes clear the cause; so that in the case of facts like these which have a cause other than themselves, universal knowledge is more precious than sense-perception ... Hence it is clear that knowledge of things demonstrable cannot be acquired by perception [...]'

Aristotle does not deny the importance of perception – on the contrary, he says the universal is 'elicited from' a series of perceptions – but a superficial reading of the above remarks can easily give the impression that he underrates perception.

'Scientific knowledge and its object differ from opinion and the object of opinion in that scientific knowledge involves universals and proceeds by necessary connections ... '

Aristotle's point here, to put it in modern terms, is that scientific knowledge involves *laws*. To notice that a particular animal has red blood is, for Aristotle, a matter of opinion – it's what we might call a mere 'factoid'. To understand that blood *has* to be red because it uses haemoglobin to transport oxygen, is genuinely *scientific* knowledge.

'So though there are things which are true and real and yet can be otherwise, *scientific knowledge* clearly does not concern them ... Nor are they any concern of *rational intuition* – by rational intuition I mean an originative source of scientific knowledge – nor of indemonstrable knowledge, which is the grasping of the immediate premiss ... opinion is in fact the grasping of a premiss which is immediate but not [understood to be] necessary [...]
    ... if a man grasps truths that cannot be other than they are, in the way in which he grasps the definitions through which demonstrations take place, he will have not opinion but knowledge: if on the other hand he apprehends these attributes as inhering in their subjects, not in virtue of the subjects' substance and essential nature, he possesses opinion and not genuine knowledge ... Knowledge is the apprehension of, e.g., the attribute 'animal' as incapable of being otherwise, opinion the apprehension of 'animal' as capable of being otherwise – e.g. the apprehension that 'animal' is an element in the essential nature of man is knowledge; the apprehension of 'animal' as predicable of man but not as an element in man's essential nature is opinion [...]'

Aristotle claims, in short, that scientific knowledge sees into the essential natures of things: knowing a mere 'accidental' fact about a thing should not qualify as real scientific knowledge. He now goes on to identify a thing's essential nature with its reason for existing.

'... in all these examples it is clear that the nature of the thing and the reason of the fact are identical: the question 'What is [a lunar] eclipse?' and its answer 'The privation of the moon's light by the interposition of the earth' is identical with the question 'What is the reason of eclipse?' or 'Why does the moon suffer eclipse?' and the reply 'Because of the failure of light through the earth's shutting it out [. . .]'

Thus, as we maintain, to know a thing's nature is to know the reason why it is . . . '

Aristotle regards this 'giving the reason why' as the most fundamental kind of explanation. The basic scientific move is to explain 'that for the sake of which' a thing exists or is the way it is. In the *Physics*, he argues for this teleological view of science, as follows:

'A difficulty presents itself: why should not nature work, not for the sake of something, nor because it is better so, but just as the sky rains, not in order to make the corn grow, but of necessity? What is drawn up must cool, and what has been cooled must become water and descend, the result of this being that the corn grows . . . Why then should it not be the same with the parts in nature, e.g. that our teeth should come up of necessity – the front teeth sharp, fitted for tearing, the molars broad and useful for grinding down the food – since they did not arise for this end, but it was merely a coincidental result . . . Wherever all the parts came about as they would have done if they had come about for an end, such things survived, being organized spontaneously in a fitting way; whereas those which grew otherwise perished and continue to perish . . . '

Against this pre-echo of Darwinian natural selection, Aristotle argues as follows:

. . . it is impossible that this should be the true view. For teeth and all other natural things either invariably or normally come about in a given way; but this is never true of the products of chance or spontaneity. We do not ascribe to chance or mere coincidence the frequency of rain in winter, but frequent rain in summer we do . . . when an event takes place always or for the most part, it is not accidental or by chance . . . If, then, it is agreed that things are either the result of coincidence or for an end, and these cannot be the result of coincidence or spontaneity, it follows that they must be for an end . . .

Further, where a series has a completion, all the preceding steps are for the sake of that. Now surely as in intelligent action, so in nature . . . The relation of the later terms to the earlier is the same in both.'

Back now to the *Posterior Analytics*:

' . . . though sense-perception is innate in all animals, in some the sense-perception comes to persist, in others it does not. So animals in which this persistence does not occur have either no knowledge at all outside the act of perceiving, or no knowledge of objects of which no impression persists; animals in which it does occur have perception and can continue to retain the sense-impression in the soul: and when such persistence is frequently repeated a further distinction at once arises between those which . . . develop a power of systematizing [sense-impressions] and those which do not. So out of sense-perception comes to be what we call memory, and out of frequently repeated memories of the same thing develops experience; for a number of memories constitute a single experience. From experience again … develop the skill of the craftsman and the knowledge of the man of science …

We conclude that these stages of knowledge are neither innate in a determinate form, nor developed from other higher states of knowledge, but from sense-perception […]'

Aristotle here says that none of our knowledge is innate – a fundamental empiricist tenet and a reaction against Plato's theory that knowledge is really recollection of a previous existence. Though he rejects evolution as an explanation of the apparent design of, for example teeth, he asserts here that *knowledge* evolves, both at the individual and at the species-to-species level.

'Thus it is clear that we must get to know the primary premisses by induction; for the method by which even sense-perception implants the universal is inductive. [However, since scientific knowledge must be demonstrative] it follows that there will be no scientific knowledge of the primary premisses, and since except intuition nothing can be truer than scientific knowledge, it will be intuition that apprehends the primary premisses … If, therefore, it is the only other kind of true thinking except scientific knowledge, intuition will be the originative source of scientific knowledge. And the originative source of science grasps the original basic premiss … '

That is, if scientific knowledge is knowledge which results from a syllogism of a certain sort (one which moves through the essential nature or final cause of something), then the premisses of such a syllogism must also be known – indeed must be better known than the conclusion. In many cases, these premisses will be derived from other syllogisms, but this cannot be the whole story (Aristotle believes). Eventually, there must be premisses which are not based on other syllogisms, but on something he calls 'induction' or 'intuition'.

Comments and questions

This notion of 'intuition' obviously plays a vital role in science as Aristotle sees it. Intuition grasps the fundamental premisses on which the whole structure of syllogisms is based. But how – we want to ask – is intuition to be justified?

Suppose two scientists have different intuitions about something, what then? For example, suppose scientists A and B both observe various things moving. A's intuition (which is a very natural one) is that objects naturally slow down and stop – their natural state is rest. B's intuition, on the other hand, is that it is as natural for a moving object to remain in motion as for an object at rest to remain at rest. Must we wait for both systems of kinetics to develop, and see which is more fruitful or economical overall? Or is there any way that the intuition itself can be assessed?

....

....

Aristotle argues:

1. Everything that happens does so either by chance or for some purpose.

— 5 —

2. It's obvious that many events in the natural world do not happen by chance, since chance events are 'one-off' and (for example) teeth coming through is not 'one-off'.
3. So if these events do not happen by chance they must happen for some end, that is, because they are directed towards some end state.

What, if anything, is wrong with this argument?

....

....

Is it helpful to represent scientific thinking in terms of syllogistic logic?

....

....

2

Francis Bacon (1561–1626) on scientific method – from *Selected Aphorisms*: **Routledge, 1905 (eds Spedding, Ellis and Heath)**

In the following remarks, Bacon distinguishes between an Aristotelian approach to science, which jumps prematurely from a few familiar examples to generalisations, and a more painstaking method which uses *experiment* to test its generalisations.

 'Man, being the servant and interpreter of Nature, can do and

understand so much and so much only as he has observed in fact or in thought of the course of nature: beyond this he neither knows nor can do anything [. . .]

There are and can be only two ways of searching into and discovering truth. The one flies from the senses and particulars to the most general axioms, and from these principles, the truth of which it takes for settled and immovable, proceeds to judgment . . . And this is the way now [= the early seventeeth century] in fashion. The other derives axioms from the senses and particulars, rising by a gradual and unbroken ascent, so that it arrives at the most general axioms last of all. This is the true way, but as yet untried [. . .]

Both ways set out from the senses and particulars, and rest in the highest generalities; but the difference between them is infinite. For the one just glances at experiment and particulars in passing, the other dwells duly and orderly among them. The one, again, begins at once by establishing certain abstract and useless generalities, the other rises by gradual steps to that which is prior and better known in the order of nature [. . .]

It cannot be that axioms established by argumentation should avail for the discovery of new works; since the subtlety of nature is greater many times over than the subtlety of argument. But axioms duly and orderly formed from particulars easily discover the way of new particulars, and thus render sciences active [. . .]

The axioms now in use, having been suggested by a scanty . . . experience and a few particulars of the most general occurrence, are made for the most part just large enough to fit and take these in: and therefore it is no wonder if they do not lead to new particulars. And if some opposite instance, not observed or known before, chance to come in the way, the axiom is rescued and preserved by some frivolous distinction; whereas the truer course would be to correct the axiom itself [. . .]

The conclusions of human reason as ordinarily applied in matters of nature, I call for the sake of distinction *Anticipations of Nature* (as a thing rash or premature). That reason which is elicited from facts by a just or methodical process, I call *Interpretations of Nature* [. . .]

For the winning of assent, indeed, anticipations are far more powerful than interpretations; because being collected from a few instances, and those for the most part of familiar occurrence, they straightway touch the understanding and fill the imagination; whereas interpretations on the other hand, being gathered here and there from very various and widely dispersed facts, cannot suddenly strike the understanding [. . .]

One method of delivery alone remains to us; which is simply this: we must lead men to the particulars themselves, and their series and order; while men on their side must force themselves for a while to lay their notions by and begin to familiarize themselves with facts.'

In the following extract, Bacon emphasises the importance of experiment (as opposed to mere observation).

'The sense fails in two ways. Sometimes it gives no information, sometimes it gives false information. For first, there are very many things which escape the sense, even when best disposed and no way obstructed . . .

And again when the sense does apprehend a thing its apprehension is not much to be relied upon. For the testimony and information of the sense has reference always to man, not to the universe . . .

To meet these difficulties . . . I endeavour to accomplish not so much by instruments as by experiments. For the subtlety of experiments is far greater than that of the sense itself, even when assisted by exquisite instruments; such experiments, I mean, as are skilfully and artificially devised for the express purpose of determining the point in question. To the immediate . . . perception of the sense therefore I do not give much weight; but I contrive that the office of the sense shall be only to judge of the experiment, and the experiment itself shall be the judge of the thing.'

Comments and questions

According to Bacon, the difference between Aristotelian science and genuinely empirical science is really a matter of degree: true science dwells longer among particulars. Well, how shall we know when we have dwelt long enough among particulars, or become familiar enough with facts?

....

....

How important is the distinction between observation and experiment? And how should the distinction be drawn?

....

....

3

David Hume (1711–76) on the concept of a cause – from *Enquiry Concerning Human Understanding*, section VII: 1748

In the *Enquiry Concerning Human Understanding*, Hume greatly shortened and simplified the ground-breaking discussion of causality from his youthful *Treatise of Human Nature*. The extract below presents the main steps of the argument.

To put it very briefly, Hume's point is that if we are serious about empiricism, then we cannot say that when a particular event, such as a push, causes another particular event, such as a stumble, the push *makes* the stumble happen. In fact, we can only understand 'That push caused that stumble' in terms of a history of push-like things and stumble-like things, or in terms of a mental habit of expectation resulting from that history. But both the history and the expectation are things which are *external* to the relationship between that particular push and that particular stumble, taken by itself. Taking that relationship strictly alone allows no concept of causality at all.

As a consistent empiricist, Hume begins by claiming that concepts (or 'ideas') only have clear meaning to the extent that they are based on experience (or 'impressions').

'There are no ideas, which occur in metaphysics, more obscure and uncertain, than those of *power, force, energy or necessary connexion* . . . We shall, therefore, endeavour, in this section, to fix, if possible, the precise meaning of these terms, and thereby remove some part of that obscurity, which is so much complained of in this species of philosophy.

It seems a proposition, which will not admit of much dispute, that all our ideas are nothing but copies of our impressions, or, in other words, that it is impossible for us to *think* of any thing, which we have not antecedently *felt*, either by our external or internal senses. I have endeavoured to explain and prove this proposition, and have expressed my hopes, that, by a proper application of it, men may reach a greater clearness and precision in philosophical reasonings, than what they have hitherto been able to attain. Complex ideas may, perhaps, be well known by definition, which is nothing but an enumeration of those parts or simple ideas, that compose them. But when we have pushed up definitions to the most simple ideas, and find still some ambiguity and obscurity; what resource are we then possessed of? By what invention can we throw light upon these ideas, and render them altogether precise and determinate to our intellectual view? Produce the impressions or original sentiments, from which the ideas are copied. These impressions are all strong and sensible. They admit not of ambiguity. They are not only placed in a full light themselves, but may throw light on their correspondent ideas, which lie in obscurity. And by this means, we may, perhaps, attain a new microscope or species of optics, by which, in the moral sciences [that is, psychology] the most minute, and most simple ideas may be so enlarged as to fall readily under our apprehension, and be equally known with the grossest and most sensible ideas, that can be the object of our enquiry.'

> This is about as clear a statement of radical empiricism as could be wished for. Trace back our concepts to their sources in experience, Hume says, and we will fully and clearly understand what they mean.

'To be fully acquainted, therefore, with the idea of power or necessary connexion, let us examine its impression; and in order to find the impression with greater certainty, let us search for it in all the sources, from which it may possibly be derived.

When we look about us towards external objects, and consider the operation of causes, we are never able, in a single instance, to discover any power or necessary connexion; any quality, which binds the effect to the cause, and renders the one an infallible consequence of the other. We only find, that the one does actually, in fact, follow the other. The impulse of one billiard-ball is attended with motion in the second. This is the whole that appears to the *outward* senses. The mind feels no sentiment or *inward* impression from this succession of objects: Consequently, there is not, in any single, particular instance of cause and effect, any thing which can suggest the idea of power or necessary connexion [. . .]

Since, therefore, external objects as they appear to the senses, give us no idea of power or necessary connexion, by their operation in particular instances, let us see, whether this idea be derived from reflection on the operations of our own minds, and be copied from any internal impression. It may be said [and *was* said, by Locke] that we are every moment conscious of internal power; while we feel, that, by the simple command of our will, we can move the organs of our body, or direct the faculties of our mind . . .

We shall proceed to examine this pretension; and first with regard to the influence of volition over the organs of the body. This influence, we may observe, is a fact, which, like all other natural events, can be known only by experience, and can never be foreseen from any apparent energy or power in the cause, which connects it with the effect, and renders the one an infallible consequence of the other. The motion of our body follows upon the command of our will. Of this we are every moment conscious. But the means, by which this is effected; the energy, by which *the will* performs so extraordinary an operation; of this we are so far from being immediately conscious, that it must for ever escape our most diligent enquiry . . .

. . . is there any principle in all nature more mysterious than the union of soul with body; by which a supposed spiritual substance acquires such an influence over a material one, that the most refined thought is able to actuate the grossest matter? Were we empowered, by a secret wish, to move mountains, or control the planets in their orbit; this extensive authority would not be more extraordinary, nor more beyond our comprehension. But if by consciousness we perceived any power or energy in the will, we must know this power; we must know its connexion with the effect; we must know the secret union of soul and body, and the nature of both these substances; by which the one is able to operate, in so many instances, upon the other [. . .]

We learn from anatomy, that the

immediate object of power in voluntary motion, is not the member itself which is moved, but certain muscles, and nerves, and animal spirits [nerve impulses] and, perhaps, something still more minute and more unknown, through which the motion is successively propagated, before it reaches the member itself whose motion is the immediate object of volition. Can there be a more certain proof that the power, by which this whole operation is performed, so far from being directly and fully known by an inward sentiment or consciousness, is, to the last degree, mysterious and unintelligible [. . .]'

So far, there have been three steps in Hume's argument. First, he argued that, in order to understand the idea of causality, we need to get clear about where in our experience the idea comes from (a typical empiricist move). Then he argued that the idea does not come from our experience of any single case of A causing B. Most recently, he has been arguing against the suggestion that the idea of force or power comes from our awareness of our own power to make our bodies move.

He is now about to claim that the idea can only come from *repeated* experiences of As causing Bs – which means that power or force is not a component of any single situation in which an A causes a B.

'It appears, then, that this idea of a necessary connexion among events arises from a number of similar instances, which occur, of the constant conjunction of these events; nor can that idea ever be suggested by any one of these instances, surveyed in all possible lights and positions. But there is nothing in a number of instances, different from every single instance, which is supposed to be exactly similar; except only, that after a repetition of similar instances, the mind is carried by habit, upon the appearance of one event, to expect its usual attendant, and to believe, that it will exist. This connexion, therefore, which we *feel* in the mind, this customary transition of the imagination from one object to its usual attendant, is the sentiment or impression, from which we form the idea of power or necessary connexion. Nothing farther is in the case. Contemplate the subject on all sides; you will never find any other origin of that idea. This is the sole difference between one instance, from which we can never receive the idea of connexion, and a number of similar instances, by which it is suggested. The first time a man saw the communication of motion by impulse, as by the shock of two billiard-balls, he could not pronounce that the one event was *connected*: but only that it was *conjoined* with the other. After he has observed several instances of this nature, he then pronounces them to be *connected*. What alteration has happened to give rise to this new idea of *connexion*? Nothing but that he now *feels* these events to be *connected* in his imagination, and can readily foretell the existence of one from the appearance of the other. When we say, therefore, that one object is connected with another, we mean only, that they have acquired a connexion in our thought, and give rise to this inference, by which they become proofs of each other's existence: A conclusion, which is somewhat extraordinary; but which seems founded on sufficient evidence. Nor will its evidence be weakened by any general diffidence of the understanding, or sceptical suspicion concerning every conclusion, which is new and extraordinary. No conclusions can be more agreeable to scepticism than such as make discoveries concerning the weakness and narrow limits of human reason and capacity.

And what stronger instance can be produced of the surprising ignorance and weakness of the understanding, than the present? For surely, if there be any relation among objects, which it imports to us to know perfectly, it is that of cause and effect. On this are founded all our reasonings concerning matter of fact or existence. By means of it alone we attain any assurance concerning objects, which are removed from the present testimony of our memory and senses. The only immediate utility of all sciences, is to teach us, how to control and regulate future events by their causes. Our thoughts and enquiries are, therefore, every moment, employed about this relation: Yet so imperfect are the ideas which we form concerning it, that it is impossible to give any just definition of cause, except what is drawn from something extraneous and foreign to it. Similar objects are always conjoined with similar. Of this we have experience. Suitably to this experience, therefore, we may define a cause to be *an object, followed by another, and where all the objects, similar to the first, are followed by objects similar to the second.* Or, in other words, where, *if the first object had not been, the second never had existed.* The appearance of a cause always conveys the mind, by a customary transition, to the idea of the effect. Of this also we have experience. We may, therefore, suitably to this experience, form another definition of cause; and call it, *an object followed by another, and whose appearance always conveys the thought to that other.* But though both these definitions be drawn from circumstances foreign to the cause, we cannot remedy this inconvenience, or attain any more perfect definition, which may point out that circumstance in the cause, which gives it a connexion with its effect. We have no idea of this connexion; nor even any distinct notion what it is we desire to know, when we endeavour at a conception of it.'

Comments and questions

We can usefully represent Hume's argument in syllogism form:

1. Concepts which are not based on experience are meaningless and to be rejected.
2. We never experience one thing *making* another happen (a central element in our ordinary concept of a cause).
3. So our ordinary concept of a cause is defective and needs to be changed.

If you disagree with Hume's conclusion 3, where do you think his argument goes wrong?

....

....

Suppose Hume is right and we have to give up the idea of A *making* B happen. How serious a loss would this be? If, for example, we have to give up the idea of some kind of transmission (of energy or power or something) from A to B, can we still cope with everyday life?

....

....

If the idea of transmission is genuinely useful in science (in simplifying theory for example), should empiricism rule it out because we don't detect it with our senses or instruments? Couldn't its role in the theory give it meaning?

....

....

Hume's second definition of a cause depends on our 'customary transition' in thought from cause to effect. When we see clouds, the thought of rain pops into our heads. But is this thought of rain a rational inference, or just a conditioned reflex?

Hume argued, in another famous passage, that there is no rational inference from causes to effects (and one development of this shocking claim follows, in the reading from Popper).

What do you think? Is it really *reasonable* to expect the effect, having witnessed the cause?

....

....

Karl Popper (1902–94) on induction – from *The Logic of Scientific Discovery*: **Hutchinson, 1959**

So there you are, gazing out over the savannah. You have certain dramatic visual and aural (and fortunately not tactile) experiences. Can these experiences justify the statement, 'That cheetah just killed that zebra'? Popper thinks not, because to call one of the things involved a 'cheetah' – to use any inherently general word – has implications beyond what you've just experienced.

Then can any number of similar experiences justify the claim 'Cheetahs kill zebras'? Again, Popper thinks not, because the claim is so general as to go beyond existing experience. It implies that unseen cheetahs have killed unseen zebras. It also implies that, left to their own devices, future cheetahs will go on killing future zebras.

So why should we believe that cheetahs kill zebras, (as opposed to, say, 'Cheetahs kiss zebras')? On Popper's account, the idea that cheetahs kill zebras pops into someone's head – by some process which Popper hands over to psychology to explain. The important point for understanding scientific method is that the idea, however produced, is then *tested* (by savannah-gazing, asking experts etc). If it survives these tests, we can scientifically proceed with it.

Popper claims two advantages for this theory-first model of science (*SP* p.18f). First, it makes science out to be rational, and it does so, using only the *deductive* thinking we understand comparatively well. In this sense, it stands with common sense against scepticism. Secondly, it allows us to distinguish genuine science from pseudo-science and metaphysics. In the case of genuine science, we make considerable efforts to prove our conjectures false. We actively look for things which would show our hypothesis to be false.

'The theory to be developed in the following pages stands directly opposed to all attempts to operate with the ideas of inductive logic. It might be described as the theory of *the deductive method of testing*, or as the view that a hypothesis can only be empirically *tested* – and then only *after* it has been advanced [...]

The initial stage, the act of conceiving or inventing a theory, seems to me neither to call for logical analysis nor to be susceptible of it. The question of how it happens that a new idea occurs to a man – whether it be a musical theme, a dramatic conflict, or a scientific theory – may be of great interest to empirical psychology; but it is irrelevant to the logical analysis of scientific knowledge [...]

Accordingly I shall distinguish sharply between the process of conceiving a new idea, and the methods and results of examining it logically. As to the task of the logic of knowledge ... I shall proceed on the assumption that it consists solely in investigating the methods employed in those systematic tests to which every new idea must be subjected if it is to be seriously entertained [...]

... the method of critically testing theories, and selecting them according to the results of tests, always proceeds on the following lines. From a new idea, put up tentatively, and not yet justified in any way ... conclusions are drawn by means of logical deduction. These conclusions are then compared with one another and with other relevant statements, so as to find what logical relations (such as equivalence, derivability, compatibility or incompatibility) exist between them ... finally, there is the testing of the theory by way of empirical applications of the conclusions which can be derived from it.

The purpose of this last kind of test is to find out how far the new consequences of the theory – whatever may be new in what it asserts – stand up to the demands of practice, whether raised by purely scientific experiments, or by practical technological applications. Here too, the procedure of testing turns out to be deductive. With the help of other statements, previously accepted, certain singular statements – which we call 'predictions' – are deduced from the theory; especially predictions that are easily testable or applicable. From these statements, those are selected which are not derivable from the current theory, and more especially those which the current theory contradicts. Next we seek a decision as regards these (and other) derived statements by comparing them with the results of practical applications and experiments. If this decision is positive, that is if the singular conclusions turn out to be acceptable, or *verified*, then the theory has, for the time being, passed its test: we have found no reason to discard it. But if the decision is negative, or in other words, if the conclusions have been *falsified*, then their falsification also falsifies the theory from which they were logically deduced.

It should be noticed that a positive decision can only temporarily support the theory, for subsequent negative decisions may always overthrow it. So long as a theory withstands detailed and severe tests and is not superseded by another theory in the course of scientific progress, we may say that it has 'proved its mettle' or that it is '*corroborated*' by past experience ...

. . . no conclusive disproof of a theory can ever be produced; for it is always possible to say that the experimental results are not reliable, or that the discrepancies which are asserted to exist between the experimental results and the theory are only apparent and that they will disappear with the advance of our understanding. (In the struggle against Einstein, both these arguments were often used in support of Newtonian mechanics, and similar arguments abound in the field of the social sciences.) If you insist on strict proof (or strict disproof) in the empirical sciences, you will never benefit from experience, and never learn from it how wrong you are [. . .]

Nothing resembling inductive logic appears in the procedure here outlined. I never assume that we can argue from the truth of singular statements to the truth of theories. I never assume that by force of 'verified' conclusions, theories can be established as 'true', or even as merely 'probable'. Those [epistemological] problems . . . to which inductive logic gives rise, can be eliminated without creating new ones in their place [. . .]

Objections are bound to be raised against my proposal to adopt falsifiability as our criterion for deciding whether or not a theoretical system belongs to empirical science. They will be raised, for example, by those who are influenced by the school of thought known as 'conventionalism' . . .

For the conventionalist, theoretical natural science is not a picture of nature but merely a logical construction . . .

According to this conventionalist point of view, laws of nature are not falsifiable by observation: for they are needed to determine what an observation and, more especially, what a scientific instrument is. It is these laws, laid down by us, which form the indispensable basis for the regulation of our clocks and the correction of our so-called 'rigid' measuring rods. A clock is called 'accurate' and a measuring rod 'rigid' only if the movements measured with the help of these instruments satisfy the axioms of mechanics which we have decided to adopt . . .

. . . I regard conventionalism as a system which is self-contained and defensible . . . Yet in spite of all this I find it quite unacceptable . . . Whenever the 'classical' system of the day is threatened by the results of new experiments which might be interpreted as falsifications according to my point of view, the system will appear unshaken to the conventionalist. He will explain away the inconsistencies which may have arisen; perhaps by blaming our inadequate mastery of the system [. . .]

I admit that my criterion of falsifiability does not lead to an unambiguous classification [of theories into genuinely scientific, and pseudo-scientific or metaphysical ones]. Indeed, it is impossible to decide, by analysing its logical form, whether a system of statements is a conventional system of irrefutable implicit definitions, or whether it is a system which is empirical in my sense . . . *Only with reference to the methods applied* to a theoretical system is it at all possible to ask whether we are dealing with a conventionalist or an empirical theory. The only way to avoid conventionalism is by taking a *decision*: the decision not to apply its methods. We decide that if our system is threatened we will never save it by any kind of *conventionalist stratagem* [. . .]

I propose the following definition. A theory is to be called 'empirical' or 'falsifiable' if it divides the class of all possible basic statements unambiguously into the two following nonempty subclasses. First, the class of all those basic statements with which it is inconsistent (or which it rules out, or prohibits): we call this the class of the *potential falsifiers* of the theory; and secondly, the class of those basic statements which it does not contradict (or which it 'permits'). We can put this more briefly by saying: a theory is falsifiable if the class of its potential falsifiers is not empty [. . .]

We must distinguish clearly between falsifiability and falsification. We have introduced falsifiability solely as a criterion for the empirical character of a system of statements. As to falsification, special rules must be introduced which will determine under what conditions a system is to be regarded as falsified.

We say that a theory is falsified only if we have accepted basic statements which contradict it. This condition is necessary but not sufficient; for non-reproducible single occurrences are of no significance to science. Thus a few stray basic statements contradicting a theory will hardly induce us to reject it as falsified. We shall take it as falsified only if we discover a *reproducible effect* which refutes the theory. In other words, we shall only accept the falsification if a low-level empirical hypothesis which describes such an effect is proposed and corroborated [. . .]

We have now reduced the question of the falsifiability of theories to that of the falsifiability of those singular statements which I have called basic statements. But what kind of singular statements are these basic statements? How can they be falsified? [. . .]

Every test of a theory, whether resulting in

its corroboration or falsification, must stop at some basic statement or other which we *decide to accept*. If we do not come to any decision, and do not accept some basic statement or other, then the test will have led nowhere. But considered from a logical point of view . . . any basic statement can again in its turn be subjected to tests . . . This procedure has no natural end. Thus if the test is to lead us anywhere, nothing remains but to stop at some point or other and say we are satisfied, for the time being.

It is fairly easy to see that we arrive in this way at a procedure according to which we stop only at a kind of statement that is especially easy to test. For it means that we are stopping at statements about whose acceptance or rejection the various investigators are likely to reach agreement . . . If some day it should no longer be possible for scientific observers to reach agreement about basic statements this would amount to a new 'Babel of Tongues': scientific discovery would be reduced to absurdity . . .

. . . so, after science has done its work of deduction or explanation, we stop at basic statements which are easily testable. Statements about personal experiences . . . are clearly not of this kind; thus they will not be very suitable to serve as statements at which we stop [. . .]

Basic statements are therefore . . . statements asserting that an observable event is occurring in a certain individual region of space and time [. . .]

The basic statements at which we stop, which we decide to accept as satisfactory, and as sufficiently tested, have admittedly the character of *dogmas*, but only in so far as we may desist from justifying them by further arguments (or by further tests). But this kind of dogmatism is innocuous since, should the need arise, these statements can easily be tested further. I admit that this too makes the chain of deduction in principle infinite. But this kind of *'infinite regress'* is also innocuous since in our theory there is no question of trying to prove any statements by means of it. And finally, as to *psychologism*: I admit, again, that the decision to accept a basic statement, and to be satisfied with it, is causally connected with our experiences – especially with our *perceptual experiences*. But we do not attempt to *justify* basic statements by these experiences. Experiences can *motivate* a *decision*, perhaps decisively, and hence an acceptance or rejection of a statement, but a basic statement cannot be justified by them – no more than by thumping the table.'

Comments and questions

Thumping a table motivates without justifying because it's not connected with the thumper's claim being true. But perceptual experiences as of a cheetah killing a zebra *are* connected – except for dreams and so on – with what makes the claim true. Is Popper right to say that perceptual experiences, such as seeing something with your own eyes, cannot rationally justify a statement like 'The house is on fire'?

....

....

Is it always unscientific to protect claims – as Popper says conventionalists do – from falsification?

Why are non-reproducible occurrences of no significance to science?

....

....

Hilary Putnam (b. 1926) against Popper – from 'The "Corroboration" of Theories' in *The Philosophy of Karl Popper*: Open Court, 1974 (ed. P. A. Schilpp)

In this reading, Hilary Putnam attacks Popper's view of science, and offers an alternative.

'Popper himself uses the term 'induction' to refer to any method for verifying or showing to be true (or even probable) general laws on the basis of observational or experimental data (what he calls 'basic statements'). His views are radically Humean: no such method exists or can exist. A principle of induction would have to be either [innate] (a possibility Popper rejects) or justified by a higher-level principle. But the latter course necessarily leads to an infinite regress.

What is novel is that Popper concludes neither that empirical science is impossible nor that empirical science rests upon principles that are themselves incapable of justification. Rather, his position is that empirical science does not really rely upon a principle of induction!

Popper does not deny that scientists state general laws, nor that they test these general laws against observational data. What he says is that when a scientist 'corroborates' a general law, that scientist does not thereby assert that law to be true or even probable. 'I have corroborated this law to a high degree' only means ' I have subjected this law to severe tests and it has withstood them'. Scientific laws are *falsifiable*, not verifiable. Since scientists are not even trying to *verify* laws, but only to falsify them, Hume's problem does not arise for empirical scientists.

A Brief Criticism of Popper's View

. . . When a scientist accepts a law, he is recommending to other men that they rely on it – rely on it, often, in practical contexts. Only by wrenching science altogether out of the context in which it really arises – the context of men trying to change and control the world – can Popper even put forward his peculiar view on induction . . .

If 'this law is highly corroborated', 'this law is scientifically accepted', and like locutions merely meant 'this law has withstood severe tests' – and there were no suggestion at all that a law which has withstood severe tests is likely to withstand further tests, such as the tests involved in an application or attempted application, then Popper would be right: but then science would be a wholly unimportant activity. It would be practically unimportant, because scientists would never tell us that any law or theory is safe to rely upon for practical purposes; and it would be unimportant for the purpose of understanding, since on Popper's view, scientists never tell us that any law or theory is true or even probable. Knowing that certain 'conjectures' (according to Popper all scientific laws are 'provisional conjectures') have not yet been refuted is *not understanding anything*.

Since the application of scientific laws does involve the anticipation of future successes, Popper is not right in maintaining that induction is unnecessary. Even if scientists do not inductively anticipate the future (and, of course, they do), men who apply scientific laws and theories do so. And 'don't make inductions' is hardly reasonable advice to give these men . . .

Kuhn's View of Science

Recently a number of philosophers have begun to put forward a rather new view of scientific activity . . . The view . . . reaches its sharpest expression in the writings of Thomas Kuhn and Louis Althusser. I believe that both of these philosophers commit errors; but I also believe that the tendency they represent (and that I also represent, for that matter) is a needed corrective to the [Popperian] deductivism we have been examining . . .

The heart of Kuhn's account is the notion of a *paradigm*. Kuhn has been legitimately criticized for some inconsistencies and unclarities in the use of this notion; but . . . a paradigm is simply a scientific theory together with an example of a successful and striking application. It is important that the application – say, a successful explanation of some fact, or a successful and novel prediction – be *striking*. What this means is that the success is sufficiently impressive that scientists – especially young scientists choosing a career – are led to try to emulate that success by seeking further explanations, predictions, or whatever on the same model. For example, once U.G. [universal gravitation] had been put forward and one had the example of Newton's derivation of Kepler's laws together with the example of the derivation of, say, a planetary orbit or two, then one had a paradigm. The most important paradigms are the ones that generate scientific fields: the field generated by the Newtonian paradigm was, in the first instance, the entire field of celestial mechanics . . .

Kuhn maintains that the paradigm that structures a field is highly immune to falsification – in particular, it can only be overthrown by a new paradigm. In one sense, this is an exaggeration: Newtonian physics would probably have been abandoned, even in the absence of a new paradigm, if the world had started to act in a markedly non-Newtonian way . . . What is true, I believe, is that in the absence of such a drastic and unprecedented change in the world, and in the absence of its turning out that the paradigmatic successes had something 'phony' about them (e.g. the data were faked, or there was a mistake in the deductions), a theory which is paradigmatic is not given up because of observational and experimental results by themselves, but because and when a better theory is available [. . .]

Kuhn's most controversial assertions have to do with the process whereby a new paradigm supplants an older paradigm. Here he tends to be radically subjectivistic (overly so, in my opinion): data, in the usual sense, cannot establish the superiority of one paradigm over another because data themselves are perceived through the spectacles of one paradigm or another. Changing from one paradigm to another requires a 'Gestalt switch'. The history and methodology of science get rewritten when there are major paradigm changes; so there are no 'neutral' historical and methodological canons to which to appeal. Kuhn also holds views on meaning and truth which are relativistic and, on my view, incorrect; but I do not wish to discuss these here [. . .]

As might be expected, there are substantial differences between Kuhn and Popper on the issue of the falsifiability of scientific theories. Kuhn stresses the way in which a scientific theory may be immune from falsification, whereas Popper stresses falsifiability as the *sine qua non* of a scientific theory . . . Kuhn sees normal science [that is, science in the quiet periods between paradigm shifts] as neither an activity of trying to falsify one's paradigm nor as an activity of trying to confirm it . . . Once a paradigm has been set up, and a scientific field has grown around that paradigm, we get an interval of what Kuhn calls 'normal science'. The activity of scientists during such an interval is described by Kuhn as 'puzzle solving' [. . .]

I have suggested that [during periods of 'normal science'] . . . we take a theory as fixed, take the facts to be explained as fixed, and seek further facts – frequently contingent facts about the particular system – which will enable us to fill out the explanation of the particular fact on the basis of the theory. I suggest that adopting this point of view will enable us better to appreciate both the relative unfalsifiability of theories which have attained paradigm status, and the fact that the 'predictions' of physical theory are frequently facts which were known beforehand [...]

... let us see how U.G. came to be accepted. Newton first derived Kepler's laws from U.G ... this was not a 'test' in Popper's sense, because Kepler's laws were already known to be true. Then he showed that U.G. could account for the tides on the basis of the gravitational pull of the moon: this also was not a 'test', in Popper's sense, because the tides were already known. Then he spent many years showing that small perturbations (which were already known) in the orbits of the planets could be accounted for by U.G. By this time the whole civilized world had accepted – and, indeed, acclaimed – U.G.; but it had not been 'corroborated' at all in Popper's sense!

If we look for a Popperian 'test' of U.G. – a derivation of a new prediction, one risky relative to background knowledge – we do not get one until the Cavendish experiment [measuring the attraction between two spheres] of 1797, roughly a hundred years after the theory had been introduced [...]

In sum, a theory is only accepted if the theory has substantial, non-*ad hoc*, explanatory successes. This is in accordance with Popper; unfortunately, it is in even better accordance with the 'inductivist' accounts that Popper rejects, since these stress *support* rather than *falsification*.'

Comments and questions

In discussions after reading an earlier version of this article, Putnam conceded that the history of the acceptance of Newton's theory of universal gravitation was more complex than he had suggested. Newton's theory made predictions about the earth's shape which were tested and confirmed in 1733, and it also gave a precise explanation of the known but hitherto mysterious phenomenon of 'precession' (the slow change in the earth's axis of rotation). Putnam also accepted that to describe even paradigm-level theories as fully unfalsifiable during periods of 'normal science' is overstating the case. He continued to believe, however, that scientific theories are often – and properly – not as falsifiable as Popper demands.

What do you think? Is it always unscientific to protect a theory from falsification?

....

....

Putnam proposes a dilemma for Popper: either surviving past tests makes it likely that a law or theory will survive future ones, or it doesn't. If it does, we have classical induction from past to future (which Popper was committed to eliminating). But if it doesn't, then there's no reason to use scientific laws or theories in real life (which is absurd). How should Popper respond to this dilemma?

....

....

6

Paul Feyerabend (1924–94) on scientific method – from 'How to Defend Society against Science': *Radical Philosophy*, vol. 2, 1975

Feyerabend here claims, against Popper, that real scientific theories are not falsifiable in the way he requires. This is part of his larger argument that there is no distinctive method belonging to science.

'. . . no new and revolutionary scientific theory is ever formulated in a manner that permits us to say under what circumstances we must regard it as endangered: many revolutionary theories are unfalsifiable. Falsifiable versions do exist, but they are hardly ever in agreement with accepted basic statements: every moderately interesting theory is falsified. Moreover, theories have formal flaws, many of them contain contradictions, ad hoc adjustments, and so on and so forth. Applied resolutely, Popperian criteria would eliminate science without replacing it by anything comparable. They are useless as an aid to science.

In the past decade this has been realised by various thinkers, Kuhn and Lakatos among them. Kuhn's ideas are interesting but, alas, they are much too vague to give rise to anything but lots of hot air. If you don't believe me, look at the literature. Never before has the literature on the philosophy of science been invaded by so many creeps and incompetents. Kuhn encourages people who have no idea why a stone falls to the ground to talk with assurance about scientific method . . . Secondly, whenever one tries to make Kuhn's ideas more definite one finds that they are *false*. Was there ever a period of normal science in the history of thought? No – and I challenge anyone to prove the contrary.

Lakatos is immeasurably more sophisticated than Kuhn. Instead of theories he considers research programmes which are sequences of theories connected by methods of modification, so-called heuristics. Each theory in the sequence may be full of faults. It may be beset by anomalies, contradictions, ambiguities. What counts is not the shape of the single theories, but the tendency exhibited by the sequence. We judge historical developments, achievements over a period of time, rather than the situation at a particular time. History and methodology are combined into a single enterprise. A research programme is said to progress if the sequence of theories leads to novel predictions. It is said to degenerate if it is reduced to absorbing facts that have been discovered without its help. A decisive feature of Lakatos' methodology is that such evaluations are no longer tied to methodological rules which tell the scientist to either retain or abandon a research programme. Scientists may stick to a degenerating programme, they may even succeed in making the programme overtake its rivals and they therefore proceed rationally with whatever they are doing (provided they continue calling degenerating programmes degenerating and progressive programmes progressive). This means that Lakatos offers *words* which *sound* like the elements of a methodology; he does not offer a methodology. There is no method according to the most advanced and sophisticated methodology in existence today ...'

Comments and questions

Bacon says that scientific progress is more to be hoped for from improvements in method than improvements in instruments. In particular, good science sets up carefully planned experiments. Feyerabend, however, suggests that there is no distinctively scientific method. Does he mean the same thing as Bacon meant by the word 'method'?

....

....

Overview of Area 1

The central concern of this 'Area' has been to say what it is about certain kinds of thinking and acting which makes them scientific.

For Aristotle the fundamental point is that the premisses in a scientific syllogism contain information about a thing's essence or *raison d'être*. For example, the syllogism:

1. All ungulates have multiple stomachs.
2. Cows are ungulates.
3. So cows have multiple stomachs.

would not be a scientific syllogism, even if it was all true.

A genuinely scientific syllogism would be something more like:

4. Multiple stomachs exist to digest grass.
5. Cows eat grass.
6. So cows have multiple stomachs.

The conclusion is the same, but 4–6 goes through the purpose or *final cause* of multiple stomachs: 1–3 does not.

This – together with Aristotle's notion of 'intuition' – eventually led people to think that scientists could simply 'intuit' the real essences of things, on the basis of everyday experience.

In the extract from Bacon, we see the seventeeth-century rejection of that mediaeval view. Bacon insists that we need to go beyond familiar experience in two ways: we need to incorporate more and perhaps unfamiliar phenomena, and we need consciously to set up *experiments*, designed to answer specific questions.

Bacon also wrote down rules for arriving at conclusions from a body of evidence gathered in these ways. It therefore became clear that these rules of induction governed a kind of thinking which was very different from the deductive thinking of logic or Euclidean geometry, though these had become accepted as the paradigms of good reasoning. This opened the way for Hume to raise questions about 'inductive' thinking. When experience leads us to form the belief that A causes B: (a) can we legitimately mean by this that A *makes* B happen? and (b) can we call this belief a *rational* belief, as opposed to a kind of conditioned response (see *SP*, ch. 2)?

Hume's questions still await good answers, and in the Reading from Popper, we saw one, radical, response to them. Popper agrees with Hume that we must answer 'No' to both questions, and argues that since scientific thinking *is* rational, it must be distinguished by its attempt to set up explanatory hypotheses or conjectures which are as falsifiable as we can make them. Those conjectures which survive our determined attempts to prove them false can rationally be accepted, at least temporarily, as scientific.

The Reading from Putnam offered some criticisms of Popper's view and suggested instead a Kuhnian approach to scientific method. According to Putnam, real scientists do not allow their theories to be falsified as readily as Popper suggests.

Our final Reading, from Feyerabend, sketches some problems with the Kuhnian approach and prefers the model of scientific progress due to Lakatos. On this model, however, Feyerabend thinks we have to say that, after all, there is *no* distinctively scientific method.

There are other important questions in

the philosophy of science. We haven't looked, for example, at the instrumentalism debate (about the extent to which scientific theories can, or should, be regarded as useful fictions). There are also lots of fascinating and difficult questions in the philosophy of physics – whether to say, for example, that space-time is *real*. But the Readings of Area 1 have at least introduced what are probably the central problems in philosophical thinking about science.

In Area 2 we will see how taking our concept of reality from science (in one way or another) impinges on our common-sense belief that our minds and their contents are real.

Mind

The reading selections in this area ask what it means to say a thing is *real*, and whether minds and their contents should be considered real.

7

B. F. Skinner (1904–90) on behaviourism – from *Science and Human Behaviour*: Macmillan, 1953

In this extract, Skinner argues that a scientific approach to human behaviour conflicts with the traditional belief that human beings act freely and spontaneously. He goes on to suggest that the scientific, deterministic view will bring large benefits in social and international planning.

 'Science is more than the mere description of events as they occur. It is an attempt to discover order, to show that certain events stand in lawful relations to other events. No practical technology can be based upon science until such relations have been discovered. But order is not only a possible end product; it is a working assumption which must be adopted at the very start. We cannot apply the methods of science to a subject matter which is assumed to move about capriciously. Science not only describes, it predicts. It deals not only with the past but with the future. Nor is prediction the last word: to the extent that relevant conditions can be altered, or otherwise controlled, the future can be controlled. If we are to use the methods of science in the field of human affairs, we must assume that behaviour is lawful and determined. We must expect to discover that what a man does is the result of specifiable conditions and that once these conditions have been discovered, we can anticipate and to some extent determine his actions.

This possibility is offensive to many people. It is opposed to a tradition of long standing which regards man as a free agent, whose behaviour is the product, not of specifiable antecedent conditions, but of spontaneous inner changes of course. Prevailing philosophies of human nature recognize an internal 'will' which has the power of interfering with causal relationships and which makes the prediction and control of behavior impossible . . . Regardless of how much we stand to gain from supposing that human behavior is the proper subject matter of a science, no one who is a product of Western civilization can do so without a struggle. We simply do not want such a science.

Conflicts of this sort are not unknown in the history of science . . . Primitive beliefs about man and his place in nature are usually flattering. It has been the unfortunate responsibility of science to paint more realistic pictures. The Copernican theory of the solar system displaced man from his pre-eminent position at the centre of things. Today we accept this theory without emotion, but originally it met with enormous resistance. Darwin challenged a practice of segregation in which man set himself firmly apart from the animals, and the bitter struggle which arose is not yet ended. But though Darwin put man in his biological place, he did not deny him a possible position as master. Special faculties or a special capacity for spontaneous, creative action might have emerged in the process of evolution. When that distinction is now questioned, a new threat arises [. . .]

Our current practices . . . are thoroughly confused. At times we appear to regard a man's behavior as spontaneous and responsible. At other times we recognize that inner determination is at least not complete, that the individual is not always to be held to account . . .

. . . We regard the common man as the product of his environment; yet we reserve the right to give credit to great men for their achievements . . . We want to believe that right-minded men are moved by valid principles even though we are willing to regard wrong-minded men as victims of erroneous propaganda . . . Though we observe that Moslem children in general become Moslems while Christian children in general become Christians, we are not willing to accept an accident of birth as a basis for belief . . .

All this suggests that we are in transition. We have not wholly abandoned the traditional philosophy of human nature; at the same time we are far from adopting a scientific point of view without reservation [. . .]

Confusion in theory means confusion in practice. The present unhappy condition of the world may in large measure be traced to our vacillation. The principal issues in dispute between nations, both in peaceful assembly and on the battlefield, are intimately concerned with the problem of human freedom and control . . . We shall almost certainly remain ineffective in solving these problems until we adopt a consistent point of view.'

Comments and questions

Skinner seems to assume that 'spontaneous' implies 'unpredictable'. But in fact, we predict what other people are going to do all the time, and mostly with considerable success. When someone utters the words, 'I'm off to work', that's usually a pretty good sign that he or she is about to leave and go to work. What is the real basis of Skinner's feeling that the 'traditional philosophy of human nature' is unscientific?

....

....

If no science could deal with 'spontaneous inner changes' (such as acts of will), does that imply that they aren't real?

....

....

C. S. Peirce (1839–1914) on reality and truth – from 'How to Make our Ideas Clear': *Popular Science Monthly 12, 1878*

In this paper, Peirce states his 'ideal limit'

theory of truth, and derives from it, a 'clear idea' of reality. For Peirce, reality is defined in terms of beliefs in the minds of ideal investigators.

'... it would probably puzzle most men, even among those of a reflective turn of mind, to give an abstract definition of the real. Yet such a definition may perhaps be reached by considering the points of difference between reality and its opposite, fiction. A figment is a product of somebody's imagination; it has such characters as his thought impresses upon it. That whose characters are independent of how you or I think is an external reality. There are, however, phenomena within our own minds, dependent upon our thought, which are at the same time real in the sense that we really think them. But though their characters depend on how we think, they do not depend on what we think those characters to be. Thus, a dream has a real existence as a mental phenomenon, if somebody has really dreamt it; that he dreamt so and so, does not depend on what anybody thinks was dreamt, but is completely independent of all opinion on the subject. On the other hand, considering, not the fact of dreaming, but the thing dreamt, it retains its peculiarities by virtue of no other fact than that it was dreamt to possess them. Thus we may define the real as that whose characters are independent of what anybody may think them to be.

But however satisfactory such a definition may be found, it would be a great mistake to suppose that it makes our idea of reality perfectly clear. Here, then, let us apply our rules. According to them, reality, like every other quality, consists in the peculiar sensible effects which things partaking of it produce [this is another version of empiricism]. The only effect which real things have is to cause belief, for all the sensations which they excite emerge into consciousness in the form of beliefs. The question therefore is, how is true belief (or belief in the real) distinguished from false belief (or belief in fiction) [...]

... all the followers of science are fully persuaded that the processes of investigation, if only pushed far enough, will give one certain solution to every question to which they can be applied ... They may at first obtain different results, but, as each perfects his method and his processes, the results will move steadily together toward a destined centre. So with all scientific research. Different minds may set out with the most antagonistic views, but the process of investigation carries them by a force outside of themselves to one and the same conclusion. This activity of thought, by which we are carried, not where we wish, but to a foreordained goal, is like the operation of destiny. No modification of the point of view taken, no selection of other facts for study, no natural bent of mind even, can enable a man to escape the predestinate opinion. This great law is embodied in the conception of truth and reality. The opinion which is fated to be ultimately agreed by all who investigate, is what we mean by the truth, and the object represented in this opinion is the real ...

But it may be said that this view is directly opposed to the abstract definition which we have given of reality, inasmuch as it makes the characters of the real to depend on what is ultimately thought about them. But the answer to this is that, on the one hand, reality is independent, not necessarily of thought in general, but only of what you or I or any finite number of men may think about it; and that, on the other hand, though the object of the final opinion depends on what that opinion is, yet what that opinion is does not depend on what you or I or any man thinks. Our perversity and that of others may indefinitely postpone the settlement of opinion; it might even conceivably cause an arbitrary proposition to be universally accepted as long as the human race should last. Yet even that would not change the nature of the belief, which alone could be the result of investigation carried sufficiently far; and if, after the extinction of our race, another should rise with faculties and disposition for investigation, that true opinion must be the one which they would ultimately come to. 'Truth crushed to earth shall rise again,' and the opinion which would finally result from investigation does not depend on how anybody may actually think. But the reality of that which is real does depend on the real fact that investigation is destined to lead, at last, if continued long enough, to a belief in it.'

Comments and questions

Peirce says that a dream is a real mental phenomenon because it is 'completely independent of all opinion on the subject'. Is it completely independent of the *dreamer's* opinion?

....

....

Peirce also says that 'every ... quality, consists in the peculiar sensible effects which things partaking of it produce'. Is this true?

....

....

Peirce notices an apparent conflict between his 'abstract definition' of reality (as independence of what anyone thinks), and his 'clear idea' of it (as whatever an ideal investigator would think). How does he propose to escape this seeming contradiction? Does his escape plan work?

....

....

Bertrand Russell (1872–1970) on sense-data – from 'The Relation of Sense-data to Physics', in *Mysticism and Logic*: Longmans, 1918

In this seminal article, Russell argues that the claims of common sense about material objects, and the claims of physics too, are ultimately verified by sensory impressions. A claim like 'There's an oscilloscope on the bench' might be verified by visual impressions of a box-like object with a screen, tactile sensations of something heavy and metallic, and so on.

Now we normally regard an object referred to by common sense or physics as some further thing whose presence is signalled by the sensory impressions we receive. But there are two problems with this. First, it seems less economical than making do with just the sensory impressions if we can manage to do so. And second, it seems to commit us to a very problematic inference (from impressions in the mind to external things which we never perceive directly). Better, therefore, to *define* the 'external things' presumed by common sense and physics in terms of sensory impressions. If this is really possible – and Russell tries in this paper to sketch how the definition would go – it would have the double advantages of economy and resistance to scepticism.

'Physics is said to be an empirical science, based upon observation and experiment.

It is supposed to be verifiable, i.e. capable of calculating beforehand results subsequently confirmed by observation and experiment.

What can we learn by observation and experiment?

Nothing, so far as physics is concerned, except immediate data of sense: certain patches of colour, sound, tastes, smells, etc., with certain spatio-temporal relations.

The supposed contents of the physical world are *prima facie* very different from these: molecules have no colour, atoms make no noise, electrons have no taste . . .

If such objects are to be verified, it must be solely through their relation to sense-data: they must have some kind of correlation with sense-data, and must be verifiable through their correlation *alone*.

But how is the correlation itself ascertained? A correlation can only be ascertained empirically by the correlated objects being constantly *found* together. But in our case, only one term of the correlation,

namely the sensible term, is ever *found*: the other term seems essentially incapable of being found. Therefore, it would seem, the correlation with objects of sense, by which physics was to be verified, is itself utterly and for ever unverifiable.

There are two ways of avoiding this result.

(1) We may say that we know some principle *a priori,* without the need of empirical verification, e.g. that our sense-data have *causes* other than themselves, and that something can be known about these causes by inference from their effects . . . but insofar as [this strategy] is adopted physics ceases to be empirical or based upon experiment and observation alone. Therefore this way is to be avoided as much as possible.

(2) We may succeed in actually defining the objects of physics as functions of sense-data [. . .]

Thus if physics is to be verifiable we are faced with the following problem: Physics exhibits sense-data as functions of physical objects [that is, tells us that if such-and-such an object is present we will probably get such-and-such sense-data], but verification is only possible if physical objects can be exhibited as functions of sense-data [. . .]

Sense-data at the times when they are data are all that we directly and primitively know of the external world [. . .]

I regard sense-data as not mental, and as being, in fact, part of the actual subject matter of physics. There are arguments . . . for their subjectivity, but these arguments seem to me only to prove *physiological* subjectivity, i.e. causal dependence on the sense-organs, nerves, and brain. The appearance which a thing presents to us is causally dependent on these . . . but continuity makes it not unreasonable to suppose that they present *some* appearance at [other, presently unoccupied] places [...]

Since the 'thing' [for example, a physical object like a table] cannot, without indefensible partiality, be identified with any single one of its appearances, it came to be thought of as something distinct from all of them and underlying them. But by the principle of Occam's razor [requiring theories to minimise the entities they postulate], if the class of appearances will fulfill the purposes for the sake of which the thing was invented by the prehistoric metaphysicians to whom common sense is due, economy demands that we should identify the thing with the class of its appearances. It is not necessary to *deny* a substance or substratum underlying these appearances; it is merely expedient to abstain from asserting this unnecessary entity [...]

... The inferred entities which I shall allow myself are of two kinds: (a) the sense-data of other people, in favour of which there is the evidence of testimony, resting ultimately upon the analogical argument in favour of minds other than my own [see *SP* pp. 40–4]; (b) the 'sensibilia' [sense-data regardless of whether they are actually present to any mind] which would appear from places where there happen to be no minds, and which I suppose to be real although they are no one's data ... It would give me the greatest satisfaction to be able to dispense with [(a)], and thus establish physics upon a solipsistic basis; but those – and I fear they are the majority – in whom the human affections are stronger than the desire for logical economy, will, no doubt, not share my desire [...]'

Russell proceeds to argue that the unified space and time of common sense can be constructed from 'sensibilia'. He then moves on to the construction of enduring material objects, and having completed that, explains illusions and dreams as constructed out of sense-data which 'have intrinsically just the same status as any others, but differ as regards their correlations or causal connections with other "sensibilia" and with "things".'

'I conclude, therefore, that no valid objection exists to the view which regards sense-data as part of the actual substance of the physical world, and that, on the other hand, this view is the only one which accounts for the empirical verifiability of physics ... I should hope that, with further elaboration, the part played by unperceived 'sensibilia' could be indefinitely diminished, probably by invoking the history of a 'thing' to eke out the inferences derivable from its momentary appearance.'

Comments and questions

Russell begins by pointing out that physics is verified by observation, usually in the context of an experiment. Is it correct to think, as Russell does, that in an observation, an individual receives 'immediate data of sense'? If it is, should we also accept that these immediate data of sense are sufficiently 'thing-like' to be correlated with physical objects, or to make up the 'actual substance of the world'? If not, why not?

....

....

Rudolf Carnap (1891–1970) on the argument from analogy – from 'Psychology in the Language of Physics': *Erkenntnis,* vol. 2, 1931

In our last reading, Russell mentioned 'the analogical argument', which concludes that other people have a mental life like mine, because they show behaviour like mine.

Carnap attacks the argument on the grounds that its conclusion is unverifiable and therefore devoid of factual content. (This depends on yet another version of the empiricist claim that the meaning of a statement consists in the difference it would make in experience if true). The argument's conclusion – that someone has a mental life – cannot possibly be directly verified by the language community at large, and so cannot really make a statement about any matter of fact.

Carnap begins by presenting the argument:

"'In my own case, when I am angry I also experience, in addition to the angry behaviour, the feeling of anger. When I observe angry behaviour in another person I may, therefore, if not with certainty then at least with probability, make the analogical inference that he too has a feeling of anger (which does not mean a physical condition), in addition to the angry behaviour''.

Rebuttal: While it is true that analogical inferences do not provide certainty, they are no doubt permissible as inferences conferring probability. Let us consider an example of an ordinary inference by analogy. I see a box of a certain shape, size and colour. I establish that it contains steel nibs. I discover another box of the same appearance. I infer by analogy that it probably also contains steel nibs. Now the [argument] maintains that the proposed analogical inference about matters pertaining to another psyche is of the same logical form. If this were the case, the inference would be legitimate. But it is not the case. The concluding sentence is meaningless, a mere pseudo-sentence. For, since it is a sentence about matters pertaining to another psyche, which is not supposed to be interpreted physically, it is in principle unverifiable . . . The difference to our present example lies precisely in the fact that the concluding sentence is unverifiable. It can in principle be verified that the second box also contains steel nibs . . . The two analogous sentences 'There are steel nibs in the first box' and 'There are steel nibs in the second box' are logically and epistemologically of the same type. Therefore, the analogical inference is legitimate here. But this is not the case with regard to the two sentences 'I am angry' and 'The other person is angry'. We consider that the first sentence makes sense while the second sentence (when the physical interpretation is ruled out) makes no sense . . .'

Carnap goes on to consider the following reply:

"'. . . [the fact that] A is actually experiencing a feeling of anger is something that I can establish simply by asking him. He will then testify that he experienced a feeling of anger. Having known him as a credible person and a good observer, why should I not consider his statement as true, or at least as probably true?'

Rebuttal: Before I can decide whether I should accept A's statement as true, false or probably true, indeed before I can even consider this question, I must first understand the statement; it must have a meaning for me. And it only makes sense if I can verify it . . . If the statement is physically interpreted, it is verifiable through . . . sentences about particular perceptions and intuitive impressions [of mine]. But since the [argument] rejects the physical interpretation of the statement, there is, in principle, no possibility of my verifying it. Consequently, it is meaningless for me. The question whether I should accept it as true or false or probably true cannot even arise [. . .]

But, it will be said, do we not need the statements of our fellow men in order to construct intersubjective science? How poor would physics, geography and history become if I had to restrict myself to the events that I had directly observed myself! This is true. But there is a fundamental difference between a statement of A about a geographical condition of China, or about a historical event of the past, and a statement of A about his anger yesterday. I can in principle verify statements of the first type through [my own] perception sentences . . . But I cannot even in principle verify the statement about the anger if, in accordance with the [argument], the physical interpretation is ruled out . . . a sentence that is not verifiable and therefore meaningless without the utterance of A, cannot become meaningful through such an utterance.

. . . the speech of our fellow men . . . cannot deliver us anything . . . that we could not in principle acquire in a different way. For

the statements of our fellow men are not of a fundamentally different type from any other physical occurrences. It is true that physical occurrences differ in that they can be used as indications of further physical occurrences to varying degrees. For those physical occurrences which we call 'statements of fellow men', this degree is especially high. Therefore, science rightly treats them as especially important. But, in principle, there exists at most a difference of degree between what the statement of a fellow human being contributes to our scientific knowledge and what a barometer contributes [. . .]'

Carnap goes on to argue that even when I say '*I* feel angry', this must also be interpreted physically, since on a non-physical interpretation, even if it would be verifiable (by me) and so meaningful (for me), it would be unverifiable and so meaningless for everybody else. Nobody would know what I meant when I said 'I feel angry'.

This surprising result – that my statements about my *own* state of mind have to be interpreted as statements about my physical condition – is confirmed (Carnap thinks) when we remember how language is learned. Other people tell the child-learner, on the basis of its behaviour, 'You're angry', or, on the basis of Mr Punch's behaviour, 'Mr Punch is angry':

'It follows that the child is taught the habit of uttering under certain conditions a sentence expressing the physical state in himself as observed (or inferred from signs observed) by another person. Hence if the child produces the same sounds again, no more may be inferred from this than that the body of the child is in the same physical state.

Summary

So-called psychological sentences are always translatable into the language of physics, be they specific sentences about matters pertaining to another psyche, about matters pertaining to one's own psyche in the past, about matters pertaining to one's own psyche in the present, or general sentences [such as 'Absence makes the heart grow fonder']. Every psychological sentence refers to physical processes of the body … psychology is a branch of physics.'

Comments and questions

Few philosophers now accept a verificationism as sharp-edged as Carnap's – but perhaps that is at least in part because of the shocking conclusions which seem to follow from it. It's important to remember how very plausible this verificationism was (is).

Here's Carnap on this point (from another *Erkenntnis* article called 'The Elimination of Metaphysics through Logical Analysis of Language'):

Let us suppose, by way of illustration, that someone invented the word 'teavy' and claimed that there are things which are teavy and things which are not teavy. In order to learn the meaning of this word, we ask him about its criterion of application: how does one ascertain in a real case whether a thing is teavy or not? Let us suppose to begin with that we get no answer from him: there are no empirical signs of teaviness, he says. In that case we would deny the legitimacy of using the word. If the person who uses the word says that, all the same, there are things which are teavy and things which are not, but it remains for the weak and finite mind of man an eternal secret which things are teavy and which are not, we shall regard this as empty verbiage. Now perhaps he insists that he really does mean something by the word 'teavy'. From this, however, we only learn the psychological fact that he associates images and feelings with the word. The word does not acquire a meaning through associations of this kind. If no criterion of application is stipulated, then nothing is asserted by sentences in which the word appears; they are only pseudo-statements …

… The (pseudo)statements of metaphysics do not *describe existing states of affairs* … They *express the general attitude of a person towards life.*

Well, the 'criterion of application' for statements like 'John is homesick' involves only John's verbal and other behaviour. Is it true, then, that psychological statements about other people, when reduced to their essential factual content, are *only* about overt behaviour?

....

....

11

A. J. Ayer (1910–89) on other minds – from 'One's Knowledge of Other Minds', in *Philosophical Essays*: St Martin's Press/Macmillan, 1954

In his splendid early manifesto for logical positivism, *Language, Truth and Logic* (1936), Ayer had maintained, like Carnap, that the argument from analogy (arguing that other people have thoughts and feelings like mine, from the fact that they behave the way I do) ended in an unverifiable and therefore factually meaningless conclusion.

In this later, less positivistic article, he tries to rehabilitate the argument from analogy. He begins by comparing scepticism about other minds with scepticism about events distant in time or space.

'We cannot really know what happened in the past [the sceptic claims], because we cannot go back and look. The best evidence we can now obtain is not the best conceivable ... So, if really knowing is to be equated with having the best evidence conceivable, it becomes, as I have said, a necessary fact that one cannot really know the truth of any statement about the past. In the same way, we cannot really know what is going on in some other part of space. This seems a smaller deprivation than the other because of the possibility of visiting the place in question. If we cannot visit it, it is for a practical and not a logical reason ...

It does not follow, however, that we are reduced to scepticism [about other places].

So long as we hold it to be theoretically conceivable that we should be in the privileged situation [of having the best conceivable evidence], the fact that we are not is not regarded as condemning us to utter ignorance. We are not inclined to say that the evidence we can obtain is good for nothing at all just because it is not, and in the circumstances cannot be, the best possible ...

When it comes, however, to the case of other minds, the fact of our being underprivileged appears, at first sight, very much more serious. For here ... to be privileged is to be the other person. Only he really knows what he thinks and feels ... it is plainly a contradiction that I should both remain myself and be someone other than myself: yet this is exactly what here seems to be required. In the other cases which we have considered, the fact that one was underprivileged was the outcome of one's situation, the position that one happened to occupy in space and time; and it could be remedied, at least in theory, by the situation's being changed. But how could a change in my situation make me someone else? ... Thus it seems that the thoughts and feelings of others are inaccessible to us, not merely because we happen to occupy the relatively unfavourable position that we do, but because we are respectively the persons that we are ...

This reasoning is plausible but I do not think that it is sound [...]

... it is necessarily true that, being the person that I am, I am not also someone else ... And if this is made the requirement for my really knowing what he thinks or feels, then it is necessarily true that this is something that I can never really know. On the other hand, with regard to any given property, which I may or may not myself in fact possess, there seems to be no logical reason why I should not test the degree of its connection with some other properties: and what I am asserting when I ascribe an experience to some other person is just that the property of having it [occurs together] with certain others. The inference is not from my experience as such to his experience as such but from the fact that certain properties have been found to be conjoined in certain contexts to the conclusion that in a further context the conjunction will still hold. This is a normal type of inductive argument; and I cannot see that it is in any degree invalidated by the fact that however far one is able to extend the positive analogy, it always remains within the compass of one's own experience.'

Comments and questions

In essence, Ayer puts this question to the sceptic: why should I assume that the difference between myself and others is a relevant difference, when I'm building up correlations between inner experiences and behaviour? This throws the burden of proof onto the sceptic – always a good strategic move.

But the obvious answer is that I never have, and it seems, never *could* have, the kind of access to others' experiences which I have to my own. This marked difference in actual and possible access is surely just the kind of thing which ought to make me suspicious about generalising from myself to others.

Is this correct? If it *is* correct, it throws us back on Ayer's interesting characterisation

of scepticism. Is it reasonable to say that we cannot really *know* X, if we are unable to get the 'best conceivable evidence' for X?

....

....

Norman Malcolm (1911–90) on other minds – from 'Knowledge of Other Minds': *The Journal of Philosophy* LV, 1958

In this article, Malcolm first argues that attempts to resuscitate the argument from analogy lead nowhere. He then goes on to explain, from a Wittgensteinian point of view, why this must be so.

'There have been various attempts to repair the argument from analogy. Mr Stuart Hampshire has argued that its validity as a method of inference can be established in the following way: others sometimes infer that I am feeling giddy from my behaviour. Now I have direct, non-inferential knowledge, says Hampshire, of my own feelings. So I can check inferences made about me against the facts, checking thereby the accuracy of the methods of inference [. . .]

. . . Hampshire has apparently forgotten the purpose of the argument from analogy, which is to provide some probability that 'the walking and speaking figures which I see and hear, have sensations and thoughts' (Mill). For the reasoning that he describes involves the assumption that other people *do* have thoughts and feelings: for they are assumed to make *inferences* about me from *observations* of my behaviour. But the philosophical problem of the existence of other minds *is* the problem of whether human figures other than oneself do, among other things, make observations, inferences, and assertions.'

> Malcolm's point is that Hampshire's version of the argument begs the question against the sceptic. The sceptic asks 'How do I know that other people have thoughts and feelings like mine?' Hampshire's reply (according to Malcolm) is, 'I can check that other people's inferences about my states of mind are accurate, and so confirm that the analogical method of inference, as used by them, works well. I can therefore use it myself with confidence.' But this presupposes that other people do think and reason. In other words, it takes for granted the very thing which was in dispute.
>
> This taking-for-granted-the-thing-to-be-proved happens so frequently in philosophy (and elsewhere) that it has a name all to itself – begging the question.

'The version of analogical reasoning offered by Professor H. H. Price is more interesting. He suggests that 'one's evidence for the existence of other minds is derived primarily from the understanding of language' . . . His idea is that if another body gives forth noises one understands, like 'There's the bus', and if these noises give one new information, this 'provides some evidence that the foreign body which uttered the noises is animated by a mind like one's own . . . ' The body from which these informative sounds proceed need not be a human body. 'If the rustling of the leaves of an oak formed intelligible words conveying new information, and if gorse bushes made intelligible gestures, I should have evidence that the oak or the gorse bush was animated by an intelligence like my own' . . .

Although differing sharply from the classical analogical argument, the reasoning presented by Price is still analogical in form: I know by introspection that when certain combinations of sounds come from me they are 'symbols in acts of spontaneous thinking'; therefore similar combinations of sounds, not produced by me, 'probably function as instruments to an act of spontaneous thinking, which in this case is not my own' . . .

I wish to argue against Price that no amount of intelligible sounds coming from an oak tree or kitchen table could create any probability that it has sensations or thoughts . . .

Since it has nothing like the human face or body it makes no sense to say of a tree, or an electronic computer, that it is looking or pointing at or fetching something . . . Therefore it would make no sense to say that it did or did not understand the above words. Trees and computers cannot either pass or fail the tests that a child is put through. They cannot even take them . . . How informative sentences and valuable predictions could emanate from a gorse bush might be a grave scientific problem, but the explanation could never be that the gorse bush has a mind. Better no explanation than nonsense [. . .]

. . . the most fundamental error of the argument from analogy . . . is present whether the argument is the classical one (the analogy between my body and other bodies) or Price's version (the analogy between my language and the noises and signs produced by other things). It is the mistaken assumption that one *learns from one's own case* what thinking, feeling, sensation are. Price gives expression to this assumption when he says: 'I know from introspection what acts of thinking and perceiving are . . . ' It is the most natural assumption for a philosopher to make and indeed seems at first to be the only possibility. Yet Wittgenstein has made us see that it leads first to solipsism and then to nonsense. I shall try to state as briefly as possible how it produces those results [. . .]

. . . one supposes that one inwardly picks out something as thinking or pain and thereafter identifies it whenever it presents itself in the soul. But the question to be pressed is, Does one make *correct* identifications? The proponent of these 'private' identifications has nothing to say here. He feels sure that he identifies correctly the occurrence in his soul; but feeling sure is no guarantee of being right. Indeed he has no idea of what being *right* could mean. He does not know how to distinguish between actually making correct identifications and being under the impression that he does, (See *Philosophical Investigations* #258–9) . . . When we see that the ideas of correct and incorrect have no application to the supposed inner identification, the latter notion loses its appearance of sense. Its collapse brings down both solipsism and the argument from analogy.

. . . A philosopher feels himself in difficulties about other minds because he assumes that first of all he is acquainted with mental phenomena 'from his own case'. What troubles him is how to make the transition from his own case to the case of others . . .

But [having accepted Wittgenstein's point] he is in danger of flying to the opposite extreme of behaviorism, which errs by believing that through observation of one's own circumstances, behavior, and utterances one can find out that one is thinking or angry. The philosophy of 'from one's own case' and behaviorism, though in a sense opposites, make the common assumption that first-person, present-tense psychological statements are verified by self-observation. According to the 'one's own case' philosophy the self-observation cannot be checked by others; according to behaviorism the self-observation would be by means of outward criteria that are available to all. The first position becomes unintelligible; the second is false for at least many kinds of psychological statements. We are forced to conclude that first-person psychological statements are not (or hardly ever) verified by self-observation. It follows that they have no verification at all; for if they had a verification it would have to be by self-observation.

But if sentences like 'My head aches' or 'I wonder where she is' do not express observations then what do they do? What is the relation between my declaration that my head aches and the fact that my head aches, if the former is not a report of an observation? The perplexity about the existence of *other* minds has, as the result of criticism, turned into a perplexity about the meaning of one's own psychological sentences about oneself. At our starting point it was the sentence '*His* head aches' that posed a problem; but now it is the sentence '*My* head aches' that puzzles us [. . .]

. . . we must conceive of first-person psychological sentences in some entirely different light. Wittgenstein presents us with the suggestion . . . that first-person sentences are to be thought of as similar to the natural nonverbal, behavioral expressions of psychological states. 'My leg hurts,' for example, is to be assimilated to crying, limping, holding one's leg. This is a bewildering comparison and one's first thought is that two sorts of things could not be more unlike. By saying the sentence one can make a *statement*; it has a *contradictory*; it is *true* or *false*; in saying it one *lies* or *tells the truth*; and so on. None of these things, exactly, can be said of crying, limping, holding one's leg. So how can there be any resemblance? . . . I think this analogy ought to be explored. For it has at least two important merits: first, it breaks the hold on us of the question 'How does one know when to say 'My leg hurts'?' for in the light of the analogy this will be as nonsensical as the question 'How does one know when to cry, limp, or hold one's leg?'; second, it explains how the utterance of a first-person psychological sentence by another person can have *importance* for us, although not as an identification – for in the light of the analogy it will have the same importance as the natural behavior which serves as our preverbal criterion of the psychological states of others.'

Comments and questions

Malcolm's central claim is that if we are supposed to know what thoughts and sensations are from our own case (from introspection), and on later occasions, recognise the same sort of thing in our mind as another thought or another sensation, then there would have to be a way of checking that we have recognised the new candidate *right*. If I believe I've identified a rare species of butterfly, it's important that I can check this against the books, or at least against the judgement of other lepidopterists. But in fact, there's no way of checking that *this* sensation really is a taste of lemon, or that *that* mental occurrence really is a thought about butterflies. The idea of checking makes no sense here.

It follows, according to Malcolm, that we don't learn what thoughts and sensations are from our own case. And it follows too, that what seem to be reports ('I have a sinking feeling in my stomach', 'I was just thinking about my childhood' and so on) cannot really be reports in the ordinary sense. We have to understand them more on the model of expressions, like a groan of apprehension, or a nostalgic sigh.

But as Malcolm also points out, a sentence like 'My leg hurts' can be true or false: groaning or limping cannot be true or false (though they *can* be genuine or pretended). And if 'My leg hurts' is true, that's presumably because it reports a fact (but see *SP* pp.170–2, against the correspondence theory of truth). So 'My leg hurts' must after all be a report of an (inner) fact. And if I report it, I have to detect and identify it – and we're right back where we started. Where should we break out of this circle?

....

....

Hume says (in the *Dialogues Concerning Natural Religion*) that if we heard a voice from the sky, or if legible and coherent books were produced not by authors but by some spontaneous process, it'd be reasonable to think that there was an intelligence responsible. In the same way, it seems to me (though Malcolm says otherwise) that if a kitchen table spoke intelligently to us, showed awareness of events around it, seemed to feel about its wooden 'body' roughly as we feel about ours, and so on, we would and should begin to regard it as intelligent. Of course we'd look for trickery, and we might well suspect hallucination too. But after a certain amount of investigation, we might reasonably rule those possibilities out.

Does Price's language-based version of the argument from analogy do the trick, then? Well, there's a difference between being 'animated by an intelligence' and having thoughts and feelings. A chess-playing computer is animated by an intelligence (the programmer's, at one remove), but it doesn't think or feel. But the kitchen table does much more than spit out decent chess moves: it sustains a proper conversation with us. We might insist that the table has become inhabited or possessed by a thinking and feeling spirit, but I suppose we would in fact take the language ability as evidence of thoughts and feelings associated *somehow* with the table. And if we'd be right to do so, wouldn't the same argument give us good reason to believe in thoughts and feelings associated with the human figures we see around us?

Yet if the argument is, 'A is correlated with B in my case: A occurs in other cases: so probably B occurs in other cases too,' it seems to be subject to a powerful objection (see, for example, *SP* p. 42). Induction from

one case to five billion different cases isn't going to justify the confidence we actually attach to the 'hypothesis' that other people have thoughts and feelings.

The alternative seems to be that language ability actually *constitutes* self-aware consciousness in some way, rather than just providing evidence of it. But this, as Malcolm says, is very close to behaviourism.

What do you think? Is Price's argument good?

....

....

Colin McGinn (b. 1950) on the mind/body problem – from 'Consciousness and Space': *Journal of Consciousness Studies* 2, **vol. 12, no. 3, 1995**

Here (to balance the optimistic conclusion of *SP*, Chapter 21) is a reasoned pessimism about making sense of the mind. McGinn argues that consciousness stands in an anomalous relation to the idea of space, neither entirely in it nor entirely out of it. We do of course associate consciousness with normally functioning human bodies, which are fully spatial. Yet the idea of putting consciousness in a bottle is nonsense. We do say that a thought or feeling is 'in' someone's head, but it's not 'in there' in the same sense that the brain is in there.

This anomalous spatial status, McGinn

believes, disqualifies consciousness from scientific treatment, unless our understanding of space changes very radically. But this kind of change is not really feasible, McGinn argues, given the profound dependence all our thinking shows on the idea of space, and on analogies derived from it.

📖 '... there is something highly misleading about the popular suggestion that mental phenomena have the same sort of status as the posits of physical science: that is, that both are unobservables postulated to make the best sense of the data. Apart from the obvious point that we also know about our mental states 'from the inside', there is a crucial disanalogy here, which underscores the *sui generis* character of the mental case. While we think of the unobservables of physics as existing in space and hence in spatial relation to the things we do observe, we do not think of the mental states that explain behaviour in this way ... It is thus far more puzzling how they relate to behaviour, especially causally, than is the relation of atomic events to the macroscopic behaviour of material bodies ... In the physical case, we have notions of contact causation and gravitational force acting across space, but in the mental case it is quite unclear how these causal paradigms are supposed to apply. *How* do conscious events cause physical changes in the body? ... Recent philosophy has become accustomed to the idea of mental causation, but this is actually much more mysterious than is generally appreciated, once the non-spatial character of consciousness is acknowledged ...

... consciousness does not, on its face, slot smoothly into the ordinary spatial world. The Cartesian intuition of unextendedness is a firm part of our ordinary conception of the mental ...

If consciousness is not constitutionally spatial, then how could it have had its origin in the spatial world?

... How can you derive the unextended from the extended? Note too that this problem has no parallel in the relation between the abstract and the physical, since, though non-spatial, the abstract is not supposed to have *emerged* from the material [...]

... There are, historically, two main lines of response to the problem, commonly supposed to be exclusive and exhaustive. One response denies ... that mind sprang from matter. Instead, mind has an autonomous existence, as independent of matter as matter is of mind. Perhaps mind has always existed ... or owes its existence to a direct act of God.

A second response questions ... that consciousness is inherently non-spatial. We may grant that we ordinarily conceive of it in this way, but [perhaps this is] ... yet another area in which common sense misconceives the true nature of reality. In fact, conscious states are just as spatially constituted as brain states, since they *are* brain states ... Thus we have classical materialism, the thesis that consciousness is nothing over and above the cellular structures and processes we observe in the brain. Since these admit of straightforward spatial characterisation, so, by identity, do conscious states ... the materialist insists that the appearance of non-spatiality that consciousness presents is a kind of illusion ...

Now it is not my intention here to rehearse any of the usual criticisms of these two venerable positions, beyond noting that both have deeply unattractive features . . . These are positions we feel driven to, rather than ones that save the phenomena in a theoretically satisfying way. My purpose is to identify a third option . . . to preserve material emergence while not denying the ordinary non-spatial conception of consciousness . . . Consciousness is an anomaly in our present world view and, like all anomalies, it calls for some more or less drastic rectification in [current theory].

I am now in a position to state the main thesis of this paper: in order to solve the mind-body problem we need, at a minimum, a new conception of space. We need a conceptual breakthrough in the way we think about the medium in which material objects exist, and hence in our conception of material objects themselves . . . That which we refer to when we use the word 'space' has a nature that is quite different from how we standardly conceive it to be; so different, indeed, that it is capable of 'containing' the non-spatial (as we now conceive it) phenomenon of consciousness. Things in space can generate consciousness only because . . . they harbour some hidden aspect or principle.

. . . Consciousness is so singular, ontologically, and such an affront to our standard spatial notions, that some pretty remarkable properties of matter will be needed in order to sustain the assumption that consciousness can come from matter. It is not likely that we need a merely local conceptual revolution [. . .]

. . . And here the bitter pill beneath the sweet coating begins to seep through. For to suggest that we need a radically new conception of space is not to imply that we

can achieve any such conception, even in principle. It may be merely to point to a place where we are incurably ignorant . . .

Viewing the matter in a properly naturalistic spirit, with the human species counted as just one evolved species among others, the overwhelming probability is that we are subject to definite limits on our powers of understanding, just as every other species is.

. . . But I think something more specific is suggested by our discussion so far: namely, that our troubles over space and consciousness arise from certain deep-seated features of the way we represent space to ourselves . . . our entire conceptual scheme is shot through with spatial notions, these providing the skeleton of our thought in general. Experience itself, the underpinning of thought, is spatial to its core . . . This is a line of thinking powerfully advocated by P. F. Strawson, who focuses particularly on the role of space in our practices of identification . . . The guiding Strawsonian thesis is that the distinction between particular and universal, and hence between subject and predicate, is founded on the idea, or experience, of spatial distinctness . . . Without that spatial resource we should not be able to frame the conception of multiple instances of a single property. This implies that the very notion of a proposition presupposes the notion of spatial separation, and hence location. At root, then, our entire structure of thought is based upon a conception of space in which objects are severally arrayed; though once this structure is in place we can extend and refine it by means of analogy and relations of conceptual dependence.

[But] how, if the Strawsonian thesis is right, do we contrive to think about consciousness at all? It ought to be impossible. The answer lies in those analogies and dependencies just mentioned. We go in for spatialising metaphors and, centrally, we exploit relations to the body in making sense of numerically distinct but similar conscious episodes . . . this is to impose upon conscious events a conceptual grid that is alien to their intrinsic nature . . . We represent the mental by relying upon our folk theory of space because that theory lies at the root of our being able to represent at all – not because the mental itself has a nature that craves such a mode of representation.

To represent consciousness as it is in itself – neat, as it were – we would need to let go of the spatial skeleton of our thought. But, according to the Strawsonian thesis, that would be to let go of the very notion of a proposition, leaving us nothing to think with. So there is no real prospect of our achieving a spatially nonderivative style of thought about consciousness . . . No doubt this lies behind the sense of total theoretical blankness that attends our attempts to fathom the nature of consciousness; we stare agape in a vacuum of incomprehension [. . .]

I have been arguing that consciousness . . . marks the place of a deep lack of knowledge about space, which is hard even to get into focus. No doubt it is difficult to accept that two of the things with which we are most familiar [consciousness and space] might harbour such intractable obscurities. Irony being a mark of truth, however, we should take seriously the possibility that what we tend to think completely transparent should turn out to transcend altogether our powers of comprehension.'

Comments and questions

McGinn emphasises the difficulty of understanding how conscious events could causally relate to material ones, due to their anomalous spatial nature. Since he also thinks they certainly do causally relate to material events, we need to change our understanding of space so that they are no longer anomalous. This, however, is *much* easier said than done.

But if (as *SP*, Chapter 21 suggested) a conscious experience is a brain event *as it appears from the inside*, it could have properties – including a strange nonspatiality – which the brain event as it appears from the outside doesn't share. The same thing, seen under different aspects, can have very different and even incompatible properties. So the brain event as it appears from the outside – spatially respectable of course – could play its full causal role, in spite of having another aspect under which its causal role is plagued with difficulty. Would this solve McGinn's problem?

....

....

McGinn considers the view that the non-spatiality of consciousness is a kind of illusion. Could consciousness as a whole be an illusion?

....

....

14

William James (1842–1910) on the reality of the mind – from 'Does "Consciousness" Exist?': *Journal of Philosophy, Psychology and Scientific Methods*, vol. 1, 1904

In this extract, James tries to overcome the common sense dualism of thoughts and things, suggesting that both consist of an underlying 'pure experience' which can be seen as consciousness when placed in one context, and as matter when placed in another. This 'neutral monism' tries to do justice to our common-sense dualist convictions, without committing us to the apparently unscientific entities or properties of dualism.

"'Thoughts'' and ''things'' are names for two sorts of object, which common sense will always find contrasted and will always practically oppose to each other. Philosophy, reflecting on the contrast, has varied in the past in her explanations of it, and may be expected to vary in the future . . . In [various neo-Kantian] writers . . . the spiritual principle attenuates itself to a thoroughly ghostly condition, being only a name for . . . [something] of which in its own right absolutely nothing can be said.

I believe that 'consciousness', when once it has evaporated to this estate of pure diaphaneity, is on the point of disappearing altogether. It is the name of a nonentity, and has no right to a place among first principles. Those who will cling to it are clinging to a mere echo, the faint rumour left behind by the disappearing 'soul' upon the air of philosophy . . . For twenty years I have distrusted 'consciousness' as an entity . . . It seems to me that the hour is ripe for it to be openly and universally discarded.

To deny plumply that 'consciousness' exists seems so absurd on the face of it – for undeniably 'thoughts' do exist – that I fear some readers will follow me no farther . . . I mean only to deny that the word stands for an entity, but to insist most emphatically that it does stand for a function . . . That function is *knowing*. 'Consciousness' is supposed necessary to explain the fact that things not only are, but get reported, are known. Whoever blots out the notion of consciousness from his list of first principles must still provide in some way for that function's being carried on.

My thesis is that if we start with the supposition that there is only one primal stuff or material in the world, a stuff of which everything is composed, and if we call that stuff 'pure experience', then knowing can easily be explained as a particular sort of relation towards one another into which portions of pure experience may enter. The relation itself is a part of pure experience; one of its terms becomes the subject or bearer of the knowledge, the knower [this 'knower' for James is not a substantive Self but just the 'passing thought'], the other becomes the object known [. . .]

. . . we are supposed by almost every one to have an immediate consciousness of consciousness itself. When the world of outer fact ceases to be materially present, and we merely recall it in memory, or fancy it, the consciousness is believed to stand out and to be felt as a kind of impalpable inner flowing . . . [James quotes G. E. Moore, who says] '. . . When we try to introspect the sensation of blue, all we can see is the blue; the other element is as if it were diaphanous. Yet it *can* be distinguished, if we look attentively enough, and know that there is something to look for.'

. . . This supposes that the consciousness is one element . . . from which, if you abstract the content, the consciousness will remain revealed to its own eye . . .

Now my contention is exactly the reverse of this. *Experience, I believe, has no such inner duplicity* . . . a given undivided portion of experience, taken in one context of associates, play[s] the part of a knower, of a state of mind, of 'consciousness'; while in a different context the same undivided bit of experience plays the part of a thing known, of an objective 'content'. In a word, in one group it figures as a thought, in another group as a thing. And, since it can figure in both groups simultaneously we have every right to speak of it as both subjective and objective at once . . . dualism, I say, is still preserved in this account, but reinterpreted, so that, instead of being mysterious and elusive, it becomes verifiable and concrete [. . .]

If the reader will take his own experiences, he will see what I mean. Let him begin with a perceptual experience . . . and let him for the present treat this complex object in the commonsense way as being 'really' what it seems to be, namely, a collection of physical things . . . Now at the same time it is just *those self-same things* which his mind, as we say, perceives; and the whole philosophy of perception from Democritus's time downwards has been just one long wrangle over the paradox that what is evidently one reality should be in two places at once, both in [external] space and in a person's mind. 'Representative'

theories of perception avoid the logical paradox, but on the other hand they violate the reader's sense of life, which knows no intervening mental image but seems to see the room and the book immediately just as they physically exist.

The puzzle of how the one identical room can be in two places is at bottom just the puzzle of how one identical point can be on two lines. It can, if it be situated at their intersection; and similarly, if the 'pure experience' of the room were a place of intersection of two processes, which connected it with different groups of associates respectively, it could be counted twice over, as belonging to either group . . .

. . . In one of these contexts it is your 'field of consciousness'; in another it is 'the room in which you sit', and it enters both contexts in its wholeness [. . .]

As 'subjective' we say that the experience represents; as 'objective' it is represented. What represents and what is represented is here numerically the same; but we must remember that no dualism of being represented and representing resides in the experience *per se*. In its pure state . . . there is no self-splitting of it into consciousness and what the consciousness is 'of'. Its subjectivity and objectivity are functional attributes solely, realized only when the experience is . . . considered along with its two differing contexts . . . '

Comments and questions

Given that we don't know anything about 'pure experience' except that it sometimes appears to us as things, sometimes as thoughts, and sometimes as both at once, it might seem that little has been gained by

— 44 —

supposing it to exist. However, James hopes to use it to explain, not only the relationship between mind and body, but also the 'directness' of perception. We feel, when we see a chair, that we are directly conscious of the chair itself and not a mental representation of the chair, *because* the chair and our consciousness of it are two aspects of the same 'pure experience'.

Still, for all we know about it, we might as well call this fundamental substance 'fairy dust'. And how explanatory is it – of the directness of perception or anything else – to bring 'fairy dust' into the equation?

Is this a serious objection or can James reply to it convincingly?

....

....

Paul Churchland (b. 1942) on the unreality of thoughts – from *Matter and Consciousness: A Contemporary Introduction to the Philosophy of Mind***: MIT Press, 1988**

One widely-held view is that thoughts, decisions, sensations and what-have-you will be found to be identical to states and processes in the brain. Brain surgeons have found, for example, that stimulating a particular area of the brain leads the patient to report a colour flash, while stimulating another area leads the patient to report a memory. So doesn't it look as if the experience of seeing the colour flash

just is neural activity in that area? Can't we say that the sensation is identical with the brain event? (For more on this, see extract 6/49 and *SP*, pp. 160–2).

In the following Reading, Churchland claims that thoughts, sensations, decisions and so on are not sufficiently well-defined to be identified with anything scientific. They form a 'radically false and misleading' explanation of human behaviour, which will simply be junked when a good brain-based account comes along.

'The identity theory was called into doubt [by functionalists – see Reading 6/51 and *SP* pp. 162–8] not because the prospects for a materialistic account of our mental capacities were thought to be poor, but because it seemed unlikely that the arrival of an adequate materialistic theory would bring with it the nice one-to-one match-ups, between the concepts of folk psychology and the concepts of theoretical neuroscience, that intertheoretic reduction requires. The reason for that doubt was the great variety of quite different physical systems that could instantiate the required functional organization. *Eliminative materialism* also doubts that the correct neuroscientific account will produce a neat reduction of our common-sense framework, but here the doubts arise from a quite different source.

As the eliminative materialists see it, the one-to-one match-ups will not be found, and our common sense psychological framework will not enjoy an intertheoretic reduction, *because our common-sense psychological framework is a false and radically misleading conception of the causes of human behavior and the nature of cognitive activity.* On this view, folk psychology is not just an incomplete representation of our inner natures; it is an outright *mis*-representation of our internal states and activities . . . we must expect that the older framework will simply be eliminated, rather than reduced, by a matured neuroscience.'

> Churchland goes on to argue that the concepts of folk psychology – concepts such as 'belief, desire, fear, sensation, pain, joy and so on' – will go the way of concepts like 'phlogiston' (a 'heat-substance' wrongly supposed, in the eighteenth century, to be given off during combustion). Our currently familiar psychological concepts will just disappear, replaced by a conceptual framework which provides superior prediction and control.

Comments and questions

Churchland says that the 'magnitude of the conceptual revolution here suggested . . . would be enormous'. He says, for example, that 'our private introspection will be transformed . . . just as the astronomer's perception of the night sky is much enhanced by the detailed knowledge of modern astronomical theory'.

Is this 'night sky' analogy *fair*, do you think? A pre-modern astronomer might misdescribe a comet's size, colour, or location, and might attribute to it causal powers it does not possess. But the comet was not an illusion. It really did pass across the night sky.

Churchland's claim, however, is that your conscious decision to buy a camera is not only subject to misdescription (as 'firm' or 'sudden' for example), and not only falsely supposed to have causal powers it does not possess (to lead you to go to a certain shop, for example). His claim is that a person of the future might realise that nothing really corresponded to the word 'decision' at all, just as we now say that nothing corresponded to the word 'phlogiston'.

Could this *possibly* be true?

....

....

If we do switch to explaining our own and others' behaviour in terms of 'neuropharmacological states' and so on, will we still be able to regard any of our actions as free and responsible?

....

....

— 46 —

Overview of Area 2

The Readings in Area 2 present a number of answers to the question 'Are minds real?', and show where these answers might lead.

For Skinner, mental phenomena are capricious, therefore unsuitable for science, and therefore destined for the dustbin of history. Overt behaviour is public and observable, and so can be accepted within science as genuinely real.

Peirce, on the other hand, argues that the very concept of reality depends on an apparently mental phenomenon, namely belief. To say that X is real is to say that at the end of an ideal process of investigation, people would believe in X. So to say, for example, that a sequence of behaviour is real, according to Peirce, *means* that an ideal investigator would believe in it.

Russell too constructs reality out of facts about observers, but for very different reasons and in a very different way. He argues that any observation or experiment comes down eventually to the sensations of the observer. It's therefore more economical, and less vulnerable to scepticism, to define external things in terms of these sensations. Russell realises that he should really limit himself strictly to his own sensations, but he allows himself to posit the sensations of other observers too. This raises the question of the reality of other people's sensations, and in general, the problem of other minds.

In our fourth selection, Carnap states – and rejects – the main argument (the argument from analogy) in favour of the existence of other minds. Statements about another's psyche must, he believes, be interpreted as saying something about that person's body. What's more, statements about my own psyche must be interpreted in the same way, or others would not be able to understand them. This rules out Russell's subjective concept of reality, even if limited to Russell's own sensations.

The Readings which follow – from Ayer and Malcolm – pursue the question of other minds. They argue respectively for, and against, versions of the argument from analogy.

The Reading from Colin McGinn accepts that mental phenomena do not fit into current science. But rather than taking this to show that they are not real, he believes that our current science must be imperfect. Accommodating consciousness within science will require a revolutionary change in our concept of space, indeed a change which may totally boggle the limited human mind. But it's better to knock our heads against this brick wall, McGinn thinks, than try to say that consciousness is not real.

The Reading from William James offers a possible exit from the problem. According to James, neither the sensation nor the external thing is ultimately 'real': they are the same underlying 'pure experience' as it occurs in different contexts. Thoughts and things are 'functional attributes' of something which is essentially neither – something which, though it can appear both as the thing known and as the process of knowing, would still be real if it didn't appear as either.

Our last Reading, from Paul Churchland, agrees with Skinner that the traditional framework for explaining human behaviour – in terms of beliefs, desires, decisions and so on – is deeply unscientific and will sooner or later disappear. He expects it to be replaced, however, by a scientific theory based on brain processes, not one based on behaviour. (In Reading 5/41, we'll see Quine suggest that reducing the mental to behaviour is a stage on the way to full reduction to physiology – which he interprets, like Churchland, as a way of repudiating mentalistic theorising.)

Overall, Area 2 looked at the mind in connection with the question 'What does it mean to say that a thing is *real*?' We'll confront the enigma of mentality again in Area 6, in connection with objectivity, and of course it's involved in the problems of knowledge and language too. Area 2 has given us a first look at some of the options which we will explore in more depth later.

Area 2 also introduces the problem of freedom. If we accept Plato's concept of reality, according to which a thing is real if it has a causal role, (see *SP*, p. 31), then it seems to follow that mental events such as decisions are *either* fully involved in the causal nexus, and so as fully determined as any other causal process, *or* non-existent. Having considered some ways of saying that they don't exist, we now consider, in Area 3, the consequences of regarding them as fully causal.

Freedom

The Reading selections in this area ask whether we have sufficient freedom to act morally, and debate what makes an action right or wrong.

16

Peter Strawson (b. 1919) on determinism – from 'Freedom and Resentment': *Proceedings of the British Academy*, **vol. XLVIII, 1962**

In this well-known article, Strawson tries to identify the central insights, both of those ('pessimists') who believe that determinism would, if true, destroy moral thinking, and of those ('optimists') who believe that determinism and morality are compatible. He begins by summarising the dispute between the two.

'Some optimists about determinism point to the efficacy of the practices of punishment, and of moral condemnation and approval, in regulating behaviour in socially desirable ways. In the fact of their efficacy, they suggest, is an adequate basis for these practices; and this fact certainly does not show determinism to be false. To this the pessimists reply, all in a rush, that *just*

punishment and *moral* condemnation imply moral guilt and guilt implies moral responsibility and moral responsibility implies freedom and freedom implies the falsity of determinism. And to this the optimists are wont to reply in turn that it is true that these practices require freedom in a sense, and the existence of freedom in this sense is one of the facts as we know them. But what 'freedom' means here is nothing but the absence of certain conditions the presence of which would make moral condemnation or punishment inappropriate . . . '

'Optimists' or compatibilists argue (roughly) that the freedom we need for moral responsibility is only absence of constraint. As long as a person is not constrained to act in a particular way, compatibilists believe, that person is morally responsible. 'Pessimists' generally insist that we have some stronger concept of freedom in mind when we hold people morally responsible.

' . . . And the general reason why moral condemnation or punishment are inappropriate when these [constraining] factors or conditions are present is held to be that the practices in question will be generally efficacious means of regulating behaviour in desirable ways only in cases where these factors are *not* present . . . Then what does the pessimist find missing? When he tries to answer this question, his language is apt to alternate between the very familiar and the very unfamiliar. Thus he may say, familiarly enough, that the man who is the subject of justified punishment, blame or moral condemnation must really deserve it; and then add, perhaps, that . . . the condition of his genuinely deserving blame is something that goes beyond the negative freedoms which the optimist concedes. It is, say, a genuinely free identification of the will with the act. And this is the condition which is incompatible with the truth of determinism [...]

...What I want to contrast is the attitude (or range of attitudes) of involvement or participation in a human relationship, on the one hand, and what might be called the objective attitude (or range of attitudes) to another human being, on the other. Even in the same situation ... they are not altogether *exclusive* of each other; but they are, profoundly, *opposed* to each other. To adopt the objective attitude to another human being is to see him, perhaps, as an object of social policy; as a subject for what, in a wide range of senses, might be called treatment; as something certainly to be taken account, perhaps precautionary account, of; to be managed or handled or cured or trained ... The objective attitude may be emotionally toned in many ways, but not in all ways: it may include repulsion or fear, it may include pity or even love, though not all kinds of love. But ... it cannot include resentment, gratitude, forgiveness, anger, or the sort of love which two adults can sometimes be said to feel reciprocally, for each other. If your attitude towards someone is wholly objective, then though you may fight him, you cannot quarrel with him, and though you may talk to him, even negotiate with him, you cannot reason with him. You can at most pretend to quarrel or reason with him [...]

...The question we have to ask is: ... would, or should, the acceptance of the truth of [determinism] ... mean the end of gratitude, resentment, and forgiveness; of all

reciprocated adult loves; of all essentially *personal* antagonisms [...]

...I am strongly inclined to think that [this] is, for us as we are, practically inconceivable. The human commitment to participation in ordinary inter-personal relationships is, I think, too thoroughgoing and deeply rooted for us to take seriously the thought that a general theoretical conviction might so change our world that, in it, there were no longer any such things as inter-personal relationships as we normally understand them ...

...A sustained objectivity of inter-personal attitude, and the human isolation which that would entail, does not seem to be something of which human beings would be capable, even if some general truth were a theoretical ground for it ... when we do in fact adopt such an attitude in a particular case, our doing so is not the consequence of a theoretical conviction which might be expressed as 'Determinism is the case', but is a consequence of our abandoning, for different reasons in different cases, the ordinary inter-personal attitudes.

It might be said that this leaves the real question unanswered ... For the real question is not a question about what we actually do, or why we do it. It is not even a question about what we would in fact do if a certain theoretical conviction gained general acceptance. It is a question about what it would be *rational* to do if determinism were true, a question about the rational justification of ordinary inter-personal attitudes in general. To this I shall reply, first, that such a question could seem real only to one who had utterly failed to grasp the purport of the preceding answer, the fact of our natural human commitment to ordinary inter-personal attitudes. This commitment is part of the general framework of human life, not something that can come up for review as particular cases come up within this general framework. And I shall reply, second, that if we could imagine what we cannot have, viz. a choice in this matter, then we could choose rationally only in the light of an assessment of the gains and losses to human life, its enrichment or impoverishment; and the truth or falsity of a general thesis of determinism would not bear on the rationality of *this* choice [...]

...it is useless to ask whether it would not be rational for us to do what it is not in our nature to (be able to) do [...]

And now we can try to fill in the lacuna which the pessimist finds in the optimist's account of the concept of moral responsibility, and of the bases of moral condemnation and punishment; and to fill it in from the facts as we know them.

... [The optimist represents the practice of punishment and condemnation] solely as instruments of policy, as methods of individual treatment and social control. The pessimist recoils from this picture ... He is apt to say, among much else, that the humanity of the offender himself is offended by *this* picture of his condemnation and punishment.

...The picture painted by the optimists is painted in a style appropriate to a situation envisaged as wholly dominated by objectivity of attitude. The only operative notions invoked in this picture are such as those of policy, treatment, control. But a thoroughgoing objectivity of attitude, excluding as it does the moral reactive attitudes, excludes at the same time essential elements in the concepts of moral condemnation and moral responsibility ... The deeper emotional shock is a reaction, not simply to an inadequate conceptual analysis, but to the suggestion of a change in our world [...]

...What is in question is the pessimist's justified sense that to speak in terms of social utility alone is to leave out something vital in our conception of these practices. The vital thing can be restored by attending to that complicated web of attitudes and feelings which form an essential part of the moral life as we know it, and which are quite opposed to objectivity of attitude. Only by attending to this range of attitudes can we recover from the facts as we know them a sense of what we mean, i.e. of all we mean, when, speaking the language of morals, we speak of desert, responsibility, guilt, condemnation, and justice [...]

...The optimist's style of over-intellectualising the facts is that of a characteristically incomplete empiricism, a one-eyed utilitarianism. He seeks to find an adequate basis for certain social practices in calculated consequences, and loses sight (perhaps wishes to lose sight) of the human attitudes of which these practices are, in part, the expression. The pessimist does not lose sight of these attitudes, but is unable to accept the fact that it is just these attitudes themselves which fill the gap in the optimist's account. Because of this, he thinks the gap can be filled only if some general metaphysical proposition is repeatedly verified in all cases where it is appropriate to attribute moral responsibility [that is, only if the agent exercises some non-empirical 'freedom of the will' every time he or she acts] [...]

... in philosophy, though it is also a

theoretical study, we have to take account of the facts in *all* their bearings; we are not to suppose that we are required, or permitted, as philosophers, to regard ourselves, as human beings, as detached from the attitudes which, as scientists, we study with detachment . . . '

Comments and questions

Strawson makes two main claims: firstly, that the objective attitude, applied generally to human life, is not a real option for us (from which it follows that we needn't ask ourselves whether, if determinism were true, it would be more rational to adopt that objective attitude); and secondly, that it's right to feel dissatisfied with the 'optimist's' (or compatibilist's) reduction of moral freedom to an objectively-conceived absence of constraint, but wrong to look towards some metaphysical 'freedom of the will' for the missing element.

In Strawson's view, an optimist who avoids an excessively objective attitude, and keeps in touch with the wider range of human responses, can provide as rich an account of morality as any pessimist can reasonably require.

In the years since Strawson wrote, fictional representation of 'inhumanly' objective characters has become commonplace. The *Star Trek* characters Spock and Data are popular examples. Is it really impossible, as Strawson claims, to imagine ourselves adopting a consistently objective attitude to other people?

....

....

Strawson's second claim is that compatibilism seems unattractive only because it tends to lose touch with the wider range of human responses. But if we accept – as the compatibilist thinks we must – that all our actions *really are* determined, won't these 'human responses' seem like mere froth, mere subjective feelings, irrelevant to the real business of prediction and control?

....

....

17

Norman Malcolm (1911–90) on determinism – from 'The Conceivability of Mechanism': *The Philosophical Review* LXXVII, 1968

Malcolm begins by defining 'mechanism' as 'a special application of physical determinism – namely, to all organisms with neurological systems'. In essence, 'mechanism' says that our voluntary bodily movements are caused by changes in the nervous system. Malcolm argues first that:

 ' . . . the postulated neurophysiological theory ['mechanism'] is comprehensive. It is assumed to provide complete causal explanations for all bodily movements that are not produced by external physical forces. It is a closed system in the sense that it does not admit, as antecedent conditions, anything other than neurophysiological states and processes. Desires and intentions have no place in it.

If the neurophysiological theory were true, then in no cases would desires, intentions, purposes be necessary conditions of any human movements. It would never be true that a man would *not* have moved as he did if he had *not* had such and such an intention. Nor would it ever be true that a certain movement of his was due to, or brought about by, or caused by his having a certain intention or purpose. Purposive explanations of human bodily movements would *never* be true [. . .]'

> This point made, and some definitional preliminaries completed, Malcolm proceeds to address:

' . . . the question whether mechanism is conceivable. Sometimes when philosophers ask whether a proposition is conceivable, they mean to be asking whether it is self-contradictory. Nothing in our examination has indicated that mechanism is a self-contradictory theory, and I am sure it is not . . .

But there is a respect in which mechanism is not conceivable. This is a consequence of the fact that mechanism is incompatible with the existence of any intentional behaviour. The speech of human beings is, for the most part, intentional behaviour. In particular, stating, asserting or saying that so-and-so is true requires the intentional uttering of some sentence. If mechanism is true, therefore, no one can state or assert anything. In a sense, no one can *say* anything. Specifically, no one can assert or state that mechanism is true. If anyone were to assert this, the occurrence of his intentional 'speech act' would imply that mechanism is false.

Thus there is a logical absurdity in

asserting that mechanism is true. It is not that the doctrine of mechanism is self-contradictory . . . The mere proposition that mechanism is true is not self-contradictory. But the conjunctive proposition, 'Mechanism is true and someone asserts it to be true' *is* self-contradictory. Thus anyone's assertion that mechanism is true is necessarily false. The assertion implies its own falsity by virtue of providing a counter-example to what is asserted [. . .]

23. A proponent of mechanism might claim that since the absurdity we have been describing is a mere 'pragmatic paradox' and not a self-contradiction in the doctrine of mechanism, it does not provide a sense in which mechanism is inconceivable. He may say that the paradox is similar to the paradox of a man's asserting that he himself is unconscious . . . His act of stating implies that what he states is false. But this paradox does not establish that a man cannot be unconscious, or that we cannot conceive that a man should be unconscious.

Now there is some similarity between the paradox of stating that oneself is unconscious and the paradox of stating that mechanism is true. But there is an important difference. *I* cannot state, without absurdity, that *I* am unconscious. But anyone else can, without absurdity, state that I am unconscious. There is only one person (myself) whose act of stating this proposition is inconsistent with the proposition. But an assertion of mechanism by any person whomsoever is inconsistent with mechanism. . . . the unstatability of mechanism is absolute.

Furthermore, no one can consistently assert that although mechanism is unstatable it may be true. For this assertion too, would require an intentional utterance (speech act)

— 53 —

and so would be incompatible with mechanism [...]'

> Malcolm goes on to discover a second reason for thinking that mechanism – which seemed at first to be perfectly conceivable – is not a conceivable theory. He asks us to imagine evidence for mechanism gradually building up:

'... suppose that in many instances when we thought the behaviour [of a boy running after a ball] was intentional, it was subsequently proved to us that ... a [neurological] technician controlled the boy's movements. We can also suppose that the technician's predictions of behaviour would be both more reliable and more accurate than are the predictions based on purposive assumptions.

If such demonstrations occurred on a massive scale, we should be learning that the principles of purposive explanation have a far narrower application than we had thought. On more and more occasions we (that is, each one of us) would be forced to regard other human beings as mechanisms. The ultimate outcome of this development would be that we should cease to think of the behaviour of others as being influenced by desires and intentions [...]

25. Having become believers in mechanistic explanations of the behaviour of others, could each of us also come to believe that mechanistic causation is the true doctrine for his own case? Not if we realized what this would imply, for each of us would see that he could not include himself within the scope of the doctrine. Saying or doing something *for a reason* (in the sense of grounds as well as in the sense of purpose)

implies that the saying or doing is intentional ... my acceptance of mechanism as true for myself would imply that I am incapable of saying or doing anything for a reason. There could be *a* reason (that is, a cause) but there could not be such a thing as *my* reason ... Thus my assertion of mechanism would involve a second paradox. Not only would the assertion be inconsistent, in the sense previously explained, but also it would imply that I am incapable of having rational grounds for asserting anything, including mechanism.

Once again, we see that mechanism engenders a form of solipsism. In asserting mechanism I must deny its application to my own case: for otherwise my assertion would imply that I could not be asserting mechanism on rational grounds [...]

The inconceivability of mechanism, in the two respects we have elucidated, does not establish that mechanism is false. It would seem, logically speaking, that a comprehensive neurophysiological theory of human behaviour ought to be confirmable by scientific investigation. Yet the assertion that this confirmation had been achieved would involve the two paradoxes we have elucidated. Mechanism thus presents a harsh, and perhaps insoluble, antimony to human thought.'

Comments and questions

In a frank postscript to this article, Malcolm confesses that he is not entirely confident of his argument that a complete mechanistic explanation of a sequence of behaviour 'knocks out' a complete purposive explanation of it.

What do you think? Could we consistently accept two explanations of the same behaviour, one in terms of the agent's neurology and the other terms of his or her desires and intentions?

....

....

Suppose a defender of mechanism said that Malcolm's paradoxes only arise because we're persisting with outmoded concepts (purpose, intention, desire, evidence etc). Presumably, as we slowly become convinced of the truth of mechanism, we would develop a new vocabulary, in which these paradoxes would not arise. Are Malcolm's paradoxes really just anachronisms, or do they have a more enduring source?

....

....

⬤18

Daniel Dennett (b. 1942) on determinism – from 'Mechanism and Responsibility', in *Essays on Freedom of Action*: Routledge and Kegan Paul (ed. Ted Honderich) 1973

Malcolm was trying to support Strawson's first claim – that a consistently objective attitude to human behaviour is, in real terms, inconceivable – but not his second. Dennett, by contrast, aims to support his second claim – that determinism is compatible with moral responsibility – while counselling caution about his first.

He writes:

📖 '... some philosophers [believe] that the mechanistic displaces the purposive, and any mechanistic (or causal) explanation of human motions takes priority over, indeed renders false, any explanation in terms of desires, beliefs, intentions ... I want to argue that this principle is false [...]

... Consider the case of the chess-playing computer, and the different stances one can choose to adopt in trying to predict and explain its behaviour. First there is the *design stance*. If one knows exactly how the computer's program has been designed (and we will assume for simplicity that this is not a learning or evolving program but a static one), one can predict the computer's designed response to any move one makes ...

Second, there is what we may call the *physical stance*. From this stance our predictions are based on the actual state of the particular system, and are worked out by applying whatever knowledge we have of the laws of nature. It is from this stance alone that one can predict the malfunction of systems (unless, as sometimes happens, a system is designed to malfunction after a certain time, in which case malfunctioning in one sense becomes part of its proper functioning). Instances of predictions from the physical stance are common enough: 'If you turn on that switch you'll get a nasty shock' ...

There is a third stance one can adopt towards a system, and that is the *Intentional stance*. This tends to be most appropriate when the system one is dealing with is too complex to be dealt with effectively from the other stances. In the case of the chess-playing

computer one adopts this stance when one tries to predict its response to one's move by figuring out what a good or reasonable response would be, given the information the computer has about the situation. Here one assumes not just the absence of malfunction, but the rationality of design or programming as well. Of course the stance is pointless, in view of its extra assumption, in cases where one has no reason to believe in the system's rationality. In weather predicting one is not apt to make progress by wondering what clever move the wise old West Wind will make next ...

Whenever one can successfully adopt the Intentional stance toward an object, I call that object an *Intentional system*. The success of the stance is of course a matter to be settled pragmatically ... some computers undeniably *are* Intentional systems, for they are systems whose behaviour can be predicted, and most efficiently predicted by adopting the Intentional stance towards them [...]

... One adopts the Intentional stance toward any system one assumes to be (roughly) rational, where the complexities of its operation preclude maintaining the design stance effectively ... to adopt a truly moral stance toward the system (thus viewing it as a person), might often turn out to be psychologically irresistible ... but it is logically distinct ... We might, then, distinguish a fourth stance, above the Intentional stance, called the *personal stance* [...]

Communication ... is not a separable and higher *stance* one may choose to adopt toward something, but a type of interaction one may attempt within the Intentional stance [...]

... our predictions of what an Intentional system will do are formed on the basis of what would be reasonable (for anyone) to do under the circumstances, rather than on what a wealth of experience with this system or similar systems might inductively suggest the system will do. It is the absence from the mechanistic stances of this presupposition of rationality that gives rise to the widespread feeling that there is an antagonism between predictions or explanations from these different stances. The feeling ought to be dissipated at least in part by noting that the absence of a presupposition of rationality is not the same as a presupposition of irrationality [...]

... the only implication that could be drawn from the *general* thesis of man's ultimately mechanistic organization would be that man must, then, be imperfectly rational ... and from any *particular* mechanistic explanation of a bit of behaviour it would not follow that that bit of behaviour was or was not a rational response to the environmental conditions at the time, for the mere fact that the response *had* to follow, given its causal antecedents, casts no more doubt on its rationality than the fact that the computer *had* to answer '108' casts doubts on the arithmetic correctness of its answer [...]

The Intentional stance toward human beings, which is a precondition of any ascriptions of responsibility, *may* coexist with mechanistic explanations of their motions. The other side of this coin, however, is that we *can* in principle adopt a mechanistic stance toward human bodies and their motion, so there remains an important question to be answered. Might we abandon the Intentional stance altogether ... in favour of a purely mechanistic world view, or is this an alternative that can be ruled out on logical or conceptual grounds? This question has been approached a number of different ways in the literature, but there is near unanimity about the general shape of the answer: for Strawson the question is whether considerations (of determinism, mechanism etc.) could lead us to look on everyone exclusively in the 'objective' way, abandoning the 'participant' attitude altogether. His decision is that this could not transpire, and he compares the commitment to the participant attitude to our commitment to induction, which is 'original, natural, non-rational (not irrational), in no way something we choose or could give up' … Sellars makes much the same point in arguing that 'the scientific image cannot replace the manifest without rejecting its own foundation' …

… it is important to see what does not follow from the consensus above. It does not follow, though Malcolm thinks it does, that there are some things in the world, namely human beings, of which mechanism as an embracing theory cannot be true, for there is no incompatibility between mechanistic and Intentional explanation. Nor does it follow that we will always characterize some things Intentionally, for we may all be turned into zombies next week … All that is the case is that we, *as persons*, cannot *adopt* exclusive mechanism (by eliminating the Intentional stance altogether) …

All this says nothing about the impossibility of dire depersonalization in the future … If the growing area of success in mechanistic explanation of human behaviour does not in itself rob us of responsibility, it does make it more pragmatic, more effective or efficient, for people on occasion to adopt less than the Intentional stance towards others … The advent of brain-washing, subliminal advertising, hypnotism and even psychotherapy (all invoking variations on the design stance), and the more direct physical tampering with drugs and surgical intervention, for the first time make the choice of stance a genuine one.'

Comments and questions

Dennett's main claim here is that mechanistic explanation is compatible with Intentional explanation. But since it often seems easier to predict the working of, say, a video recorder from how it should rationally work rather than from detailed knowledge of its design or physical state, and since it seems to follow from this that a video recorder qualifies as an Intentional system, it's natural to wonder how relevant Dennett's claim really is to the human predicament. The compatibility of mechanistic with Intentional explanation may be reassuring to video recorders – if they worry about these things – but is it reassuring to *us*? What we want to know is whether the *moral* stance is compatible with mechanism.

Dennett's view seems to be that we can cheerfully admit that we're irrational in persevering with the Intentional stance in cases where the design or physical stances provide better explanations. We're 'imperfectly rational' – but we knew that already of course.

But is persevering with the *moral* stance just a matter of using fond, old-fangled methods when better ones are available? Is the main purpose of the *moral* or *personal* stance – as of the other stances – prediction? Wouldn't the triumph of mechanism destroy something essential for seeing other people as *persons*?

....

....

19

Max Black (1909–88) on causality – from 'Making Something Happen', in *Determinism and Freedom*: New York University Press, 1958 (ed. S. Hook)

In this article, Max Black examines – in the Wittgensteinian manner – the real ordinary use of the word 'cause'. He rejects a Humean analysis (see Reading 1/3), on the grounds that the concept of a cause is based on clear paradigm cases and so requires no single, overarching definition (*SP*, p. 177). And he concludes that, because the meaning of the term radiates out from these paradigm cases by means of metaphor and analogy, it has no single, clear meaning to serve in any statement of determinism. Determinism has no clear meaning.

Black begins by presenting some simple, stereotypical cases of making something happen – lifting a glass of beer to one's lips, for example. He stresses that in the paradigm cases:

 'There would be an absurdity in saying that evidence could be provided for or against the view that he had moved the glass . . .

For what could be the goal of the supposed investigation? If somebody is not already satisfied that the familiar episode is a case of what we ordinarily call 'making something happen', it is inconceivable that further empirical evidence would satisfy him. The supposed investigation would have no terminus [. . .]'

Black's point here is that in the simplest cases it makes no sense to ask for evidence or proof that A caused X. If we see someone move a glass along a table with our own eyes, no further evidence can be required. Anyone who asks for proof in this context, only shows that he or she does not understand the word 'cause' in the way we do. So if someone (influenced by Hume) says, 'Well I saw the hand move and I saw the glass move, but I still need proof that the hand moved the glass', that only shows a failure of understanding, not an acute sense of evidence.

Black goes on to isolate some common features of these paradigm cases of making something happen. Here is what he says about the feature Hume called 'necessary connexion' (see Reading 1/3 and *SP*, ch. 2).

'*When pushed, the glass* had *to move.* Certainly, it is natural to say this, and there must be some sense in which it is true. No doubt mythology plays a part: there is a discernible inclination to think of the moving object as animate – a manikin, helpless in our grasp, 'having no choice' but to move. But good sense remains when mythology has been discarded. We need only remind ourselves of the circumstances in which we say that an object acted on by an external force does *not* have to move. We say so when the given force is insufficient to produce the desired motion . . . Again, a penny tossed in the air *has* to come down again, but it does not *have* to come down tails. Here and elsewhere, the relevant contrast is between what sometimes happens and what invariably happens. To generalize: we say that M had to happen when A happened, only if M would always ensue, given an unchanged setting and the same concomitant . . . we might say that A is a part of a certain sufficient condition for the occurrence of M.

In this cursory examination of some features of a paradigm case of making something happen, I have had little occasion to refer to any 'constant conjunction' between producing action and induced motion. The omission has been deliberate. The assertion 'P made M happen by doing A' does not mean the same as 'If P were to repeat actions sufficiently like A, then, other things being equal, motions like M would invariably ensue'. If the [Humean] analysis were correct, the original causal statement would include as part of its meaning a generalization whose verification would need repeated observation and an induction upon an indefinite number of situations resembling the original situation. The original statement ('P made something happen, etc') [would be] so far from being verifiable by inspection that a lengthy inquiry would be needed to establish its truth . . . But I think the truth of the matter is much simpler: in order to be sure that P made O move, we need only look. The verifying situation is right before our eyes.

. . . In using the language of 'making something happen' we take for granted that the episode in view has a special and appropriate character. Should we be challenged to specify these conditions in full detail, we should eventually have to talk about constant conjunctions . . . But such investigation would establish the *presuppositions* for the proper use of causal language, not the meaning of the assertions made by means of language [. . .]

There is a sense, therefore, in which 'P made M happen by doing A' can be said to mean the same as 'While P did A, M happened' – the sense in which both statements would be verified by the same state of affairs. But there is also an important sense in which the two are strikingly different – because they imply different presuppositions and are connected with diverse linguistic practices.

. . . When we order someone to do something, we envisage his making something happen. If our language contained no provision for isolating causal episodes, we could issue no orders, give no commands . . . All that part of our life concerned with getting things done, or with anticipating and controlling the consequences of our actions, uses the language of 'making things happen' and is inconceivable without it.

Another connection is with moral language. To say that somebody made M happen is to hold him responsible for it . . . a language containing no provision for linking persons with events for whose occurrence they are held responsible would be one in which moral judgments as we now know them would be impossible.'

Black is claiming here that the Humean analysis of causality removes from language a resource it needs for moral judgements. The reason moral thinking is imperilled is not that (if determinism is true) we are compelled to do what we do, but that we lose the vocabulary of *making* something happen.

He now moves on to emphasise the variety of uses of the word 'cause':

'. . . I have been confining myself to cases where some person causes a *motion*. But it is natural to extend the language to cases where the agent produces a cessation of motion . . . it is equally natural to talk of 'making something happen' when what is produced is a *qualitative* change. And so we pass, by easy transitions, from the material realm to that of the affections and sentiments. We talk of making somebody laugh, of making somebody reconsider, or making somebody happy – without always realising how far we have strayed from the prototypes [. . .]

Anybody with a logician's desire for clear-cut distinctions may well be exasperated by the lack of systematic principle in these patterns of analogical and metaphorical extensions of causal language [. . .]

I have been arguing that 'cause' is an essentially schematic word, tied to certain more or less stable criteria of application but permitting wide variation of specific determination according to context and the purposes of investigation. Now, if this is so, any attempt to state a 'universal law of causation' must prove futile. To anybody who insists that 'nothing happens without a sufficient cause' we are entitled to retort with the question "What do you *mean* by 'cause'?" . . . The fatal defect of determinism is its protean capacity to elude refutation – by the same token, its informative content is

negligible. Whatever virtues it may have in encouraging scientists to search for comprehensive laws and theories, there can be no rational dispute about its truth value.'

Comments and questions

Is determinism really a general injunction to scientists – saying 'Search for general laws' or something like that – rather than a statement of fact? Does the apparent statement 'Every event has sufficient causes' really tell us nothing factual?

....

....

Does the underlying threat to moral thinking derive, not from determinism (whether interpreted as a statement of fact or an injunction), but from Hume's claim that when we say 'A made X happen' that can only legitimately mean that A-like things are constantly conjoined with X-like things?

....

....

Frederick Dretske (b. 1932) on the reality of meaning – from 'Does Meaning Matter?', in *Information, Semantics and Epistemology*: Blackwell, 1990 (ed. E. Villaneuva)

In this essay, Dretske tries to reconcile materialism ('only matter really exists') with our conviction that reasons for actions do genuinely explain them. Dretske wants to show that meanings do matter – that is, do genuinely explain actions – that they *are* matter (because identical with brain states), and yet that they explain in virtue of their meaning, not in virtue of their material properties.

📖 'The prevailing wisdom among materialists is that even if . . . some events have a meaning, and even if, as physical events in good standing, they have an impact on their material surroundings, the fact that they mean what they do won't help explain why they do what they do.

This doctrine about what Dennett (1983) calls the *impotence* of meaning should not be taken to imply that the objects having meaning are causally inert. It only means that that it is not their intentional properties, their content or meaning, from which they derive their causal powers . . . [This standard materialist view holds that] although events in the brain, those we might want to identify with a particular thought *about* Hoboken, are *about* Hoboken, their power to stimulate glands and regulate muscle tension – and thus to control behavior – derive, not from what they mean, not from the fact that they are about Hoboken, but from their electrical and chemical properties [. . .]

. . . The explanatory gulf between those properties of events that make them mental and those properties (of the same events) that explain their causal impact on other material events – in particular motor output – constitutes a dualism, a property-dualism, that exists *within* a materialistic metaphysics.

This, it seems to me, is an unacceptable position for any theory of the mind to occupy. If the mind . . . is not . . . . good for helping one understand why the system possessing it does what it does, then I don't see the point in having a mind. Why bother thinking if the fact that you think, and facts about what you think, do not – sometimes at least – explain why you behave the way you do?

. . . it is no good having a theory of meaning if the meaning in question doesn't *do* something, something that both needs to be done and will, without the help of meaning, not be done . . . People stopped talking about the soul when they realized that there was nothing for the soul to do. Information and meaning [if they don't genuinely explain behaviour] deserve the same fate [. . .]

Materialists have painted themselves into this corner . . . by misidentifying what meaning and content, the what-it-is we believe, desire, fear and intend, are supposed to explain . . . [It is true that] if A causes B, the fact, if it is a fact, that A means M will not – indeed, cannot – figure in a causal explanation of B. It cannot because, in similar circumstances, an event lacking this meaning, but otherwise the same, will have exactly the same effects . . . Nonetheless, the fact that A means M, though it fails to explain why B occurred, may help explain a closely related fact: the fact that events of type A, when they occur, cause events of type B . . . And this fact, especially when we are trying to explain the behavior of a system, is a fact eminently worth explaining [. . .]

I have argued elsewhere (Dretske 1988) that the behavior of a system should not be identified with its bodily movements. What distinguishes the movement of my arm (an event) from my moving my arm (behavior), even when my arm moves because I move it, is the fact that the behavior, my moving my arm, consists in arm movements being caused by some internal event or process. The behavior, let me repeat, is not a movement *which is caused* by some internal event or process; it is, rather, this movement's *being caused* by some internal event or process. Hence ... to explain a person's behavior (in contrast to explaining the bodily movements in which behavior typically culminates) one must explain, not why this or that event occurs (not why the arm moves) but why one event is causing another (why the arm is being caused to move) [...]

The meaning of neural events *is*, I agree, epiphenomenal [= not causally efficacious] if all we are trying to explain is why bodily movements occur. It *is not* ... epiphenomenal if what we are trying to explain is something else ... why this or that movement is *being caused* to occur [...]

... I move my arm ... *in order* to frighten away a pesky fly. With such a purpose I am, let us say, *shooing away a fly*. That is my *action*. My biological twin [a molecule-for-molecule copy of me produced artificially], though he moves his arm in the same way (with the same result) does not shoo away a fly. He doesn't have wants or beliefs, the kind of purposes I have in moving my arm. He isn't, therefore, performing the same action. Though there *is* a fly there, and it *is* frightened away by the movement of his arm, he isn't shooing it away ... though my twin and I behave in the same way (we both move our arm, we both frighten away the fly) the explanation of my twin's behavior is much different than the explanation of my behavior ... I perform an action – shooing away a fly – and he doesn't ... I did it *in order* to get the fly to

move. He didn't ... my twin, though he may remain indistinguishable from me, cannot *do* many of the things I do [...]

... biologically indistinguishable organisms can not only be in psychologically different states, this psychological difference can help to explain their respective *bodily* behaviors. They are both moving their arm – moving it, in fact, in exactly the same way. Yet they may have quite different reasons for moving their arms in this way: the one person is waving goodbye [or copying another's action] the other brushing away a pesky fly. This means, in turn, that insofar as otherwise identical behaviors can qualify as different *actions* because the corresponding movements are produced with different intentions ... biologically identical organisms can *act* in much different ways. These results are achieved by identifying an organism's behavior, not with the surface changes – including bodily movements – that are internally produced, but with the *process* in which such changes are brought about.'

Comments and questions

Suppose a thought about Hoboken is identical with some brain state. That brain state will of course have a hugely complex set of intrinsic and relational chemical and electrical properties. Could the thought's property of being about Hoboken be identical to some subset of these (standing in some relation of raised excitation, for example, to the cells that activate when the person visualises or remembers Hoboken)? And if this property-identity held, would that give causal efficacy to the thought's meaning?

Dretske's response to this move is to

make a sharp distinction between predictability and explanation. A statement like, 'The subject uttered the sounds 'Ah, Hoboken' because of raised excitation levels connecting c1-c101, c2-c102 etc. etc. etc.' might be predictively more powerful than, 'She said 'Ah, Hoboken' because she had been thinking about Hoboken.' But, Dretske feels, the neurological statement doesn't *explain* why she said what she said.

Well, suppose the neurological approach gives us good predictability. It is reasonable to want more?

....

....

Suppose, as before, that mental properties are identical with (very complex) sets of neurological properties. It seems to follow that if A is waving goodbye to a departing aunt and B is shooing away a fly, then A's brain will be in a different state from B's. Even if they're looking at, and focussing on, the same thing (so that their basic visual cortex activity is the same), A's 'Auntie Edna' cells will be highly excited, while B's will be quiescent. B's 'fly memory' and 'fly language' cells will be ready to leap into action, while A's are on regular standby. So if Dretske holds that A and B might be biologically indistinguishable, must he deny that mental properties might be identical with material ones? In other words, must he accept property-dualism? (In a good article in the same book, Jaegwon Kim argues that Dretske's approach is 'fundamentally dualistic'.)

....

....

Thomas Hobbes (1588–1679) on human nature – from *Leviathan*, chs 11, 13, 17: 1651

Hobbes was an early materialist, identifying thoughts and sensations with activity in the nervous system. This mechanistic picture seems to have encouraged a view of human beings as essentially selfish, striving always for 'Power after Power'.

Our innate selfishness makes it natural, Hobbes thought, for everyone to be in a constant state of violent competition with everyone else. Fortunately however, realising that this would be disastrous for everyone, people agree to submit to a government which will control their rapaciousness.

Hobbes presents this dark picture of human nature with splendid pungency and verve.

'. . . the Felicity of this life [does not consist] in the repose of a mind satisfied. For there is no utmost aim, nor greatest Good, as is spoken of in the Books of old Moral Philosophers. Nor can a man any more live, whose Desires are at an end, than he whose Senses and Imagination are at a stand. Felicity is a continual progress of desire, from one object to another . . . The cause [of this] is, That the object of man's desire is not to enjoy once only, and for one instant of time; but to assure for ever the way of his future desire. And therefore the voluntary actions and inclinations of all men tend, not only to the procuring, but also the assuring of a contented life . . .

So that in the first place, I put for a general

inclination of all mankind, a perpetual and restless desire of Power after Power, that ceases only in Death. And the cause of this is not always that a man hopes for a more intensive delight, than he has already attained to; or that he cannot be content with a moderate power: but because he cannot assure the power and means to live well . . . without the acquisition of more . . .

Competition for Riches, Honour, Command, or other power, [creates] Contention, Enmity, and War: Because the way of one Competitor, to the attaining of his desire, is to kill, subdue, supplant, or repel the other [. . .]

Nature has made men so equal, in the faculties of body and mind . . . that though there [may] be found one man sometimes manifestly stronger in body or of quicker mind than another; yet when all is reckoned together, the difference between man and man is not so considerable, as that one man can thereupon claim to himself any benefit, to which another man may not pretend as well as he. For as to strength of body, the weakest has strength enough to kill the strongest, either by secret machination, or by confederacy with others, that are in the same danger as himself [. . .]

From this equality of ability arises equality of hope in the attaining of our Ends. And therefore if any two men desire the same thing, which nevertheless they cannot both enjoy, they become enemies; and . . . endeavour to destroy or subdue one another. And hence it comes to pass that . . . if one plant, sow, build, or possess a convenient [home], others may be expected to come prepared with forces united, to dispossess and deprive him, not only of the fruit of his labour, but also of his life, or liberty. And the invader again is in the like danger of another.

And from this [fear] of one another, there is no way for any man to secure himself, so reasonable, as Anticipation; that is, by force, or wiles, to master the persons of all men he can . . . till he sees no other power great enough to endanger him . . .

Again, men have no pleasure, (but on the contrary a great deal of grief) in keeping company, where there is no power able to over-awe them all. For every man [expects that] his companion should value him, at the same rate he sets upon himself: And upon all signs of contempt, or undervaluing, naturally endeavours . . . to extort a greater value from [those who insulted him] . . . and from others, by the example [. . .]

So that in the nature of man, we find three principal causes of quarrel. First, Competition; Secondly, [Fear]; Thirdly, Glory.

The first makes men invade for Gain; the second, for Safety; and the third, for Reputation . . .

Hereby it is manifest, that during the time men live without a common Power to keep them all in awe, they are in that condition which is called War; and such a war, as is of every man, against every man. For War [does not consist in] Battle only, or other acts of fighting; but in a tract of time [during which] the will to contend by Battle is sufficiently known . . . the nature of War [does not consist] in actual fighting; but in the known disposition thereto, during all the time there is no assurance to the contrary. All other time is Peace.

Whatsoever therefore is consequent to a time of War, where every man is Enemy to every man; the same is consequent to the time, wherein men live without other security than what their own strength, and their invention shall furnish them with. In [this] condition, there is no place for Industry; because the fruit thereof is uncertain; and consequently no [agriculture]; no Navigation, nor use of the commodities that may be imported by Sea; no commodious Building; no Instruments of moving and removing such things as require much force; no Knowledge of the face of the Earth; no account of Time; no Arts; no [Literature]; no Society; and which is worst of all, continual fear, and danger of violent death; And the life of man, solitary, poor, nasty, brutish, and short [. . .]

. . . The Desires, and other Passions of man, are in themselves no Sin. No more are the Actions, that proceed from those Passions, till they know a Law that forbids them: which till Laws be made they cannot know: nor can any Law be made, till they have agreed upon the Person that shall make it [. . .]

To this war of every man against every man, this also is consequent; that nothing can be Unjust. The notions of Right and Wrong, Justice and Injustice have there no place. Where there is no common Power, there is no Law: where no Law, no Injustice. Force and Fraud are in war the two Cardinal Virtues. Justice and Injustice . . . are Qualities that relate to men in Society, not in Solitude. It is consequent also . . . that there is no Property, no Dominion, no *Mine* and *Thine* distinct; but only that to be every man's that he can get; and for so long, as he can keep it [. . .]

The only way to erect such a Common Power, as may be able to defend [people] from the invasion of Foreigners, and the injuries of one another . . . is to confer all their power and strength upon one Man, or upon one Assembly of men, to bear their

person; and every one to [admit] and acknowledge himself to be Author of whatsoever he that . . . bears their person shall Act, or cause to be Acted, in those things which concern the common Peace and Safety; and . . . to submit their Wills, every one to his Will, and their Judgments, to his Judgment. This is more than Consent, or Concord; it is a real Unity of them all, in one and the same Person, made by covenant of every man with every man . . . as if every man should say to every man, *I Authorise and give up my Right of Governing my self, to this Man, or to this Assembly of men, on this condition, that you give up your right to him, and Authorise all his actions in like manner.* This done, the Multitude so united in one person is called a COMMON-WEALTH. This is the Generation of that great LEVIATHAN, or rather (to speak more reverently) of that *Mortal God*, to which we owe under the *Immortal God*, our peace and defence . . .

. . . he that carries this Person is called SOVEREIGN, and is said to have *Sovereign Power*, and every one besides, his SUBJECT.

Comments and questions

One response to Hobbes' account is this: if there is no right and wrong until there is law, no law until there is government, and no government until there is a mutual promise or contract, then the whole process cannot get started, because a promise or contract must be something which people think it would be *wrong* to break. Is this just a logical quibble, or is there a serious problem here for Hobbes?

....

....

Is it true that law creates right and wrong? If so, how do we know which laws to enact?

....

....

Hume said that:

> it cannot without the greatest absurdity be disputed, that there is some benevolence, however small, infused into our bosom; some spark of friendship for humankind; some particle of the dove kneaded into our frame, along with the elements of the wolf and the serpent.

Is human nature really as *appalling* as Hobbes says?

....

....

Immanuel Kant (1724–1804) on duty – from *Groundwork of the Metaphysic of Morals*: 1785

Reacting against Hobbes' view of morality as based on self-interest, Hume said that moral judgement 'arises chiefly from that regard which the natural sentiment of benevolence engages us to pay to the interests of mankind and society'. Kant, however, rejected mere sentiment as a basis for morality, essentially because he thought moral laws should be binding even on someone who happens to have no natural sentiments of benevolence. Someone who has no particle of the dove kneaded into his frame is still subject to what's right and wrong.

If Kant is right about this, morality must be based on something which even this 'unsentimental' individual retains – mere rationality. This leads Kant to the surprising claim that the only genuinely *moral* motive is the motive of duty (see *SP*, ch. 10).

'This distinction [between duty and self-interest] is far more difficult to perceive when the action accords with duty and the subject has in addition an *immediate* inclination to the action. For example, it certainly accords with duty that a shopkeeper should not overcharge an inexperienced customer; and where there is much competition a sensible shopkeeper refrains from this . . . Thus people are served *honestly*; but this is not nearly enough to justify us in believing that the shopkeeper has acted from duty or from principles of fair dealing; his interests required him to behave in this way . . .

On the other hand, to preserve one's life is a duty, and besides this every one has also an immediate inclination to do so . . . [People] do protect their lives *in conformity with duty* but not *from the motive of duty* . . .

To help others where one can is a duty, and besides this there are many spirits so sympathetic that, without any further motive of vanity or self-interest, they find an inner pleasure in spreading happiness around them . . . Yet I maintain that in such a case an action of this kind, however right and however amiable it may be, still has no genuinely moral worth. It stands on the same footing as other inclinations – for example, the inclination for honour which if fortunate enough to hit on something beneficial and right and consequently honourable, deserves praise and encouragement, but not moral esteem; for its maxim [the principle underlying the action] lacks moral content, namely, the performance of such actions, not from inclination, but *from duty* [. . .]'

So an action only has *moral* value, Kant believes, if it is performed from duty. He now claims that actions done from duty have their value, not in any consequences which result – because the action would still be morally good even if the intended consequences were somehow blocked. An action's moral value derives from the *maxim* in accordance with which it was performed. (A 'consequentialist' theory of morality holds, by contrast, that the moral value of an action is determined by the consequences which result from it.)

Kant's idea seems to be that when we perform an action, we envisage it as an action of a certain kind. I might see one and the same action of writing my signature on a cheque, for example, as making a donation, fighting my own selfishness, creating good publicity, renouncing my past and so on. Kant writes:

'. . . an action done from duty has to set aside altogether the influence of inclination, and along with inclination every object of the will; so there is nothing left able to determine the will except objectively the *law* and subjectively *pure reverence* for this practical law . . .

But what kind of law can this be, if the thought of it, without regard to any results expected from it, has to determine the will (when the will can be called good absolutely and without qualification)? Since I have robbed the will of every inducement that might arise for it as a consequnece of obeying a given law, nothing is left but the conformity of actions to universal law as such . . . That is to say, I ought never to act except in such a way *that I can also will that my maxim should become a universal law* . . .

Take this question, for example. May I not, when hard pressed, make a promise with the intention of not keeping it? Here I readily distinguish two senses to the question – Is it prudent, or is it right, to make a false promise? The first can no doubt often be the case . . . Yet it becomes clear to me at once that such a maxim [of prudent false-promising] is always founded solely on fear of consequences. To tell the truth for the sake of duty is something entirely different from doing so out of concern for inconvenient results . . . [In order] to learn in the quickest way and yet unerringly the answer to 'Does a lying promise accord with duty?' I have to ask myself 'Would I really be content that my maxim (the maxim of getting out of difficulty by a false promise) should hold as a universal law (one valid for others as well as myself)?' Could I really say to myself that everyone may make a false promise if he finds himself in difficulty . . . ? I then become aware that I can indeed will to lie, but that I can by no means will a universal law of lying; for by such a law there could properly be no promises at all [. . .] '

That is, if everyone knew about a universal law of lying, no one would trust *any* promises – the whole institution of making promises would be undermined.

Kant next claims that rational nature

exists as an end in itself. All the 'objects of inclination', Kant says, have a conditional value: they're only valuable because there are certain needs and inclinations directed towards them. But rational nature itself has an unconditional value:

'. . . Persons are not merely subjective ends whose existence as an object of our actions has a value for us; they are *objective ends* – that is, things whose existence is in itself an end . . . unless this were so, nothing at all of *absolute* value would be found anywhere. But if all value were conditioned . . . then no supreme principle could be found for reason at all.

. . . Rational nature exists as an end in itself. This is the way in which a man necessarily conceives of his own existence . . . But it is also the way in which every other rational being conceives of his existence on the same rational ground which is also valid for me; it is therefore at the same time an *objective* principle . . . The practical imperative will therefore be as follows: *Act in such a way that you always treat humanity, whether in your own person or in the person of any other, never simply as a means, but always at the same time as an end*.'

Comments and questions

Kant refuses to base morality on inclinations (even an inclination like sympathy or desire to make others happy) because an individual who happened to lack that inclination could then reject morality. So why can't a purely rational individual reject reverence for the law and the unconditioned value of other rational beings?

....

....

23

Jeremy Bentham (1748–1832) on utilitarianism – from *An Introduction to the Principles of Morals and Legislation*, chs 1 and 13: 1789

Diametrically opposed to Kant's strict concept of duty is Bentham's concept of morality as a way of maximising pleasure. In the following extracts, he sets out very clearly a utilitarian standard of right and wrong.

'Nature has placed mankind under the governance of two sovereign masters, *pain* and *pleasure*. It is for them alone to point out what we ought to do, as well as to determine what we shall do . . . They govern us in all we do, in all we say, in all we think: every effort we can make to throw off our subjection, will serve but to demonstrate and confirm it. In words a man may pretend to abjure their empire: but in reality he will remain subject to it all the while. The *principle of utility* recognizes this subjection . . . Systems which attempt to question it, deal in sounds instead of sense, in caprice instead of reason, in darkness instead of light [. . .]

. . . By the principle of utility is meant that principle which approves or disapproves of every action whatsoever, according to the tendency which it appears to have to augment or diminish the happiness of the party whose interest is in question: or, what is the same thing in other words, to promote or oppose that happiness. I say of every action whatsoever; and therefore not only of every action of a private individual, but of every measure of government.

By utility is meant that property in any object, whereby it tends to produce benefit, advantage, pleasure, good, or happiness (all this in the present case comes to the same thing) or (what comes again to the same thing) to prevent the happening of mischief, pain, evil or unhappiness to the party whose interest is considered: if that party be the community in general, then the happiness of the community: if a particular individual, then the happiness of that individual.

The interest of the community is one of the most general expressions that can occur in the phraseology of morals: no wonder that the meaning of it is often lost. When it has a meaning, it is this. The community is a fictitious *body*, composed of the individual persons who are considered as constituting as it were its *members*. The interest of the community then is, what? – the sum of the interests of the several members who compose it.

It is in vain to talk of the interest of the community, without understanding what is the interest of the individual. A thing is said to promote the interest, or to be *for* the interest, of an individual, when it tends to add to the sum total of his pleasures: or, what comes to the same thing, to diminish the sum total of his pains.

An action then may be said to be conformable to the principle of utility . . . when the tendency it has to augment the happiness of the community is greater than

any it has to diminish it [. . .]

Of an action which is conformable to the principle of utility one may always say either that it is one that ought to be done, or at least that it is not one that ought not to be done. One may say also, that it is right that it should be done; at least that is not wrong it should be done: that it is a right action; at least that it is not a wrong action. When thus interpreted, the words *ought*, and *right* and *wrong*, and others of that stamp, have a meaning: when otherwise, they have none [. . .]'

Bentham is in earnest when he says that moral terms are meaningless unless interpreted as the utilitarian recommends. Utilitarianism provides a basis in experience for deciding whether an action is right or wrong, and Bentham believes – as a good empiricist – that any term which lacks this kind of basis in experience, lacks meaning.

This rigorous approach to meaning finds a counterpart in Bentham's rigorous, and radical, approach to law. Here are some remarks from later in the *Introduction*, on punishment:

'The general object which all laws have, or ought to have, in common, is to augment the total happiness of the community; and therefore, in the first place, to exclude, as far as may be, everything that tends to subtract from that happiness: in other words, to exclude mischief.

But all punishment is mischief: all punishment in itself is evil. Upon the principle of utility, if it ought at all to be admitted, it ought only to be admitted in so far as it promises to exclude some greater evil [. . .]

It is plain, therefore, that in the following cases punishment ought not to be inflicted.

Where it is *groundless*: where there is no mischief for it to prevent; the act not being mischievous upon the whole.

Where it must be *inefficacious*: where it cannot act so as to prevent the mischief.

Where it is *unprofitable*, or too *expensive*: where the mischief it would produce would be greater than what it prevented.

Where it is *needless*: where the mischief may be prevented, or cease of itself, without it: that is, at a cheaper rate.'

Comments and questions

Is it true that, when deciding whether to punish a wrong-doer, we should think only about 'excluding future mischief'? Don't people sometimes *deserve* to be punished? And should a wrong-doer's suffering in receiving his punishment be counted as 'mischief'?

....

....

Is it true that the interests of a community reduce to the pleasures of the individuals who constitute it?

....

....

Is it true that pleasure and pain determine all our actions?

....

....

Thomas Nagel (b. 1937) against utilitarianism – from 'War and Massacre', in *Mortal Questions*: Cambridge University Press, 1979

In this well-known essay, Nagel writes with honesty and realism about our moral thinking about war.

'I propose to discuss the most general moral problem raised by the conduct of warfare: the problem of means and ends. In one view, there are limits on what may be done even in the service of an end worth pursuing – and even when adherence to that restriction may be very costly. A person who acknowledges the force of such restrictions can find himself in very acute moral dilemmas. He may believe, for example, that by torturing a prisoner he can obtain information necessary to prevent a disaster, or that by obliterating one village with bombs he can halt a campaign of terrorism. If he believes that the gains from a certain measure will clearly outweigh its costs, yet still suspects that he ought not to adopt it, then he is in a dilemma produced by the conflict between two disparate categories of moral reason: categories that may be called *utilitarian* and *absolutist*.

Utilitarianism gives primacy to a concern with what will *happen*. Absolutism gives primacy to a concern with what one is *doing* . . .

Few of us are completely immune to either of these types of moral intuition, though in some people, either naturally or for doctrinal reasons, one type will be dominant and the other suppressed or weak. But it is perfectly possible to feel the force of both types of reason very strongly: in that case the moral dilemma in certain situations of crisis will be acute, and it may appear that every possible course of action or inaction is unacceptable [. . .]

Utilitarianism says that one should try, either individually or through institutions, to maximize good and minimize evil (the definition of these categories need not enter into the schematic formulation of the view), and that if faced with the possibility of preventing a great evil by producing a lesser, one should choose the lesser evil . . . [Utilitarianism] continues to leave large portions of ethics unaccounted for. I do not suggest that some form of absolutism can account for them all, only that an examination of absolutism will lead us to see the complexity, and perhaps the incoherence, of our moral ideas [. . .]

While not every conflict between absolutism and utilitarianism creates an insoluble dilemma, and while it seems to me certainly right to adhere to absolutist restrictions unless the utilitarian considerations favouring violation are overpoweringly weighty and extremely certain – nevertheless, when that special condition is met, it may become impossible to adhere to an absolutist position. What I shall offer, then, is a somewhat qualified defence of absolutism. I believe it underlies a valid and fundamental type of moral judgement – which cannot be reduced to or overridden by other principles. And while there may be other principles just as fundamental, it is particularly important not to lose confidence in our absolutist intuitions, for they are often the only barrier

before the abyss of utilitarian apologetics for large-scale murder [. . .]

The philosopher who has done most to advance contemporary discussion of such a view . . . is G.E.M. Anscombe. In 1958 Miss Anscombe published a pamphlet entitled *Mr Truman's Degree*, on the occasion of an award by Oxford University of an honorary doctorate to Harry Truman. The pamphlet explained why she had opposed the decision to award that degree, recounted the story of her unsuccessful opposition, and offered some reflections on Truman's decision to drop atom bombs on Hiroshima and Nagasaki, and on the difference between murder and allowable killing in warfare. She pointed out that the policy of deliberately killing large numbers of civilians either as a means or as an end in itself did not originate with Truman, and was common practice among all parties during World War II for some time before Hiroshima. The Allied bombings of German cities by conventional explosives included raids which killed more civilians than did the atomic attacks; the same is true of certain fire-bomb raids on Japan.

The policy of attacking the civilian population in order to induce an enemy to surrender, or to damage his morale, seems to have been widely accepted in the civilized world, and seems to be accepted still, at least if the stakes are high enough [Nagel completed this paper in 1971, during the Vietnam war]. It gives evidence of a moral conviction that the deliberate killing of non-combatants – women, children, old people – is permissible if enough can be gained by it. This follows from the more general position that any means can in principle be justified if it leads to a sufficiently worthy end. Such an attitude is evident not only in the more spectacular current weapons systems, but also in the day-to-day conduct of the non-global war in Indo-China ... An absolutist position opposes to this the view that certain acts cannot be justified no matter what the consequences. Among those acts is murder – the deliberate killing of the harmless [...]

Many people feel, without being able to say much more about it, that something has gone seriously wrong when certain measures are admitted into consideration in the first place. The fundamental mistake is made there ... An account of absolutism might help us to understand this. If it is not allowable to *do* certain things, such as killing unarmed prisoners or civilians, then no argument about what will happen if one does not do them can show that doing them would be all right.

Absolutism does not, of course, require one to ignore the consequences of one's acts. It operates as a limitation on utilitarian reasoning, not as a substitute for it. An absolutist can be expected to try to maximize good and minimize evil, so long as this does not require him to transgress an absolute prohibition like that against murder. But when such a conflict occurs, the prohibition takes complete precedence over any consideration of consequences ...

... Once the door is opened to calculation of utility and national interest, the usual speculations about the future of freedom, peace and economic prosperity can be brought to bear to ease the consciences of those responsible for a certain number of charred babies.

For this reason alone it is important to decide what is wrong with the frame of mind which allows such arguments to begin.

But it is also important to understand absolutism in the cases where it genuinely conflicts with utility. Despite its appeal, it is a paradoxical position, for it can require that one refrain from choosing the lesser of two evils when that is the only choice one has. And it is additionally paradoxical because, unlike pacifism, it permits one to do horrible things to people in some circumstances but not in others [...]

... let me remark on a frequent criticism of absolutism that depends on a misunderstanding. It is sometimes suggested that such prohibitions depend on a kind of moral self-interest, a primary obligation to preserve one's own moral purity, to keep one's hands clean no matter what happens to the rest of the world. If this were the position, it might be exposed to the charge of self-indulgence. After all, what gives one man a right to put the purity of his soul or the cleanness of his hands above the lives or welfare of large numbers of other people? It might be argued that a public servant like Truman has no right to put himself first in this way; therefore if he is convinced that the alternatives would be worse, he must give the order to drop the bombs, and take the burden of those deaths on himself, as he must do other distasteful things for the general good.

But there are two confusions behind the view that moral self-interest underlies moral absolutism. First, it is a confusion to suggest that the need to preserve one's moral purity might be the *source* of an obligation. For if by committing murder one sacrifices one's moral purity or integrity, that can only be because there is *already* something wrong with murder. The general reason against committing murder cannot therefore be merely that it makes one an immoral person. Secondly, the notion that one might sacrifice one's moral integrity justifiably, in the service of a sufficiently worthy end, is an incoherent notion. For if one were justified in making such a sacrifice (or even morally required to make it), then one would not be sacrificing one's moral integrity by adopting that course: one would be preserving it [...]

Absolutist restrictions in warfare appear to be of two types: restrictions on the class of persons at whom aggression or violence may be directed and restrictions on the manner of attack, given that the object falls within that class. These can be combined, however, under the principle that hostile treatment of any person must be justified in terms of something *about that person* which makes the treatment appropriate. Hostility is a personal relation, and it must be suited to its target [...]

There seems to be a perfectly natural conception of the distinction between fighting clean and fighting dirty. To fight dirty is to direct one's hostility or aggression not at its proper object, but at a peripheral target which may be more vulnerable, and through which the proper object can be attacked indirectly. This applies in a fist fight, an election campaign, a duel, or a philosophical argument. If the concept is general enough to apply to all these matters, it should apply to war – both to the conduct of individual soldiers and to the conduct of nations [...]

The importance of such restrictions may vary with the seriousness of the case; and what is unjustifiable in one case may be justified in a more extreme one. But they all derive from a single principle: that hostility or aggression should be directed at its true object. This means both that it should be directed at the person or persons who provoke it and that it should aim more specifically at what is provocative about them. The second condition will determine what form the hostility may appropriately take.

It is evident that some idea of the relation in which one should stand to other people underlies this principle, but the idea is difficult to state. I believe it is roughly this: whatever one does to another person intentionally must be aimed at him as a subject, with the intention that he receive it as a subject. It should manifest an attitude to *him* rather than just to the situation, and he should be able to recognize it and identify himself as its object [...]

If absolutism is to defend its claim to priority over considerations of utility, it must hold that the maintenance of a direct inter-personal response to the people one deals with is a requirement which no advantages can justify one in abandoning. The requirement is absolute only if it rules out any calculation of what would justify its violation. I have said earlier that there may be circumstances so extreme that they render an absolutist position untenable. One may find then that one has no choice but to do something terrible. Nevertheless, even in such cases absolutism retains its force in that one cannot claim *justification* for the violation. It does not become *all right*.

As a tentative effort to explain this, let me try to connect absolutist limitations with the possibility of justifying *to the victim* what is being done to him. If one abandons a person in the course of rescuing several others from a fire or a sinking ship, one *could* say to him, 'You understand, I have to leave you to save the others.' Similarly, if one subjects an unwilling child to a painful surgical procedure, one can say to him, 'If you could understand, you would realize that I am doing this to help you.' One could *even* say, as one bayonets an enemy soldier, 'It's either you or me.' But one cannot really say while torturing a prisoner, 'You understand, I have to pull out your finger-nails because it is absolutely essential that we have the names of your confederates'; nor can one say to the victims of Hiroshima, 'You understand, we have to incinerate you to provide the Japanese government with an incentive to surrender.'

...The suggestion needs much more development; but it may help us to understand how there may be requirements which are absolute in the sense that there can be no justification for violating them. If the justification for what one did to another person had to be such that it could be offered to him specifically, rather than just to the world at large, that would be a significant source of restraint [...]

...the same conditions of appropriateness to the true object of hostility should limit the scope of attacks on an enemy country: its economy, agriculture, transportation system, and so forth. Even if the parties to a military conflict are considered to be not armies or governments but entire nations (which is usually a grave error), that does not justify one nation in warring against every aspect or element of another nation. That is not justified in a conflict between individuals, and nations are even more complex than individuals, so the same reasons apply. Like a human being, a nation is engaged in countless other pursuits while waging war, and it is not in those respects that it is an enemy [...]

Having described the elements of the absolutist position, we now must return to the conflict between it and utilitarianism. Even if certain types of dirty tactics become acceptable when the stakes are high enough, the most serious of the prohibited acts, like murder and torture, are not just supposed to require unusually strong justification. They are supposed *never* to be done, because no quantity of resulting benefit is thought capable of *justifying* such treatment of a person.

The fact remains that when an absolutist knows or believes that the utilitarian cost of refusing to adopt a prohibited course will be very high, he may hold to his refusal to adopt it, but he will find it difficult to feel that a moral dilemma has been satisfactorily resolved. The same may be true of someone who rejects an absolutist requirement and adopts instead the course yielding the most acceptable consequences. In either case, it is possible to feel that one has acted for reasons insufficient to justify violation of the opposing principle. In situations of deadly conflict, particularly where a weaker party is threatened with annihilation or enslavement by a stronger one, the argument for resorting to atrocities can be powerful, and the dilemma acute [...]

Given the limitations on human action, it is naïve to suppose that there is a solution to every moral dilemma with which the world can face us. We have always known that the world is a bad place. It appears that it may be an evil place as well.'

Comments and questions

According to Nagel, some people typically think like utilitarians and others typically think in a more absolutist way. Do you

— 74 —

detect a pattern of either kind in your own moral thinking?

....

....

Nagel says that absolutism cannot be reduced to any other principle. However, a utilitarian might claim that it is best for human happiness overall if we accept rules forbidding certain actions in all normal circumstances (see Glossary or *SP*, p. 75). On this view, apparently absolute prohibitions would derive from considerations of utility. Do you think Nagel's absolutism can be derived from utilitarianism in this way?

....

....

Suppose we accept Nagel's idea that absolute prohibitions are based on the idea of treating people as 'subjects'. Can we then argue that this principle underlies utilitarianism, since it is only when we see people as subjects that their happiness becomes an end worth striving for? Would this argument – if correct – show absolutism to be more fundamental than utilitarianism?

....

....

If neither of these attempted derivations works, does that mean that there are real situations of unresolvable moral conflict – in which *anything* we do will be morally wrong in a fundamental way?

....

....

G.E.M. Anscombe (b. 1919) on 'ought' and 'should' – from 'Modern Moral Philosophy': *Philosophy* XXXIII, 1958

In this bold and subtle essay, Anscombe suggests that 'the concepts of *moral* obligation and *moral* duty . . . and of what is *morally* right and wrong, and of the *moral* sense of 'ought', ought to be jettisoned if this is psychologically possible.' Anscombe takes her lead from a famous remark by Hume, to the effect that writers on moral questions, at some point in their argument, shift from statements which use 'is' and 'is not', to statements which use 'ought' and 'ought not'. Hume claims to be puzzled about the relation between these two kinds of statements. People write, he says, as if we can logically infer from 'is' to 'ought', though deduction here is 'altogether inconceivable'.

Anscombe believes that one of the ideas underlying Hume's remark is that the specifically moral sense of the word 'ought' (and related words) has lost contact with the kind of reasoning which made it possible.

'The terms 'should' or 'ought' or 'needs' relate to good and bad: e.g. machinery needs oil, or should or ought to be oiled, in that running without oil is bad for it, or it runs badly without oil. According to this conception, of course, 'should' and 'ought' are not used in a special 'moral' sense . . . But they have now acquired a special so-called 'moral' sense – i.e. a sense in which they imply some absolute verdict . . .

The ordinary (and quite indispensable) terms 'should', 'needs', 'ought', 'must' – acquired this special sense by being equated in the relevant contexts with 'is obliged', or 'is bound', or 'is required to', in the sense in which one can be obliged or bound by law . . .

How did this come about? The answer is in history: between Aristotle and us came Christianity, with its *law* conception of ethics. For Christianity derived its ethical notions from the Torah . . .

In consequence of the dominance of Christianity for many centuries, the concepts of being bound, permitted or excused became deeply embedded in our language and thought . . .

To have a law conception of ethics is to hold that what is needed [to be good] . . . is required by divine law. Naturally it is not possible to have such a conception unless you believe in God as a law-giver; like Jews, Stoics, and Christians. But if such a conception is dominant for many centuries, and then is given up, it is a natural result that the concepts of 'obligation', of being bound or required as by a law, should remain though they had lost their root; and if the word 'ought' has become invested in certain contexts with the sense of 'obligation' it too will remain to be spoken with a special emphasis and a special feeling in these contexts.

It is as if the notion 'criminal' were to remain when criminal law and criminal courts had been abolished and forgotten. A Hume discovering this situation might conclude that there was a special sentiment, expressed by 'criminal', which alone gave the word its sense. So Hume discovered the situation in which the notion 'obligation' survived, and the notion 'ought' was invested with that peculiar . . . 'moral' sense, but in which the belief in divine law had long since been abandoned: for it was substantially given up among Protestants at the time of the Reformation. The situation, if I am right, was the interesting one of the survival of a concept outside the framework of thought that made it a really intelligible one.

. . . it *must* be impossible to infer 'needs' or 'ought to be' from 'is' [as Hume claimed]. But in the case of a plant, let us say, the inference from 'is' to 'needs' is certainly not in the least dubious. It is interesting and worth examining; but not at all fishy . . .

. . . [there is] a transition from 'is' to 'owes' and from 'is' to 'needs': but only [if] 'owes' and 'needs' sentences express a *kind* of truths, a *kind* of facts. And it remains impossible to infer '*morally ought*' from 'is' sentences.'

Anscombe is saying that we *can* properly infer from, for example, 'This is a nasturtium' to 'This needs water twice a week' without using any hidden evaluative premises such as 'Nasturtiums are lovely' or 'It's important that this nasturtium should thrive.' Any hidden premises (about the prevailing conditions, variety of nasturtium etc) can be purely factual.

She also agrees with the usual view, that we *cannot* properly infer from 'He committed murder' to 'He (morally) ought to be punished' without some hidden evaluative premiss such as 'Murderers ought to be punished' or 'It's not right for murderers to escape punishment'.

Anscombe now goes further than this, however, claiming that this inference (even with the evaluative premiss made explicit) is not really possible:

'[For inference,] a real predicate is required, not just a word containing no intelligible thought: a word retaining the suggestion of force, and apt to have a strong psychological effect, but which no longer signifies a real concept at all [is useless for inference] . . .

. . . where one does not think there is a judge or a law, the notion of a verdict may retain its psychological effect, but not its meaning . . .

I should judge that Hume and our present-day ethicists had done a very considerable service by showing that no content could be found in the notion 'morally ought'; if it were not that the latter philosophers try to find an alternative (very fishy) content and to retain the psychological force of the term. It would be most reasonable to drop it. It has no reasonable sense outside a law conception of ethics; they are not going to maintain such a conception; and you can do ethics without it, as is shown by the example of Aristotle. It would be a great improvement if, instead of 'morally wrong', one always named a genus such as 'untruthful', 'unchaste', 'unjust' . . .'

Anscombe now argues that this 'very fishy' alternative is consequentialism of one kind or another – the view, namely, that '"the right action" is the action which produces the best possible consequences'.

She writes that:

'. . . all these [modern] philosophies are quite incompatible with the Hebrew-Christian ethic. For it has been characteristic of that ethic to teach that there are certain things forbidden whatever *consequences* threaten, such as: choosing to kill the innocent for any purpose, however good; vicarious punishment; treachery . . . ; idolatry; sodomy; adultery; making a false profession of faith . . . [However], every academic philosopher since Sidgwick has written in such a way as to exclude this ethic [. . .]

[Against consequentialism] I should contend that a man is responsible for the bad consequences of his bad actions, but gets no credit for the good ones; and contrariwise is not responsible for the bad consequences of good actions [. . .]

. . . if, [to give an example of an action which is unjust regardless of the consequences], a procedure is one of judicially executing a man for what he is clearly understood not to have done, there can be absolutely no argument about the description of this as unjust. No circumstances, and no expected consequences, which do not modify the description of the procedure as one of judicially executing a man for what he is known not to have done, can modify the description of it as unjust. Someone who attempted to dispute this would only be pretending not to know what 'unjust' means: for this is a paradigm case of injustice.

And here we see the superiority of the term 'unjust' over the terms 'morally right' and 'morally wrong' . . . it appears legitimate to discuss whether it *might* be 'morally right' in some circumstances to adopt that procedure; but it cannot be argued that the procedure would in any circumstances be just.

...if someone really thinks, *in advance*, that it is open to question whether such an action as procuring the judicial execution of the innocent should be quite excluded from consideration – I do not want to argue with him; he shows a corrupt mind [...]

It may be possible, if we are resolute, to discard the notion 'morally ought', and simply return to the ordinary 'ought' ... Now if we do return to it, can't it reasonably be asked whether one might ever need to commit injustice? Of course it can. And the answers will be various ...

[But in none of these answers will it be debatable whether] the man who says 'We need such-and-such, and will only get it this way' may be a virtuous character [or] ... whether such a procedure as the judicial execution of the innocent may not in some circumstances be the 'right' one to adopt ...'

Comments and questions

Do you agree that words like 'ought' and 'should' are meaningless without belief in divine law? (Someone might argue, in favour of this claim, that a crucial part of understanding the meaning of a statement is knowing how to use it in inferences, and that we can only *infer* to statements involving 'morally ought' from statements like 'God commands it'.)

....

....

Is it a sign of a 'corrupt mind' to think that it might be morally right to procure the judicial killing of a person you know to be innocent? Can't you tell a story in which this would seem to be the 'right' thing to do?

....

....

Is it true that an agent deserves no credit for foreseen good consequences of a bad action, or blame for foreseen bad consequences of a good action?

....

....

Overview of Area 3

Area 3 deals with the related ideas of freedom and moral goodness.

In the Reading from Strawson, we saw it argued that though we cannot take a purely 'scientific' attitude to human life, neither is it necessary to posit some mysterious, unscientific agency called 'free will'. Strawson's claim is that if we stay in touch with the richness and complexity of human responses, and avoid a 'one-eyed utilitarianism' which sees human beings simply as pleasure-maximisers, we can reconcile the need for freedom with the truth of determinism.

Malcolm tried to sharpen the sense in which 'mechanism' is not a real option for us, by showing that it leads to paradoxes. If any speech act has to be understood in non-mechanistic, intentional terms, then even the speech act 'Mechanism is true' would show that mechanism is false. This leaves us with a truth we cannot state – 'a harsh, and perhaps insoluble, antinomy to human thought'.

In the next Reading, Dennett agreed with Strawson that we can compatibly accept determinism *and* an intentional attitude to human life. On the other hand, he suggested that a mechanistic stance towards human beings is not impossible for us. His opinion is that as science gets better at predicting and controlling our behaviour, the choice of stance will become increasingly open.

Max Black approaches the problem from a different angle. He believes that there is no single concept of a cause to give univocal meaning to a statement of determinism: we use many connected concepts of causality. It is therefore a mistake to suppose – as Strawson, Malcolm and Dennett do – that determinism is true. Determinism is too vague to be called either true or false. Black makes another interesting point, when he claims that the idea of 'making happen' does not threaten moral thinking, but is essential for it. If this is correct, Hume's attack on the idea of a 'necessary connexion' (in Reading 1/3) does not help reconcile determinism and freedom, as some people have thought, but profoundly undermines the idea of a human agent acting responsibly in the world.

Dretske's article makes the important point that, if we hope to rescue intentionality, it is not enough to say that a decision explains why a certain action occurred. The decision must explain the action *in virtue of* its semantic properties, not in virtue of any material properties it may happen to have. And this is possible, Dretske argues, if the thing to be explained is not that certain bodily movements occurred, but the fact that these movements were caused to occur by some internal processes. In effect, Dretske hopes to reconcile intentional explanation with determinism, by giving them different facts to explain.

Relations between these five Readings are rather complex, and the same is true of relations between the five as a group, and the other group of five Readings which make up Area 3. One way to make a connection is through the idea that an agent always does, and cannot help but do, whatever he or she perceives to be in his or her best interest. Just as our first five Readings debated whether determinism is essential or inimical to morality, so our second five put the same question about selfishness.

Hobbes, for example, believes that when we consider the consequences of an action, deciding whether to do it or not, appetites and aversions pass one after another through the mind. Hobbes claims that these are simply 'motions' (excitations) in the nervous system, which determine the resulting action.

It's natural, then, for Hobbes to make self-interest essential to morality. According to Hobbes, self-interest produces the social contract, which establishes a government, which produces laws, which create morality.

Bentham takes a similar view, arguing that the two 'sovereign masters', Pleasure and Pain, alone 'determine what we shall do'. We accept utilitarianism as the most efficient way to get as much pleasure and avoid as much pain as we can, given that there are other people around us pursuing the same goals for themselves. This is the kind of view Strawson called 'one-eyed', the kind of view which wilfully ignores real human complexity and in doing so, makes us puppets of our desires.

Against this morality of calculation and consequences, Kant set out a moral system which ascribes to us the greatest possible freedom – the freedom of a purely rational agent acting on purely rational grounds. Inclinations of any sort, even if they were self-developed or altruistic, would for Kant be irrelevant to genuinely *moral* action.

Area 3 closes with two contemporary philosophers who try to articulate in different ways what they find unacceptable in a morality of consequences. For Nagel, utilitarianism is at best incomplete, a 'one-eyed' model of only part of moral thinking. For Anscombe, the attempt to use the concept of moral goodness, based not on divine law but on consequences, results in moral thinking which is either meaningless or corrupt. Both feel that there is something inhuman about consequentialism, just as Strawson found the objective attitude 'not in our nature' and 'emotionally shocking'.

In Area 4 we will look at an equally shocking and unacceptable idea, the sceptical claim that we cannot trust our senses.

AREA 4

Knowledge

 The readings in this area discuss the sources, and the limits, of human knowledge.

26

Galileo Galilei (1564–1642) on perception – from *The Assayer*, in *Discoveries and Opinions of Galileo*: Anchor, 1957 (ed. S. Drake)

In this short extract, Galileo explains why certain properties which we take to be real and objective 'reside only in consciousness'.

'... first I must consider what it is that we call heat, as I suspect that people in general have a concept of this which is very remote from the truth. For they believe that heat is a real phenomenon, or property, or quality, which actually resides in the material by which we feel ourselves warmed. Now I say that whenever I conceive any material or corporeal substance, I immediately feel the need to think of it as bounded, and as having this or that shape; as being large or small in relation to other things, and in some specific place at any given time; as being in motion or at rest; as

touching or not touching some other body; and as being one in number, or few, or many. From these conditions I cannot separate such a substance by any stretch of my imagination. But that it must be white or red, bitter or sweet, noisy or silent and of sweet or foul odor, my mind does not feel compelled to bring in as necessary accompaniments. Without the senses as our guides, reason or imagination unaided would probably never arrive at qualities like these. Hence I think that tastes, odors, colors, and so on are no more than mere names so far as the object in which we place them is concerned, and that they reside only in consciousness. Hence if the living creatures were removed, all these qualities would be wiped away and annihilated. But since we have imposed upon them special names, distinct from those of the other and real qualities mentioned previously, we wish to believe that they really exist as actually different from those [...]

I may be able to make my notion clearer by means of some examples ... A piece of paper or a feather drawn lightly over any part of our bodies performs intrinsically the same operations of moving and touching, but by touching the eye, the nose, or the upper lip it excites in us an almost intolerable titillation, even though elsewhere it is scarcely felt. The titillation belongs entirely to us and not to the feather; if the living and sensitive body were removed it would remain no more than a mere word. I believe that no more solid an existence belongs to many qualities which we have come to attribute to physical bodies – tastes, odors, colors, and many more [...]

To excite in us tastes, odors, and sounds I believe that nothing is required in external bodies except shapes, numbers, and slow or rapid movements. I think that if ears, tongues, and noses were removed, shapes and numbers and motions would remain, but not odors or tastes or sounds. The latter, I believe, are nothing more than names when separated from living beings, just as tickling and titillation are nothing but names in the absence of such things as noses and armpits.'

Comments and questions

Is Galileo right? Are his reasons good?

....

....

27

René Descartes (1596–1650) on doubt – from *Discourse on Method*: 1637

Both the *Discourse* and the *Meditations* have an autobiographical flavour, Descartes modestly presenting his mental spring-cleaning as something he himself did, rather than as something everyone ought to do. He explains how the idea for this program occurred to him while still a young man:

 'I was then in Germany, drawn by the wars in that country, which have not yet ended; and while I was returning to the army from the coronation of the emperor, winter weather held me up and ... I remained the whole day in a room heated by a stove, attending only to my own thoughts [...]'

... I had become aware, even during my college life, that there is no opinion, however absurd and incredible, which has not been maintained by some philosopher [= scientist]; and in the course of my travels I had come to realise that some of those whose opinions are very different from ours are not barbarians or savages, but use their reason as well as we do. I remembered also that a person brought up in France or Germany will show a very different character from the same person brought up among the Chinese or among savages ... and I was thus led to believe that the ground of our opinions is far more a matter of custom and example than any certain knowledge [...]

I knew of course that, in practical matters, it is sometimes necessary to adopt, as if beyond doubt, opinions which we know to be very uncertain ... but as I then wanted to give all my attention solely to the search for truth, I thought I should adopt just the opposite principle, and reject as false all opinions I could regard as being in the least doubtful, as a way of discovering any beliefs I had which were absolutely indubitable. Accordingly, seeing that our senses sometimes deceive us, I decided to suppose that nothing really existed such as the senses present to us; and because people sometimes err in reasoning, even in the simplest matters of geometry, I decided to reject as false all the reasonings I had previously accepted as demonstrations; and finally, considering that the very same thoughts which we experience when awake may also be experienced when we are asleep and not one of them is true, I decided to suppose that everything in my mind had no more truth than the illusions of my dreams. But immediately, I saw that, though I was trying to think that everything was false, it was absolutely necessary that I, who thought this, should be something; and I realised that this truth *I think, therefore I am* was so certain that no sceptic however extravagant could possibly shake it. I concluded, therefore, that I could accept this truth as the first principle of the philosophy I was searching for.

Next, I carefully considered what I was, and as I was able to suppose that I had no body, and that there was no world in which I might exist; but at the same time I could not suppose that I did not exist, the mere fact of my thinking proving that I did exist, I concluded that I was something whose whole essence or nature consists in thinking, something which needs no place or any material thing in order to exist. In other words, this 'I', by which I am what I am, is entirely distinct from the body, is more easily known than the body, and would continue to be what it is if the body did not exist.

After this, I asked myself about the truth and certainty of a proposition; for since I had discovered one which I knew to be true, I thought I must be able to discover what gave this proposition its certainty. And as I saw in the words *I think, therefore I am* nothing which assures me of their truth except that I see with a special clarity that in order to think I must exist, I decided that I might accept it as a general principle that those things we very clearly and distinctly conceive are true – with the proviso that we must be careful to determine correctly which things we conceive distinctly.

Next, reflecting on the fact that I doubted, and that I was consequently imperfect (since I saw very clearly that it is better to know than to doubt), I began to wonder where I had got the idea of something more perfect than myself. Now thoughts of external objects, such as the sky, the earth, light, heat, and so on are not superior to me and so could depend on me . . . But the thought of something superior to me must come, not from me, but from some nature which really is more perfect than me. To receive the idea from nothing is impossible, and it's equally impossible that something more perfect should derive from something less perfect, so the idea could not have been created by me. Accordingly, it must have been placed in me by a nature more perfect than mine, and which contains within itself all the perfections I can form an idea of. The source of the idea, in a word, must have been God [. . .]

Now it is clear that falsity or imperfection cannot proceed from a perfect being . . .

And once the knowledge of God and the soul has made us certain of this rule, we can easily understand that the truth of the thoughts we experience when awake, ought not in the least to be called in question because of the illusions of our dreams . . . it is not clear to reason that what we see or imagine really exists, but it *is* clear that all our ideas or notions contain in them some truth; for otherwise it could not be that God, who is wholly perfect and truthful, would have placed them in us. And because our reasonings are never so clear or complete when we are asleep as when we are awake . . . reason further dictates that since all our thoughts cannot be true because of our partial imperfection, those possessing truth must certainly be found in the experiences of our waking moments rather than in those of our dreams.'

Comments and questions

Descartes begins, very sensibly, from the fact that many of our beliefs are not very strongly grounded. We believe lots of things, as he says, on the basis of custom and example. But instead of simply *reviewing* his beliefs and trying to find evidence for them, Decartes decides to *reject* them – in imagination at least – and demand indubitable grounds before re-admitting them. Does this pretended wholesale rejection have any advantages over a simple case-by-case review?

....

....

Are any of the steps in Descartes' reconstruction of common sense belief – from a thought to a thinker, from clarity of conception to truth, from imperfection to a perfect being, and from a perfect being to the reliability of common sense – are *any* of these steps persuasive?

....

....

In the *Meditations*, Descartes embellishes the reasons for doubt with the idea of an evil demon. He says, 'I will suppose, then, not that God who is absolutely good and the fountain of truth [rules over us], but that some evil demon, who is at the same time extremely powerful and cunning, has employed every means to deceive me.'

Is there any way to prove that this demon is not deceiving you right now?

....

....

John Locke (1632–1704) on knowledge – from *Essay Concerning Human Understanding*, **bk 4, chs 1–4, 11: 1689**

Locke believes that in all cases of knowledge or belief, the mind deals, in the first instance, only with its own ideas. A turnip does not and cannot enter your mind: when you look at one, or remember or imagine one, what appears in your mind is a *mental representation* of the turnip. Locke therefore has to say that all knowledge is, in the first place, knowledge of mental representations.

Common sense tells us, however, that we know about *turnips*, not turnip-ideas. Most of the important passage which follows, consists of attempts by Locke to get back in touch with his turnips.

'Since the mind, in all its thoughts and reasonings, has no other immediate object but its own ideas, which alone it does or can contemplate; it is evident, that our knowledge is only conversant about them.

Knowledge then seems to me to be nothing but the perception of the connexion and agreement, or disagreement and repugnancy, of any of our ideas. In this alone it consists. Where this perception [exists], there is knowledge; and where it is not, there, though we may fancy, guess, or believe, yet we always come short of knowledge [. . .]

. . . There is, indeed, another perception of the mind, employed about the particular existence of finite beings [outside] us; which going beyond bare probability . . . passes under the name of knowledge. There can be nothing more certain, than that the idea we receive from an external object is in our minds; this is intuitive knowledge. But . . . whether we can thence certainly infer the existence of any thing without us, which corresponds to that idea, is [questionable] some men think . . . because men may have such ideas in their minds, when . . . no such object affects their senses. But yet here, I think, we are provided with an evidence, that puts us past doubting: For I ask any one, whether he [is] not invincibly conscious to himself of a different perception, when he looks on the sun by day, and thinks on it by night; when he actually tastes wormwood, or smells a rose, or only thinks on that savour or odour? We as plainly find the difference there is between any idea revived in our minds by our own memory, and actually coming into our minds by our senses, as we do between any two distinct ideas. If any one say, a dream may do the same thing, and all these ideas may be produced in us without any external objects; he may please to dream that I make him this answer: 1. That it is no great matter, whether I remove his scruple or no: Where all is but dream, reasoning and arguments are of no use, truth and knowledge nothing. 2. That I believe he will allow a very manifest difference between dreaming of being in the fire, and being actually in it. But yet if he be resolved to appear so sceptical, as to maintain, that what I call being actually in the fire is nothing but a dream; and that we cannot thereby certainly know, that any such thing as fire actually exists [outside] us: I answer, that we certainly [find] that pleasure or pain follows upon the application of certain objects to us, whose existence we perceive, or dream that

we perceive by our senses; this certainty is as great as our happiness or misery, beyond which we have no concernment to know or to be. So that, I think, we may add to the two former sorts of knowledge [the mind's immediate intuition of its own ideas, and demonstration of relations between ideas] this also of the existence of particular external objects, by that perception and consciousness we have of the actual entrance of ideas from them, and allow these three degrees of knowledge, viz. intuitive, demonstrative, and sensitive: In each of which there are different degrees and ways of evidence and certainty [. . .]

. . . all the simple ideas we have, are confined (as I have shown) to those we receive from corporeal objects by sensation, and from the operations of our own minds as the objects of reflection. But how [disproportionate] these few and narrow inlets are . . . to the vast whole extent of all beings, will be [obvious to any] who are not so foolish as to think their span the measure of all things. What other simple ideas it is possible the creatures in other parts of the universe may have, by the assistance of senses and faculties more, or perfecter, than we have, or different from ours, it is not for us to determine [. . .]

It is evident the mind [does not] know . . . things immediately, but only by the intervention of the ideas it has of them. Our knowledge therefore is real, only so far as there is a conformity between our ideas and the reality of things. But what shall be here the criterion? How shall the mind, when it perceives nothing but its own ideas, know that they agree with things themselves? This, though it seems [difficult], yet, I think, there

[are] two sorts of ideas, that, we may be assured, agree with things.

. . . the first are simple ideas, which since the mind, as has been showed, can by no means make . . . must necessarily be the product of things operating on the mind in a natural way, and producing . . . those perceptions which by the wisdom and will of our maker they are ordained and adapted to. From [this] it follows, that simple ideas are not fictions of our fancies, but the natural and regular productions of things [outside] us, really operating upon us, and so carry with them all the conformity which is intended, or which our state requires . . . And this conformity between our simple ideas, and the existence of things, is sufficient for real knowledge.

Secondly, all our complex ideas, except those of substances, being archetypes of the mind's own making, not intended to be the copies of any thing, nor referred to the existence of any thing, as to their originals; cannot [lack] any conformity necessary to real knowledge. For that which is not designed to represent any thing but itself, can never be capable of a wrong representation, nor mislead us from the true apprehension of any thing, by its [unlikeness] to it . . . So that in these we cannot miss of a certain and undoubted reality . . .'

> The problem is: if all our knowledge is of ideas, how can we possibly know that these ideas represent or conform to things which are not ideas (external objects)?
>
> Locke replies that simple ideas such as the taste of pineapple or the colour green cannot be created by the mind (and we know this because, for example, a blind person has no idea of colours or a deaf person of sounds). Since these simple ideas cannot be created by the mind, they must be produced in us by something external. They may or may not *resemble* the external thing but they do at least *co-vary* with it – and that's enough to give us real knowledge of external things.
>
> Unfortunately, this looks question-begging (see p. 36). Locke takes it for granted that we have knowledge of blind people and external objects which are green – just the kind of thing he is supposed to be proving.
>
> Locke also thinks that complex ideas created by us and not intended to copy anything real, provide real knowledge. The idea of a unicorn or Mr Pickwick doesn't mislead us about the real world. But the problem was to prove conformity between ideas and things, so the fact that some ideas don't *aim* for this conformity hardly helps.

'The knowledge of our own being we have by intuition. The existence of a God reason clearly makes known to us, as has been shown.

The knowledge of the existence of any other thing, we can have only by sensation: . . . . no particular man can know the existence of any other being, [except] when by actual operating upon him, it makes itself perceived by him. For having the idea of any thing in our mind, no more proves the existence of that thing, than the picture of a man evidences his being in the world, or the visions of a dream make thereby a true history.

It is therefore the actual receiving of ideas from without, that gives us notice of the existence of other things, and makes us know that something [exists] at that time [outside] us, which causes that idea in us, though perhaps we neither know nor consider how it does it: For it [does not diminish] the certainty of our senses, and the ideas we receive by them, that we [do not] know the manner [by which] they are produced . . . I can no more doubt, whilst I write this, that I see white and black, and that something really exists, that causes that sensation in me, than that I write or move my hand; which is a certainty as great as human nature is capable of, concerning the existence of any thing, but a man's self alone, and of God.

. . . I think nobody can, in earnest, be so sceptical, as to be uncertain of the existence of those things which he sees and feels. At least, he that can doubt so far (whatever he may have with his own thoughts) will never have any controversy with me; since he can never be sure I say any thing contrary to his own opinion. As to myself, I think God has given me assurance enough of the existence of things [outside] me; since by their different application I can produce in myself both pleasure and pain, which is one great concernment of my present state. This is certain; the confidence that our faculties do not . . . deceive us is the greatest assurance we are capable of, concerning the existence of material beings . . . But besides the assurance we have from our senses themselves, that they do not err in the information they give us, of the existence of things [outside] us, when they are affected by them, we are farther confirmed in this assurance by other concurrent reasons.

First, it is plain those perceptions are produced in us by exterior causes affecting our senses; because those that [lack] the organs of any sense, never can have the ideas belonging to that sense produced in their minds. This is too evident to be doubted: And therefore we cannot but be assured, that they come in by the organs of that sense, and no other way. The organs themselves, it is plain, do not produce them, for then the eyes of a man in the dark would produce colours, and his nose smell roses in the winter: But we see nobody gets the [taste] of a pine-apple, till he goes to the Indies, where it is, and tastes it.

Secondly, because sometimes I find, that I cannot avoid having those ideas produced in my mind . . . if I turn my eyes at noon towards the sun, I cannot avoid the ideas, which the light, or sun, then produces in me . . . And therefore it must needs be some exterior cause, and the brisk acting of some objects [outside] me, whose efficacy I cannot resist, that produces those ideas in my mind, whether I [wish it or not]. Besides, there is nobody who does not perceive the difference in himself between contemplating the sun, as he has the idea of it in his memory, and actually looking upon it: . . . his perception [of this difference] is so distinct, that few of his ideas are more distinguishable one from another. And therefore he has certain knowledge that they are not both memory, or the actions of his mind, and fancies only within him; but that actual seeing has [an external] cause.

Thirdly, add to this, that many of those ideas are produced in us with pain, which afterwards we remember without the least offence. Thus the pain of heat or cold, when the idea of it is revived in our minds, gives us no disturbance; which, when felt, was very troublesome, and is again, when actually repeated . . . And we remember the pains of hunger, thirst, or the head-ache, without any pain at all; which would either never disturb us, or else constantly do it, as often as we thought of it, were there nothing more but ideas floating in our minds . . . without the real existence of things affecting us from [outside] . . .

Fourthly, our senses in many cases bear witness to the truth of each other's report, concerning the existence of sensible things [outside] us. He that sees a fire, may, if he doubt whether it be any thing more than a bare fancy, feel it too; and be convinced by putting his hand in it . . .

Thus I see, whilst I write this, I can change the appearance of the paper: And by designing the letters tell beforehand what new idea it shall exhibit the very next moment, by barely drawing my pen over it: Which will neither appear (let me fancy as much as I will) if my hands stand still; or though I move my pen, if my eyes be shut: Nor when those characters are once made on the paper, can I choose afterwards but see them as they are; that is, have the ideas of such letters as I have made. [This makes it obvious] that they are not barely the sport and play of my own imagination, when I find that the characters, that were made at the pleasure of my own thoughts, do not obey them; nor yet cease to be, whenever I shall fancy it; but continue to affect my senses constantly and regularly . . . To which if we will add, that the sight of those shall, from another man, draw such sounds, as I beforehand design they shall stand for; there will be little reason left to doubt, that those words I write do really exist [outside] me, when they cause a long series of regular sounds to affect my ears, which could not be the effect of my imagination, nor could my memory retain them in that order.

But yet, if after all this any one will be so sceptical, as to distrust his senses, and to affirm that all we see and hear, feel and taste, think and do, during our whole [life], is but the . . . deluding appearances of a long dream, [with no corresponding] reality; and therefore will question the existence of all things, or our knowledge of any thing; I must desire him to consider, that if all be a dream, then he [only] dreams that he makes the question; and so it is not [very important], that a waking man should answer him. But yet, if he pleases, he may dream that I make him this answer, that the certainty of things existing [in the natural world], when we have the testimony of our senses for it, is not only as great as our frame can attain to, but as our condition needs. For our faculties being suited not to the full extent of [existence] nor to a perfect, clear, comprehensive knowledge of things free from all doubt and scruple; but to the preservation of us, in whom they are; and accommodated to the use of life; they serve to our purpose well enough, if they will but give us certain notice of those things, which are convenient or inconvenient to us. For he that sees a candle burning, and [has tested] the force of its flame, by putting his finger in it, will little doubt that this is something existing without him, which does him harm, and puts him to great pain: Which is assurance enough, when no man requires greater certainty to govern his actions by, than what is as certain as his actions themselves. And if our dreamer pleases to try, whether the glowing heat of a glass furnace be barely a wandering imagination in a drowsy man's fancy; by putting his hand into it, he may perhaps be wakened into a certainty greater than he could wish, that it is something more than bare imagination. So that this evidence is as great as we can desire, being as certain to us as our pleasure or pain, i.e. happiness or misery; beyond which we have no concernment, either of knowing or being. Such an assurance of the existence of things [outside] us is sufficient to direct us in attaining the good, and avoiding the evil, which is caused by them; which is [what concerns us in] being made acquainted with them.

In [conclusion] then, when our senses do actually convey into our understandings any idea, we cannot but be satisfied that . . . something [does] at that time really exist [outside] us, which does affect our senses, and by them give notice of itself to our apprehensive faculties, and actually produce that idea which we then perceive: And we cannot so far distrust their testimony, as to doubt, that such collections of simple ideas, as we have observed by our senses to be united together, do really exist together.'

Comments and questions

According to Locke, sensations of touch or pain are also ideas. If you put your finger into a candle flame, you have, in addition to the visual ideas of the colour and movement of the flame, tactile ideas of heat and pain. Does the addition of these tactile ideas prove that the visual ideas of colour and movement have a real external cause?

....

....

Locke several times asserts that if we

know enough to 'attain the good' and avoid evil, that's all the knowledge we can reasonably ask for. On Locke's account, this comes down to an ability to generate pleasant ideas in our own minds, and avoid unpleasant ones. Does this 'cognitive hedonism' really constitute *knowledge*?

....

....

Throughout this passage, Locke pictures the sceptic as a pretentious and foolish adversary, whose questions he can barely be bothered with. Would it be more accurate to say that scepticism is an unwelcome consequence of Locke's own position, which he would much prefer to disown?

....

....

Hilary Putnam (b. 1926)/Noam Chomsky (b. 1932) on innate ideas – from a series of papers reprinted in Readings in the Philosophy of Psychology, **vol. 2: Harvard University Press, 1981 (ed. Ned Block)**

There's a fundamental division in philosophy, between rationalists and empiricists. Rationalists hold that we have some information about the world, perhaps of a very general nature, which we did not acquire through experience. Empiricists hold that all our information about the world comes to us through experience (which means sensory experience of course, but also, as Locke said, our introspective experience of our own thoughts and feelings). Empiricists accept innate *capacities* and *dispositions*, but draw the line at innate *ideas*.

Both parties to this dispute regard it as fundamentally important. Locke, for example, devoted the first book of his *Essay concerning Human Understanding* entirely to arguments intended to show that we have no innate ideas, that a new-born baby is a *tabula rasa*.

Why does the disagreement matter? Because the whole empiricist programme of showing how our concepts derive from experience is a waste of time, if they *aren't* all derived, or aren't entirely derived, from experience. In case after case, the empiricist finds that a concept we seem to use cannot be derived from experience. So much the worse for the concept, the empiricist concludes. We have to give it up in favour of a concept whose derivation from experience *can* be shown.

Rationalists like Descartes and Leibniz, on the other hand, even if they have to concede that a given concept cannot be derived from experience, can stoutly refuse to give it up. We have it, they can argue, because God or evolution gave it to us. We can hold on to it, even though we cannot show where in our own experience we acquired it.

For about 250 years, the empiricists seemed to have the upper hand. Then Noam Chomsky tipped the balance in favour of innate ideas, as necessary to account for language acquisition. In very general terms, his claim was that a baby could not learn its native language if it didn't have some innate knowledge about *all* languages. Chomsky argued persuasively that learning a native language – on the basis of limited and imperfect exposure – is such an intellectual feat, that the baby needs the head start of prior knowledge. Against this, empiricists such as Hilary Putnam insisted that the same general intelligence which explains the baby's other feats of learning is enough to explain the learning of language too. Here are some extracts from their debate:

Putnam: '. . . the 'innateness hypothesis' (I.H.) is the hypothesis that the human brain is 'programmed' at birth in some quite specific and structured aspects of human natural language . . . [it says that] we should assume that the speaker has 'built in' a function which assigns weight to the grammars G1, G2, G3 . . . in a certain class S of transformational grammars [featuring 'linguistic universals' such as] 'the *active-passive* distinction . . . the presence of such major categories as *concrete noun, verb taking an abstract subject* etc.'

In short, a baby is supposed to come into the world knowing in advance that whatever language it meets will have, for example, an active-passive distinction. Putnam goes on to consider whether babies show special aptitude for learning language:

'A typical. . . . college student seriously studying a foreign language spends three hours a week in lectures. In fourteen weeks of term he is thus exposed to forty-two hours of the language. In four years he may pick up over 300 hours of the language, very little of which is actual listening to native informants. By contrast, direct method teachers estimate that 300 hours of direct-method teaching will enable one to converse fluently in a foreign language. Certainly, 600 hours ... will enable any adult to speak and read a foreign language with ease, and to use an incomparably larger vocabulary than a young child.

It will be objected that the adult does not acquire a perfect accent. So what? The adult has been speaking one way all of his life and has a huge set of habits to unlearn ...

Now the child by the time it is four or five has been exposed to vastly more than 600 hours of direct-method instruction ...'

> Putnam's argument is that learning a native language is no great feat, and so requires no improbable innate knowledge. Chomsky replied:

Chomsky: 'It seems to me that Hilary Putnam's arguments are inconclusive ... he enormously under-estimates, and in part misdescribes, the richness of structure ... the detailed properties of grammatical form ... that are acquired by the normal speaker-hearer.

Putnam's discussion of the ease of language-learning seems to me beside the point ... Suppose that Putnam were correct in believing that '... 600 hours [of direct method instruction] will enable any adult to speak and read a foreign language with ease.' We would then face the problem of explaining how, on the basis of this restricted data, the learner has succeeded in acquiring the specific and detailed knowledge that enables him to use the language with ease,

and to produce and use a range of structures of which the data presented to him constitute a minute sample.'

> Chomsky's reply, then, is to suggest that an adult learning a foreign language is *also* an intellectual feat inexplicable without prior knowledge. He goes on to consider Putnam's 'alternative approach to the problem of language acquisition':

Chomsky: '[Putnam] argues that instead of postulating an innate schematism one should attempt to account for this achievement in terms of 'general multi-purpose learning strategies'. It is these that must be innate ... Putnam is convinced, on what grounds he does not say, that the innate basis for the acquisition of language must be identical with that for acquiring any other form of knowledge, that there is nothing 'special' about the acquisition of language. A nondogmatic approach to this problem can be pursued, through the investigation of specific areas of human competence ... If we discover that the same 'learning strategies' are involved in a variety of cases, and that these suffice to account for the acquired competence, then we will have good reason to believe that Putnam's empirical hypothesis is correct ... At the moment, the only concrete proposal that is at all plausible, in my opinion, is the one sketched above. When some 'general learning strategy' is suggested, we can look into the relative adequacy of these alternatives, on empirical grounds.'

> Chomsky here claims that the difference between Putnam's 'general intelligence' and his own innate schematism is open to empirical decision. In fact, this is

rather difficult to believe, since each has already accused the opposing hypothesis of vagueness and emptiness. What empirical discovery really would swing the balance in favour of an innate schematism or general intelligence, if both can be redefined to meet such contingencies?

Putnam: '... we may well be able to discover interesting facts and laws about general intelligence without being able to describe it completely, or to model it by, say, a computer program. There may be progress in studying general intelligence without its being the case that we ever succeed in writing down a 'general learning theory' in the sense of a mathematical model of multipurpose learning [...]

It is one thing to say that we cannot scientifically explain how certain structures were produced ... and quite another to say that we now have scientific reason to postulate a large number of 'mental organs' ... Such a mental organisation would not be scientifically explicable at all; it would mean that God simply decided to produce these structures at a certain point in time because they were the ones we would need half a million (or whatever) years later ... (Why should he pack our heads with a billion different 'mental organs' instead of just making us smart?) On the other hand, if our language capacity did develop bit by bit, even with jumps ... we will have conceded that *some* internalisation of linguistic rules (at least in prototype form) can be accounted for without innateness.'

Putnam's point here is that if our supposed innate language 'wiring' evolved

gradually, then it was presumably built on a degree of primitive language competence which needed no innate wiring. However, if it is supposed to have jumped into existence more or less complete, it's scientifically inexplicable. Chomsky replies:

Chomsky: '... if it can be shown that all properties of [the initial state for language learning] can be attributed to 'general intelligence', once this mysterious notion is somehow clarified, I will cheerfully agree that there are no special properties of the language faculty. But Putnam offers not even the vaguest and most imprecise hints as to the nature of 'general intelligence' or 'multipurpose learning strategies' that he believes to exist ... his claim ... has the form of an empirical hypothesis, but not the content of one [...]

... Where a rich and intricate system of belief and knowledge is rapidly attained in a uniform way on the basis of limited and degenerate evidence, it makes sense to suppose that some 'mental organ' with special design is involved, and to try to determine the nature and properties of this 'organ' ...'

Commenting on Putnam's claim that it would require a miracle for evolution to endow us with highly specific skills, Chomsky writes:

Chomsky: 'I see no miracle here ... These skills may well have arisen as a concomitant of structural properties of the brain that developed for other reasons. Suppose that there was selection for bigger brains, more cortical surface, hemispheric specialization ...

The brains that evolved might well have all sorts of special properties that are not individually selected; there would be no miracle in this, but only the normal working of evolution . . . there are innumerable problems here, but I see no need to appeal to miracles.'

Let's end with a final comment from Putnam:

Putnam: 'Chomsky admits that not all our abilities need be task-specific and specifically selected for by natural selection . . . In connection with mathematics, he speaks of 'analytic processing' ('analytic processing' is apparently all right, although 'general intelligence' is taboo), and says that our abilities in this area 'may well have arisen as a concomitant of structural properties of the brain that developed for other reasons.' I agree emphatically . . . But if this is true of mathematical ability, it could be true of linguistic ability as well.'

Comments and questions

A fundamental part of Chomsky's case is that learning a language is, not just something we want to explain, but something astonishing. It has to be something so astonishing that we could not possibly accomplish it without the help of a built-in instruction manual. Is this difference – between 'requiring explanation' and 'astonishing' – an *empirical* difference? Can it be right to say that something every normal person can do is astonishing?

·······································
·······································

Suppose the innate instruction manual contained the statement 'All human languages contain an active/passive distinction.' Can we really imagine evolution providing this information? Suppose, by contrast, that normal human beings are innately disposed to re-conceptualise, for example Katy chasing a pigeon, as a pigeon being chased by Katy. It's easier to imagine this disposition as something evolution might provide – but does the disposition contain innate knowledge about language?

·······································
·······································

George Berkeley (1685–1753) on Idealism – from *The Principles of Human Knowledge*: **1710**

Berkeley's central idea in the following extract is this: the representative theory of perception, advanced by Locke and others, claims that we know the external world indirectly, by means of ideas in our minds which *represent* external things. This is incoherent in itself, Berkeley argues, because the only existence it allows us to know of necessarily involves perception, and in spite of this, external things are supposed to exist whether they are perceived or not. It is also an invitation to scepticism, since there is no way to prove that our ideas really do represent the external things we never access directly. Fortunately, both of these crushing problems can be solved – and without any real loss or inconvenience according to Berkeley – by simply omitting the claim that there is an external world (see *SP*, pp. 90–3).

'III. That neither our thoughts, nor passions, nor ideas formed by the imagination, exist [outside] the mind, is [something] *every body will allow*. And (to me) it seems no less evident that the various sensations or ideas imprinted on the sense, however blended or combined together (that is, whatever objects they compose), cannot exist otherwise than in a mind perceiving them. I think an intuitive knowledge may be obtained of this, by any one that shall attend to *what is meant by the term exist*, when applied to sensible things. The table I write on, I say, exists, that is, I see and feel it; and if I were out of my study I should say it existed, meaning thereby that if I was in my study I might perceive it, or that some other spirit actually does perceive it. There was an odour, that is, it was smelled; there was a sound, that is to say, it was heard; a colour or figure, and it was perceived by sight or touch. This is all that I can understand by these and the like expressions. For as to what is said of the absolute existence of unthinking things without any relation to their being perceived, that seems perfectly unintelligible. Their esse [existence] is *percipi* [being perceived], nor is it possible they should have any existence, out of the minds of thinking things which perceive them.

IV. It is indeed an opinion *strangely* prevailing amongst men, that houses, mountains, rivers, and in a word sensible objects have an existence natural or real,

distinct from their being perceived by the understanding. But [no matter] how great an assurance and acquiescence . . . this principle may [enjoy] in the world; yet whoever shall find in his heart to call it in question, may, if I mistake not, perceive it to involve a manifest contradiction. For what are the forementioned objects but the things we *perceive* by sense, and what do we perceive *besides our own ideas or sensations*; and is it not plainly [impossible] that any one of these or any combination of them should exist unperceived [. . .]

VI. Some truths . . . are so near and obvious to the mind, that a man need only open his eyes to see them. Such I take this important one to be, to wit, that all the choir of heaven and furniture of the earth, in a word all those bodies which compose the mighty frame of the world, have not any subsistence without a mind, that their *being* (esse) is to be perceived or known; that consequently so long as they are not actually perceived by me, or do not exist in my mind or that of any other *created spirit*, they must either have no existence at all, *or else subsist in the mind of some eternal spirit* [. . .]

VIII. But say you, though the ideas themselves do not exist [outside] the mind, yet there may be things *like* them [of which] they are copies or resemblances, which things exist [outside] the mind, in an unthinking substance. I answer, an idea can be like nothing but an idea; a colour or figure can be like nothing but another colour or figure. If we look but ever so little into our thoughts, we shall find it impossible for us to conceive a likeness except only between our ideas. Again, I ask whether those supposed originals or external things, of which our ideas are the pictures or representations,

[are] themselves perceivable or not? If they are, *then they are ideas*, and we have gained our point; but if you say they are not, I appeal to any one whether it [makes] sense, to assert a colour is like something which is invisible; hard or soft, like something which is intangible; and so [on].

IX. Some [people] make a *distinction* between *primary* and *secondary* qualities: by the former, they mean extension, figure, motion, rest, solidity or impenetrability, and number: by the latter they denote all other sensible qualities, [such] as colours, sounds, tastes, and so forth. The ideas we have of these they acknowledge not to be the resemblances of any thing existing [outside] the mind or unperceived; but they [believe] our ideas of the primary qualities to be patterns or images of things which exist [outside] the mind, in an unthinking substance which they call *matter*. By *matter* therefore we are to understand an inert, senseless substance, in which extension, figure and motion, *do actually subsist*. But it is evident from what we have already shown, that extension, figure, and motion, are *only ideas existing in the mind*, and that an idea can be like nothing but another idea, and that consequently neither they nor their archetypes can exist in an *unperceiving* substance. Hence it is plain, that the very notion of what is called *matter*, or *corporeal substance*, involves a contradiction in it [. . .]

XIV. I shall further add, that [in the same way that] modern philosophers prove certain sensible qualities to have no existence in matter, or [outside] the mind, the same thing may be likewise proved of all other sensible qualities whatsoever. Thus, for instance, it is said that heat and cold are affections only of the mind, and not at all patterns of real beings, existing in the corporeal substances which excite them, [because] the same body which appears cold to one hand, seems warm to another. Now why may we not as well argue that figure and extension are not patterns or resemblances of qualities existing in matter, because to the same eye at different stations, or eyes of a different texture at the same station, they appear various, and cannot therefore be the images of any thing *settled and determinate* [outside] *the mind*? Again, it is proved that *sweetness* is not really in the sapid thing, because, the thing remaining unaltered, the sweetness is changed into bitter, as in case of a fever or otherwise vitiated palate. Is it not as reasonable to say, that *motion* is not [outside] the mind, since if the succession of ideas in the mind become swifter, the motion, it is acknowledged, shall appear slower without any alteration in any external object?

XV. In short, let any one consider those arguments which are thought manifestly to prove that colours and tastes exist only in the mind, and he shall find they may with equal force be brought to prove the same thing of extension, figure, and motion. Though it must be confessed, this method of arguing does not so much prove that there is no extension or colour in an outward object, as that we do not know by *sense* which is the *true* extension or colour of the object. But the arguments foregoing plainly show it to be impossible that any colour or extension at all, or other sensible quality whatsoever, should exist in an *unthinking* subject [outside] the mind, or in truth, that there should be any such thing as an outward object [. . .]

XVIII. But though, [even if] it were possible that solid, figured, moveable substances [could exist outside] the mind, corresponding to the ideas we have of bodies, yet *how is it possible for us to know this*? Either we must know it by sense, or by reason. As for our senses, by them we have the knowledge *only of our sensations*, ideas, or those things that are immediately perceived by sense, call them what you will: but they do not inform us that things exist [outside] the mind, or unperceived . . . This the materialists themselves acknowledge. It remains therefore that if we have any knowledge at all of external things, it must be by *reason*, inferring their existence from what is immediately perceived by sense. But [I do not see] what reason can induce us to believe the existence of bodies [outside] the mind, from what we perceive, since the very patrons of matter themselves do not pretend, there is *any necessary connexion betwixt them and our ideas*. I say, it is granted on all hands (and what happens in dreams, frenzies, and the like, puts it beyond dispute) that *it is possible we might be affected with all the ideas we have now, though no bodies existed* [outside us], *resembling them*. Hence it is evident the supposition of external bodies is not necessary for producing our ideas: since it is granted they are produced sometimes, and might possibly be produced always, in the same order we see them in at present, without [external bodies].

XIX. But though we might possibly have all our sensations without them, yet perhaps it may be thought *easier* to conceive and explain the *manner* of their production, by supposing external bodies in their likeness rather than otherwise; and so it might be at least probable there are such things as bodies that excite their ideas in our minds. But neither can this be said; for though we give the materialists their external bodies, they, by their own confession, are never the nearer knowing how our ideas are produced: since they own themselves unable to comprehend in what manner *body can act upon spirit*, or how it is possible it should imprint any idea in the mind. Hence it is evident, the production of ideas or sensations in our minds, can be no reason why we should [postulate] matter or corporeal substances, *since that is acknowledged to remain equally inexplicable with or without this supposition*. If therefore it were possible for bodies to exist [outside] the mind, yet to hold they do so must needs be a very precarious opinion; since it is to suppose, without any reason at all, that God has created innumerable beings *that are entirely useless, and serve to no manner of purpose* . . .

XX. In short, if there were external bodies, it is impossible we should ever come to know it; and if there were not, we might have the very same reasons to think there were that we have now. Suppose, what [is undeniably] possible, an intelligence, without the help of external bodies, to be affected with the same train of sensations or ideas that you are, imprinted in the same order and with like vividness in his mind. I ask, whether that intelligence has not all the reason to believe the existence of corporeal substances, represented by his ideas, and exciting them in his mind, that you can possibly have for believing the same thing? Of this there can be no question; which one consideration is enough to make any reasonable person suspect the strength of whatever arguments he may think himself to have for the existence of bodies [outside] the mind [. . .]

XXXVI. If any man thinks this detracts from the existence or reality of things, he is very far from understanding what has been [suggested] in the plainest terms I could think of. Take here an abstract of what has been said. There are spiritual substances, minds, or human souls, which [produce] or excite ideas in themselves at pleasure: but these are faint, weak, and unsteady in respect of others they perceive by sense, which being impressed upon them according to certain rules or laws of nature, speak themselves the effects of a mind more powerful and wise than human spirits. These latter are said to have more *reality* in them than the former: by which is meant that they are affecting, orderly, and distinct, and that they are not fictions of the mind perceiving them. And in this sense, the sun that I see by day is the real sun, and that which I imagine by night is the idea of the former. In the sense here given of *reality*, it is evident that every vegetable, star, mineral, and in general each part of the mundane system, is as much a *real being* by our principles as by any other. Whether others mean any thing by the term *reality* different from what I do, I entreat them to look into their own thoughts and see [. . .]'

Berkeley now states and answers about a dozen objections to his Idealism. He concludes:

'LXXXVIII. So long as we attribute a real existence to unthinking things, distinct from their being perceived, it is not only impossible for us to know with evidence the nature of any real unthinking being, but even that it exists. Hence it is, that we see philosophers distrust their senses, and doubt of the existence of heaven and earth, of every thing they see or feel, even of their own bodies [. . .]

CVII. After what has been [said], I think we may lay down the *following conclusions. First*, it is plain [scientists] amuse themselves in vain, when they inquire for any natural efficient cause distinct from a *mind* or *spirit. Secondly*, [since] the whole creation is the workmanship of a *wise and good agent*, it should seem to become [scientists] to employ their thoughts (contrary to what some hold) about the *final causes* [purposes, see *SP*, pp. 30–1] *of things*: and I must confess, I see no reason why pointing out *the various ends* to which natural things are adapted, and for which they were originally with unspeakable wisdom contrived, should not be thought one good way of accounting for them, and altogether worthy a [scientist]. *Thirdly* . . . no reason can be drawn [from what I have said], why the *history of nature* should not still *be studied*, and observations and experiments made . . . *Fourthly*, by a diligent observation of the phenomena within our view, we may *discover the general laws of nature, and from them deduce the other phenomena*, I do not say *demonstrate*; for all deductions of that kind depend on a supposition that the Author of nature always operates uniformly, and in a constant observance of those rules we take for principles: *which we cannot evidently know.*'

Comments and questions

When we say that something is *real*, does that only mean – as Berkeley contends – that our ideas of it are more 'affecting, orderly and distinct' than the ideas of memory or imagination? If it means more, *what* more?

....

....

Is our perception of external things mediated by internal, mental, representations of them? If it is, how do we know this?

....

....

Could Berkeley possibly be right to say that there is no external world, or is the fact that this claim is surprising to common sense enough to rule it out?

....

....

31

Thomas Reid (1710–96) against scepticism – from *An Inquiry into the Human Mind on the Principles of Common Sense*, section VII: 1764

In this section, Reid tries to balance common sense against the radical scepticism of Berkeley and Hume (see *SP*, ch. 15).

 'Bishop Berkeley has proved, beyond the possibility of reply, that we cannot by reasoning infer the existence of matter from our sensations; and the author of the 'Treatise of Human Nature' [Hume] has proved no less clearly, that we cannot by reasoning infer the existence of our own or other minds from our sensations. But are we to admit nothing but what can be proved by reasoning? Then we must be sceptics indeed, and believe nothing at all [. . .]

All reasoning must be from first principles; and for the first principles no other reason can be given but this, that, by the constitution of our nature, we are under a necessity of assenting to them. Such principles are parts of our constitution, no less than the power of thinking: reason can neither make nor destroy them; nor can it do anything without them; it is like a telescope, which may help a man to see farther, who has eyes; but, without eyes, a telescope shows nothing at all. A mathematician cannot prove the truth of his axioms, nor can he prove anything, unless he takes them for granted. We cannot prove the existence of our minds, nor even of our thoughts and sensations. A historian, or a witness, can prove nothing, unless it is taken for granted that the memory and senses may be trusted. A [scientist] can prove nothing, unless it is taken for granted that the course of nature is steady and uniform.

How or when I got such first principles, upon which I build all my reasoning, I [do not] know; for I had them before I can remember: but I am sure they are parts of my constitution, and that I cannot throw them off. That our thoughts and sensations must have a subject, which we call *ourself*, is not therefore an opinion got by reasoning, but a natural principle. The belief in it, and the very conception of it, are equally parts of our constitution. If we are deceived in it, we are deceived by Him that made us, and there is no remedy.'

Comments and questions

People have been absolutely sure of all sorts of things. Descartes and many others have thought that belief in God is part of our constitution. Kant was sure that Euclidean geometry was part of our constitution. Reid thinks that belief in a self is part of our constitution – though Buddhists believe it's a natural illusion. Is there any test for what really is part of our constitution?

....

....

We know from various animal examples that evolution sometimes puts routines into an animal's constitution which work in most cases but don't really track reality. Frogs, apparently, will eat any moving object which is roughly the shape and size of a fly. Park a frog in front of a conveyor belt of air gun pellets and it will eat them till it bursts. So even if a belief really is part of our constitution, is that a conclusive reason for accepting it?

....

....

Immanuel Kant (1724–1804) on causality – from *Prolegomena to Any Future Metaphysics*: 1783

We begin with some background information on Kant's general project in the *Prolegomena*, then give a longer extract summarising Kant's argument, against Hume, that our belief in causality has objective validity (see *SP*, ch. 14).

The *Prolegomena* is Kant's short 'popularising' account of the *Critique of Pure Reason*, giving a schematic picture of his reply to Humean scepticism. According to Hume – as Kant reads him – causal judgements and the concept of causality itself have only subjective validity: we find ourselves compelled to think in these ways, but we cannot rationally justify them. Against this, Kant wants to show that causality and the other central elements of our thinking have an *objective* validity.

In a nutshell, his reply to Hume is that these elements are valid for the world of appearances – not for the world of things as they really are – *because we supply them* in order to make the world of appearances possible. Whether this is genuinely anti-sceptical, or whether Kant deserves his title of 'the Prussian Hume', I leave to the reader to decide. (I should perhaps say that I can't see much anti-sceptical force in it myself, but others do, and there may be other ideas in Kant which promise more).

In the *Prolegomena*, Kant begins from what seems to him the indubitable fact that there are synthetic *a priori* judgements. An *a priori* judgement (opposite, *a posteriori*) is one which is not made true by something we experience: it 'carries with it apodeictical certainty, i.e. absolute necessity, [and] therefore rests on no empirical grounds.' A *synthetic* judgement (opposite, *analytic*) is one which does not merely repeat in the predicate what was already tacitly present in the subject: its predicate adds some new information to what is already presupposed in the subject. A synthetic *a priori* judgement, then, is one which carries information *about* the world, but which is not derived from experience *of* the world.

These technical terms are important because Kant is going to argue that we do have synthetic *a priori* knowledge, and that our task is to explain how this kind of knowledge is possible – the answer being that it's possible because we *bring* it to the world of appearances in order to make that world intelligible.

It might be objected here that the distinction between the world of appearances and a world of unknowable things as they really are, lets scepticism in by the back door. But Kant rejects this, saying, 'The existence of the thing that appears is thereby not destroyed, as in genuine Idealism, but it is only shown, that we cannot possibly know it by the senses, as it is in itself.'

We now need some examples of these synthetic *a priori* judgements, and for this purpose, Kant turns to mathematics and to what he calls pure natural science. He believes that a mathematical judgment like '7+5=12' is synthetic, in other words, that being equal to twelve is not part of what is already posited by summing seven and five. He writes:

'It might at first be thought that the proposition 7+5=12 is a mere analytical judgment, following from the concept of the sum of seven and five ... But on closer examination it appears that the concept of the sum of 7+5 contains merely their union in a single number, without its being at all thought what the particular

number is that unites them. The concept of twelve is by no means thought by merely thinking of the combination of seven and five; and analyse this possible sum as we may, we shall not discover twelve in the concept. We must go beyond these concepts, by calling to our aid some visualisation (*Anshauung*)' [...]

Kant thinks the same applies to the basic principles of geometry, such as the proposition that a straight line is the shortest distance between two points. The concept of 'straightness', he says, is a quality, and contains in itself nothing about a quantity like 'shortness' (implying that the predicate is not contained in the subject, and the judgement is not analytic). He writes:

'... the space of the geometer is exactly the form of sensuous intuition which we find *a priori* in us, and [which makes possible] all external appearances (according to their form), and the latter must necessarily and most rigidly agree with the propositions of the geometer, which he draws not from any fictitious concept, but from the subjective basis of all external phenomena, which is sensibility itself. In this and no other way can geometry be made secure as to the undoubted objective reality of its propositions [...]'

As for 'pure natural science', Kant thinks that although concepts like 'motion', 'impenetrability', and 'inertia' are 'not quite pure and independent of empirical sources', nevertheless, some principles of physics do 'have the required universality; for instance, the propositions that "substance is permanent", and that "every event is determined by a cause according to constant laws", and so on. These are actually universal laws of nature which subsist completely *a priori*'.

Without going into detail, we can say that history has been decidedly unkind to all these purported examples of synthetic *a priori* knowledge. And not only history – on purely philosophical grounds, Kant's examples are open to severe attack.

Why, then, does he turn to these controversial examples to establish that synthetic *a priori* knowledge exists? Simply because it would be question-begging to use as examples the judgements he's hoping to defend against Humean scepticism. Hume would obviously not accept that any of these disputed judgements 'carries with it apodeictical certainty' and so would not accept that they can properly be called *a priori*.

Kant hoped to redefine Hume's question – whether our fundamental beliefs are produced in us by Reason or the Imagination – as the question: How is synthetic *a priori* knowledge possible? Kant says, 'Metaphysics stands or falls with the solution of this problem.' There's considerable doubt, however, whether any synthetic *a priori* knowledge really exists.

So much by way of preparation. Here, at last, is Kant's summary of his argument against Hume on causality.

'27. Now we are prepared to remove Hume's doubt. He justly maintains that we cannot comprehend by reason the possibility of Causality, that is, of the reference of the existence of one thing to the existence of another, which is necessitated by the former

. . . I am very far from holding these concepts to be derived merely from experience, and the necessity represented in them, to be imaginary and a mere illusion produced in us by long habit. On the contrary, I have amply shown that they and the theorems derived from them are firmly established *a priori*, or before all experience, and have their undoubted objective value, though only with regard to experience.

28. Though I have no notion of such a connexion of things in themselves, that they can either exist as substances, or act as causes, or stand in community with others (as parts of a real whole), and I can just as little conceive such properties in appearances as such (because those concepts contain nothing that lies in the appearances, but only what the understanding alone must think): we have [nevertheless] a notion of such a connexion of representations in our understanding, and in judgments generally; consisting in this, that representations appear in one sort of judgments as subject in relation to predicates, in another as reason in relation to consequences, and in a third as parts, which constitute together a total possible cognition. Besides, we know *a priori* that without considering the representation of an object as determined in some of these respects, we can have no valid cognition of the object, and, if we should occupy ourselves about the object in itself, there is no possible attribute, by which I could know that it is determined under any of these aspects, that is, under the concept either of substance, or of cause, or (in relation to other substances) of community, for I have no notion of the possibility of such a connexion of existence. But the question is not how things in

themselves, but how the empirical cognition of things is determined, as regards the above aspects of judgments in general, that is, how things, as objects of experience, can and shall be subsumed under these concepts of the understanding. And then it is clear, that I completely comprehend not only the possibility, but also the necessity of subsuming all phenomena under these concepts, that is, of using them for principles of the possibility of experience.'

> So far, Kant has said (if I represent him correctly) that we do and must organise our experience by regarding things as holders of properties, as causes, and as parts of wholes. These points would be entirely acceptable to Hume.

'29. When making an experiment with Hume's problematical concept . . . the concept of cause, we have, in the first place, given *a priori*, by means of logic, the form of a conditional judgment in general, i.e. we have one given cognition as antecedent and another as consequence. But it is possible that in perception we may meet with a rule of relation, which runs thus: that a certain phenomenon is constantly followed by another (though not conversely), and this is a case for me to use the hypothetical judgment, and, for instance, to say, if the sun shines long enough upon a body, it grows warm. Here there is indeed as yet no necessity of connexion, or concept of cause. But I proceed and say, that if this proposition, which is merely a subjective connexion of perceptions, is to be a judgment of experience, it must be considered as necessary and universally valid. Such a proposition would be, 'the sun is by its light

the cause of heat'. The empirical rule is now considered as a law, and as valid not merely of appearances but valid of them for the purposes of a possible experience which requires universal and therefore necessarily valid rules. I therefore easily comprehend the concept of cause, as a concept necessarily belonging to the mere form of experience, and its possibility as a synthetical union of perceptions in consciousness generally; but I do not at all comprehend the possibility of a thing generally as a cause, because the concept of cause denotes a condition not at all belonging to things, but to experience. It is nothing in fact but an objectively valid cognition of appearances and of their succession, so far as the antecedent can be conjoined with the consequent according to the rule of hypothetical judgments.

30. Hence if the pure concepts of the understanding do not refer to objects of experience but to things in themselves (*noumena*), they have no significance whatever. They serve, as it were, only to decipher appearances, that we may be able to read them as experience. The principles which arise from their reference to the sensible world only serve our understanding for empirical use. Beyond this they are arbitrary combinations, without objective validity, and we can neither cognise their possibility *a priori*, nor verify their reference to objects, let alone make it intelligible by any example; because examples can only be borrowed from some possible experience, consequently the objects of these concepts can be found nowhere but in possible experience.'

> Here, Kant seems to suppose that Hume's scepticism about causality arises only if

we try to apply causal thinking to things in themselves. Hume, however, avoids the notion of things in themselves altogether, dealing only with impressions and ideas (which are, roughly speaking, mental representations arising from the senses, and mental representations arising from the memory and imagination). Kant continues:

'This complete (though to its originator unexpected) solution of Hume's problem rescues for the pure concepts of the understanding their *a priori* origin, and for the universal laws of nature their validity, as laws of the understanding, yet in such a way as to limit their use to experience, because their possibility depends solely on the reference of the understanding to experience, but with a completely reversed mode of connexion which never occurred to Hume, not by deriving them from experience, but by deriving experience from them.

This is therefore the result of all our foregoing inquiries:"All synthetical principles *a priori* are nothing more than principles of possible experience, and can never be referred to things in themselves, but to appearances as objects of experience. And hence pure mathematics as well as a pure science of nature can never be referred to anything more than mere appearances, and can only represent either that which makes experience generally possible, or else that which, as it is derived from these principles, must always be capable of being represented in some possible experience."'

Comments and questions

Suppose we grant for the sake of argument that we cannot make sense of our perceptions unless we organise them using the idea of causality, as Kant says. And suppose we tell ourselves – as forcefully as possible – that the judgements which involve this idea deal only with things as they appear to us, not with things as they really are in themselves. Does a belief become rational, or objectively valid, because:

1. You really need it

or

2. You don't pretend it's ultimately real?

For example, suppose it's not rational of me to believe that Jemima loves me. She doesn't send me Valentine's Day cards, or provide any other evidence of devotion. Does it become rational to believe that Jemima loves me after all, if:

1. I'll go literally mad with despair if she doesn't

or

2. I apply my belief only to a 'seeming-Jemima', not to the (unknowable) real girl

or

3. Both of the above?

....

....

33

David Hume (1711–76) on miracles – from *An Enquiry Concerning Human Understanding***, section X: 1748**

The following extract gives the main steps

of Hume's influential argument, in his 'Essay on Miracles', that it can never be reasonable to believe someone who tells you that a miracle has occurred. It provides a striking example, not only of scepticism carried into the heart of accepted belief, but also of Hume's poised and ironic style.

📖 'Nothing is so convenient [in matters of religion] as a decisive argument . . . which must at least silence the most arrogant bigotry and superstition, and free us from their impertinent solicitations. I flatter myself, that I have discovered an argument of [this] nature, which, if just, will, with the wise and learned, be an everlasting check to all kinds of superstitious delusion, and consequently, will be useful as long as the world endures. For so long, I presume, will the accounts of miracles and prodigies be found in all history, sacred and profane [. . .]

Though experience be our only guide in reasoning concerning matters of fact; it must be acknowledged, that this guide is not altogether infallible, but in some cases is apt to lead us into errors. One, who in our climate, should expect better weather in any week of June than in one of December, would reason justly, and conformably to experience; but it is certain, that he may happen, in the event, to find himself mistaken [. . .]

A wise man, therefore, proportions his belief to the evidence. In such conclusions as are founded on an infallible experience, he expects the event with the last degree of assurance, and regards his past experience as a full proof of the future existence of that event. In other cases, he proceeds with more caution: He weighs the opposite experiments: He considers which side is supported by the greater number of experiments: To that side he inclines, with doubt and hesitation; and when at last he fixes his judgment, the evidence exceeds not what we properly call probability [. . .]

To apply these principles to a particular instance; we may observe, that there is no species of reasoning more common, more useful, and even necessary to human life, than that which is derived from the testimony of men, and the reports of eye-witnesses and spectators . . . It will be sufficient to observe, that our assurance in any argument of this kind is derived from no other principle than our observation of the veracity of human testimony, and of the usual conformity of facts to the reports of witnesses [. . .]

And as the evidence, derived from witnesses and human testimony, is founded on past experience, so it varies with the experience, and is regarded either as a proof or a probability, according as the conjunction between any particular kind of report and any kind of object has been found to be constant or variable . . . Where this experience is not entirely uniform on any side, it is attended with an unavoidable contrariety in our judgments, and with the same opposition and mutual destruction of argument as in every other kind of evidence. We frequently hesitate concerning the reports of others. We balance the opposite circumstances, which cause any doubt or uncertainty; and when we discover a superiority on any side, we incline to it; but still with a diminution of assurance, in proportion to the force of its antagonist [. . .]

The INDIAN prince, who refused to believe the first relations concerning the effects of frost, reasoned justly; and it naturally required very strong testimony to engage his assent to facts, that arose from a state of nature, with which he was unacquainted, and which bore so little analogy to those events, of which he had had constant and uniform experience [...]

But in order to increase the probability against the testimony of witnesses, let us suppose, that the fact, which they affirm, instead of being only marvellous, is really miraculous; and suppose also, that the testimony, considered apart and in itself, amounts to an entire proof; in that case, there is proof against proof, of which the strongest must prevail, but still with a diminution of its force, in proportion to that of its antagonist [...]

A miracle is a violation of the laws of nature; and as a firm and unalterable experience has established these laws, the proof against a miracle, from the very nature of the fact, is as entire as any argument from experience can possibly be imagined. Why is it more than probable, that all men must die; that lead cannot, of itself, remain suspended in the air; that fire consumes wood, and is extinguished by water; unless it be, that these events are found agreeable to the laws of nature, and there is required a violation of these laws, or in other words, a miracle to prevent them? Nothing is esteemed a miracle, if it [happens] in the common course of nature. It is no miracle that a man, seemingly in good health, should die on a sudden: because such a kind of death, though more unusual than any other, has yet been frequently observed to happen. But it is a miracle, that a dead man should come to life; because that has never been observed, in any age or country. There must, therefore, be an uniform experience against every miraculous event, otherwise the event would not merit that appellation. And as a uniform experience amounts to a proof, there is here a direct and full proof, from the nature of the fact, against the existence of any miracle; nor can such a proof be destroyed, or the miracle rendered credible, but by an opposite proof, which is superior [...]

The plain consequence is (and it is a general maxim worthy of our attention), 'That no testimony is sufficient to establish a miracle, unless the testimony be of such a kind, that its falsehood would be more miraculous, than the fact, which it endeavours to establish: And even in that case there is a mutual destruction of arguments, and the superior only gives us an assurance suitable to that degree of force, which remains, after deducting the inferior.' When any one tells me, that he saw a dead man restored to life, I immediately consider with myself, whether it be more probable, that this person should either deceive or be deceived, or that the fact, which he relates, should really have happened. I weigh the one miracle against the other; and according to the superiority, which I discover, I pronounce my decision, and always reject the greater miracle. If the falsehood of his testimony would be more miraculous, than the event which he relates; then, and not till then, can he pretend to command my belief or opinion [...]

In the foregoing reasoning we have supposed, that the testimony, upon which a miracle is founded, may possibly amount to an entire proof, and that the falsehood of that testimony would be a real prodigy: But it is easy to show, that we have been a great deal too liberal in our concession, and that there never was a miraculous event established on so full an evidence [. . .]'

> Hume goes on to list, with examples, some of the factors which weaken the credibility of testimony. He then emphasises the extra weakness of testimony in religious cases.

'Upon the whole, then, it appears, that no testimony for any kind of miracle has ever amounted to a probability, much less to a proof; and that, even supposing it amounted to a proof, it would be opposed by another proof, derived from the very nature of the fact, which it would endeavour to establish. It is experience only, which gives authority to human testimony; and it is the same experience, which assures us of the laws of nature. When, therefore, these two kinds of experience are contrary, we have nothing to do but subtract the one from the other, and embrace an opinion, either on one side or the other, with that assurance which arises from the remainder. But according to the principle here explained, this subtraction, with regard to all popular religions, amounts to an entire annihilation; and therefore we may establish it as a maxim, that no human testimony can have such force as to prove a miracle, and make it a just foundation for any such system of religion [. . .]

I beg the limitations here made may be [noted], when I say, that a miracle can never be proved, so as to be the foundation of a system of religion. For I [admit], that otherwise, there may possibly be miracles, or violations of the usual course of nature, of such a kind as to admit of proof from human testimony; though, perhaps, it will be impossible to find any such in all the records of history. Thus, suppose, all authors, in all languages, agree, that, from the first of January 1600, there was a total darkness over the whole earth for eight days: Suppose that the tradition of this extraordinary event is still strong and lively among the people: That all travellers, who return from foreign countries, bring us accounts of the same tradition, without the least variation or contradiction: It is evident, that our [scientists], instead of doubting the fact, ought to receive it as certain, and ought to search for the causes [. . .]

But suppose, that all the historians who treat of England, should agree, that, on the first of January 1600, Queen Elizabeth died; that both before and after her death she was seen by her physicians and the whole court, as is usual with persons of her rank; that her successor was acknowledged and proclaimed by the parliament; and that, after being interred a month, she again appeared, resumed the throne, and governed England for three years: I must confess that I should be surprized at the concurrence of so many odd circumstances, but should not have the least inclination to believe so miraculous an event. I should not doubt of her pretended death, and of those other public circumstances that followed it: I should only assert it to have been pretended, and that it neither was, nor possibly could be real. You would in vain object to me the difficulty, and almost impossibility of deceiving the world in an affair of such consequence; the wisdom and solid judgment of that renowned queen; with the little or no advantage which she could reap from so poor an artifice: All this might astonish me; but I would still reply, that the knavery and folly of men are such common phenomena, that I should rather believe the most extraordinary events to arise from their concurrence, than admit of so signal a violation of the laws of nature [. . .]

But should a miracle be ascribed to any new system of religion; men, in all ages, have been so much imposed on by ridiculous stories of that kind, that this very circumstance would be a full proof of a cheat, and sufficient, with all men of sense, not only to make them reject the fact, but even reject it without farther examination. Though the Being to whom the miracle is ascribed, be, in this case, Almighty, it does not, upon that account, become a whit more probable; since it is impossible for us to know the attributes or actions of such a Being, otherwise than from the experience which we have of his productions, in the usual course of nature. This still reduces us to past observation, and obliges us to compare the instances of the violation of truth in the testimony of men, with those of the violation of the laws of nature by miracles, in order to judge which of them is most likely and probable. As the violations of truth are more common in testimony concerning religious miracles, than in that concerning any other matter of fact; this must diminish very much the authority of the former testimony, and make us form a general resolution, never to lend any attention to it, with whatever specious pretence it may be covered [. . .]

I am the better pleased with the method of reasoning here delivered, as I think it may serve to confound those dangerous friends or disguised enemies to the Christian Religion, who have undertaken to defend it by the principles of human reason. Our most holy religion is founded on Faith, not on reason; and it is a sure method of exposing it to put it to such a trial as it is, by no means,

fitted to endure. To make this more evident, let us examine those miracles, related in scripture; and not to lose ourselves in too wide a field, let us confine ourselves to such as we find in the Pentateuch, which we shall examine, according to the principles of these pretended Christians, not as the word or testimony of God himself, but as the production of a mere human writer and historian. Here then we are first to consider a book, presented to us by a barbarous and ignorant people, written in an age when they were still more barbarous, and in all probability long after the facts which it relates, corroborated by no concurring testimony, and resembling those fabulous accounts, which every nation gives of its origin. Upon reading this book, we find it full of prodigies and miracles. It gives an account of a state of the world and of human nature entirely different from the present: Of our fall from that state: Of the age of man, extended to near a thousand years: Of the destruction of the world by a deluge: Of the arbitrary choice of one people, as the favourites of heaven; and that people the countrymen of the author: Of their deliverance from bondage by prodigies the most astonishing imaginable: I desire any one to lay his hand upon his heart, and after a serious consideration declare, whether he thinks that the falsehood of such a book, supported by such a testimony, would be more extraordinary and miraculous than all the miracles it relates; which is, however, necessary to make it be received, according to the measures of probability above established [. . .]

What we have said of miracles may be applied, without any variation, to prophecies; and indeed, all prophecies are real miracles, and as such only, can be admitted as proofs of any revelation. If it did not exceed the capacity of human nature to foretell future events, it would be absurd to employ any prophecy as an argument for a divine mission or authority from heaven. So that, upon the whole, we may conclude, that the Christian Religion not only was at first attended with miracles, but even at this day cannot be believed by any reasonable person without one. Mere reason is insufficient to convince us of its veracity: And whoever is moved by Faith to assent to it, is conscious of a continued miracle in his own person, which subverts all the principles of his understanding, and gives him a determination to believe what is most contrary to custom and experience.'

Comments and Questions

Hume is surely right about the general unreliability of testimony – we do need to listen *critically* to the things people tell us. But there's something else here too. Hume seems not to allow for the fact that a good report can sometimes have advantages over the evidence of our own eyes. Good reporters can select what's significant from the mass of incidental observations, bring out the event's connections with other things, filter events through their own informed scepticism. When we accept someone as a good reporter, we sometimes *do* trust what they tell us, even over the evidence of our own eyes.

So the question is: Should we trust someone as a good reporter *only and strictly* on the basis of his or her previous reliability? In point of fact, we are often more persuaded by the person's moral character, charisma, intelligence, expertise and so on, probably because previous reliability is in many cases difficult to establish. Are we irrational to allow ourselves to be influenced by these factors?

....

....

Is it true to say that a wise man (or woman) proportions his or her belief to the evidence? Are there any cases in which it's wise to believe something more strongly than the currently available evidence suggests?

....

....

Is it correct to define a miracle as a violation of a law of nature? Would it be better to define a miracle, for example, as a very surprising or unexpected happening which has moral or religious meaning?

....

....

Bertrand Russell on knowledge – from *My Philosophical Development*, ch. 11 (Theory of Knowledge): Routledge, 1993 reprint

In this autobiographical passage, Russell explains the general requirements, as he sees them, of a satisfactory account of knowledge.

'Among the prejudices with which I had started [working on the theory of knowledge], I should enumerate six as specially important:

First. It seemed to me desirable to emphasise the continuity between animal and human minds . . . I thought that the methods adopted in interpreting animal behaviour have much more scope than is usually admitted in interpreting what in human beings would be regarded as 'thought' or 'knowledge' or 'inference' . . .

There was one region where there was a very considerable body of precise experimental knowledge. It was the region of Pavlov's observations on conditioned reflexes in dogs. These experiments led to a philosophy called Behaviourism which had a considerable vogue. The gist of this philosophy is that in psychology we are to rely wholly upon external observations and never to accept data for which the evidence is entirely derived from introspection. As a philosophy, I never felt any inclination to accept this view, but, as a method to be pursued as far as possible, I thought it valuable. I determined that I would push it as far as possible while remaining persuaded that it had very definite limits.

Second . . . I have always been deeply persuaded that, from a cosmic point of view, life and experience are causally of little importance. The world of astronomy dominates my imagination and I am very conscious of the minuteness of our planet [. . .]

. . . I cannot, like Kant, put the moral law on the same plane as the starry heavens . . . I expect, though without complete confidence, that a thorough understanding will reduce the more important causal laws to those of physics . . .

Third. I feel that the concept of 'experience' has been very much over-emphasised . . . I found, when I began to think about theory of knowledge, that none of the philosophers who emphasise 'experience' tells us what they mean by the word . . .

Fourth. I had, and have, another prejudice which works in the opposite direction from the one we have just been considering. I think that all knowledge as to what there is in the world, if it does not directly report facts known through perception or memory, must be inferred from premises of which one, at least, is known by perception or memory. I do not think that there is any wholly *a priori* method of proving the existence of anything, but I do think there are forms of probable inference which must be accepted although they cannot be *proved* by experience.

Fifth. One of the things that I realised in 1918 was that I had not paid enough attention to 'meaning' and to linguistic problems generally. It was then that I began to be aware of the many problems concerned with the relation between words and things . . . Many philosophers speak critically of the 'correspondence theory' of truth, but it has always seemed to me that, except in logic and mathematics, no other theory had any chance of being right.

I thought, also, as a consequence of my desire to preserve continuity with animal intelligence, that the importance of language, great as it is, has been over-emphasised. It seemed to me that belief and knowledge have pre-verbal forms, and that they cannot be rightly analysed if this is not realised [. . .]

Sixth. This brings me to the last of my

initial prejudices, which has been perhaps the most important in all my thinking. This is concerned with method . . . There are many who decry analysis, but it has seemed to me evident . . . that analysis gives new knowledge without destroying any of the previously existing knowledge. This applies not only to the structure of physical things, but quite as much to concepts. 'Knowledge', for example, as commonly used is a very imprecise term covering a number of different things and a number of stages from certainty to slight probability . . . '

Comments and questions

Russell's list of 'prejudices' sets out many of the tensions which still make epistemology difficult. How is the empiricism of Four to be reconciled with the apparently 'unscientific' nature of 'experience' (emphasised in Two and Three)? How is the naturalism of One to be reconciled with the importance of language stressed in Five?

....

....

Against his own second prejudice, Russell quotes the mathematician Frank Ramsay, who says, 'I don't feel the least humble before the vastness of the heavens. The stars may be large, but they cannot think or love; and these are qualities which impress me far more than size . . . '

Russell comments, 'There is no arguing about feelings.' Is that true? Do you side with Russell or Ramsay on this point?

....

....

L. Jonathan Cohen (b. 1923) on empiricism – from 'Why Should the Science of Nature be Empirical?', in *Impressions of Empiricism*: Macmillan, 1976 (ed. G. Vesey)

In this wide-ranging essay, Cohen distinguishes two kinds of empiricism and asks how the second – which holds that all our beliefs about the world must be justified by sense perception – might itself be justified.

'In the past empiricist philosophy has urged one or other or both of two interconnected, and sometimes interconfused, theses. The first has been a thesis about the causal origins of certain beliefs, the second a thesis about the proper criteria for appraising these beliefs. The causal thesis is that all beliefs about the structure and contents of the natural world are the end-product of a process that originates wholly in individual experiences of seeing, hearing, smelling, tasting, and touching. The criterial thesis is that all these beliefs are ultimately to be appraised for their truth, soundness or acceptability in terms of the data afforded by such perceptual acts . . .

. . . No small part of the point of *causal* empiricism, from the time of Hume onwards, has been to justify *criterial empiricism*. If all our knowledge originates in sensory perceptions, then – it may be argued – claims to knowledge must always be checked against appropriate perceptual data . . .

. . . I am now calling [criterial empiricism] into question in order to see how defensible it is. The more widely a principle is taken for granted, the more important that philosophers should sometimes examine its credentials [. . .]

One classical argument for criterial empiricism ran from a thesis about the nature of human thinking. According to this thesis, thinking, in its full dress form, involves a kind of imaginative recreation of perceptual experience. The elements composing our thoughts are copies of previous perceptions, and the patterns in which those elements are combined mirror actual or possible patterns in the world of our sensory experience. It follows, if this is correct, that the truth of a thought must always be appraised by reference to the perceptual realities which it purports to represent.

But, notoriously, this thesis about the nature of human thinking turned out to be untenable. Not only could it afford no satisfactory account of thoughts about logical or temporal relations, or of the difference between entertaining, affirming, questioning or desiderating the truth of a particular thought. It also failed altogether to allow for the unambiguous representation of sorts or qualities . . .

Another classical argument ran from a thesis about the nature of existence, rather than about that of thinking. At its strongest this thesis was that existence consists in being perceived, and weaker versions held, in various ways, that assertions of existence were assertions of the availability of certain perceptions under appropriate conditions. If such a phenomenalist doctrine were true, every statement about existent entities would be a statement about perceivables and thus exposed to empirical checks. Criterial empiricism would be well-founded. But even the weaker form of phenomenalist

doctrine is too difficult to reconcile with the actual course of scientific development for the doctrine to be able to underwrite the criteria of appraisal by which that development is normally assessed.

First, one has to recognise that even in its weaker form the doctrine inherits an anthropocentric point of view from its theistic origins in the philosophy of Bishop Berkeley . . . In the older, teleological framework nature existed primarily for the use and enjoyment of man . . . But a science that can locate the human species in just one of very many millions of niches within the vast ladder of terrestrial evolution, and can then locate this particular ladder of evolution within just one of very many millions of solar systems within the universe – such a science hardly coheres with the thesis that human perceptual powers are the measure of natural reality. Once the cosmological status of man has been cut down by modern science to its proper size, it is absurd to suppose that human sensory organs have any special privilege in determining what exists [. . .]

Nor will it do to generalise the doctrine of phenomenalism, in an attempt to avoid excessive anthropocentrism and allow for the exotic sensory potentials that alien intelligences may possess elsewhere in the universe and some terrestrial animals, like elephant fish, are already known to have . . . this kind of [generalised] phenomenalism would be correspondingly useless for buttressing a defence of the normal form of criterial empiricism . . . And in any case the . . . new phenomenalism is biocentric, just as the old one was anthropocentric. When one considers how small a part living organisms actually play – so far as we know – in the vast drama of the cosmos, there seems no good reason to suppose that every existence must be perceivable by some living organism [. . .]

Since therefore neither of the two classical arguments for criterial empiricism is acceptable, we must now turn to consider some other defences that have been, or might be, proposed [. . .]'

> Cohen goes on to discuss the verification principle – which claims that the meaning of a statement resides in the method by which it would be verified. He defends Ayer's verification principle from attacks by Church and Hempel, but argues that the verification of theoretical entities in science will require 'bridging propositions', linking these unobservable entities with observable experimental data. Since these bridging propositions will change as science develops, Cohen argues, verificationism cannot set fixed criteria for appraisal. What is not verifiable this year, might be verifiable next, and this means that 'the verificationist enterprise can afford no support or defence for criterial empiricism'.

'[Another line of defence] is to argue from the very great apparent success that has so far attended the orientation of science towards criterial empiricism. If – it might be said – appraisal by reference to empirical criteria has endorsed so many fruitful hypotheses, especially in the past three or four centuries, and has thus underwritten the triumphs of modern technology, there can hardly be much amiss with it as a method of checking theories about the structure and contents of the natural world.

Such an argument has an impressive force

. . . But as a defence of criterial empiricism its logic is unfortunately rather weak. First, it is inherently question-begging so far as it is concerned with scientific predictions, since the alleged successes to which it appeals are themselves apparently to be attested by empirical evidence . . . the argument would [also] be open to criticism by anyone who wanted to account for scientific achievement in a way that did not attach so much importance to procedures of empirical verification . . .

One sometimes hears criterial empiricism defended by reference to the need for scientists to employ inter-personally acceptable standards of evidence. Introspection, intuition, self-evidence, etc. all suffer, it may be claimed, from the disadvantage that on controversial issues they often tend to produce different judgments in different people . . . Perceptual sensations, on the other hand, and, above all, visual sensations, tend towards unanimity . . . Hence the validity of criterial empiricism depends, it may be said, on the indisputable objectivity of perceptual evidence . . .

But if the aim of scientific enquiry is to get as near as possible to the truth, i.e. to the description of things and their connections as they actually are, it is not at all clear why human unanimity should be intrinsic to the process. Certainly people have often in the past agreed about propositions that we should now take to be false . . .

Moreover, unanimity at the perceptual level by no means guarantees unanimity of preference in relation to theories about fundamental structures and hidden causes. An indefinitely wide variety of theories can be made to fit any given set of perceptual data, as has been remarked by Popper, Goodman and many other philosophers of science . . .

I have now examined in turn five possible defences, or justifications, of criterial empiricism. None of them, as it turns out, is tenable. So what are we to say? Is criterial empiricism some ultimate principle of human thought ... incapable of rational justification?

My argument for [criterial empiricism] will rest essentially on ... the generally accepted need for maximum comprehensiveness of scope, and economy in number, in regard to our theories about any subject-matter whatever. This is a principle that almost all modern philosophers of science, from Bacon and Whewell to Popper and Nagel, have propounded and almost all theoretical scientists have implicitly accepted. It is a principle which can be shown to be integral to all inductive reasoning [...]

... if considerations of comprehensiveness and economy are overriding, then whatever support ... may be available for a hypothesis, the overriding consideration will always be: how many different species of observable facts does it explain? The overriding criteria of merit will be empirical ones – which is what had to be shown ...

... I am not trying to labour the obvious point that this is in practice how fundamental theories are taken to be confirmed. My point is rather that the overriding need for such empirical confirmation ... follows directly from the methodological requirement of comprehensiveness and economy in the construction of fundamental hypotheses. *The need to invoke empirical criteria for the validity of our fundamental explanations is forced on us by the desire to make our explanations as unified and comprehensive as possible ...* The defence of criterial empiricism may, it seems, be based securely on the requirement of maximum comprehensiveness and economy ... it is thus inductive logic that, at bottom,

justifies empiricism, not empiricism that needs to justify the use of inductive logic or to demonstrate the rationality of inductive reasoning.'

Comments and questions

In the splendid 'sting in the tail' to this paper, Cohen suggests that Hume's problem of justifying induction is insoluble because *induction justifies empiricism*, not the other way round.

Still, Hume's dilemma can – perhaps – be resurrected. We like our theories to be as unified and as comprehensive as possible. Granted. Now, is that preference justified by empirical success, or is it just an innate hankering we find in ourselves? If it's justified by the fact that theories of that type do better in coping with the real world, then induction has been assumed after all (since we're saying in effect, 'Theories of this type have done better in the past, so they can be expected to help us in the future too'). If it's just an innate preference, perhaps evolved over the millennia, then as Cohen says, it seems like rampant anthropocentrism to suppose that the preference justifies anything objective at all. Or have I missed the point?

....

....

If Cohen's defence of criterial empricism doesn't succeed, why *do* we think all beliefs about the world have to be checked by perception?

....

....

Overview of Area 4

The general tendency of Area 4 has been a coming to terms with the fact that we know much less than we thought we did.

One aspect of the scientific revolution – evident in the Reading from Galileo – was a renewed awareness of the unreliability of our uncorrected senses. This unreliability extends, shockingly, even to our perception of colours. In truth, Galileo says, colours exist only in our minds. (In the same way, Newton refused to say that a ray of light might be red: we should say instead, he urged, that it is 'rubrific, or red-making . . . for the rays, to speak properly, are not coloured').

But if the testimony of the senses is as unreliable as this, it becomes quite natural to subject all our beliefs to severe examination. Perhaps other, equally plausible beliefs need correction too. Descartes adopts universal doubt as his method of examination, and finds his touchstone of correction, not in measurement or experiment, but in a special subjective experience of 'clarity and distinctness'.

Locke takes Descartes' extravagant doubt less seriously, and so perceives less need either for infallible foundations of knowledge, or for innate ideas as a source of knowledge. We saw a modern reprise of Locke's empiricist rejection of innate ideas in Putnam's reaction against Chomsky.

Locke also advances a representative theory of perception, according to which all our knowledge is in the first instance of our own ideas. Unfortunately, Locke didn't really see that this makes knowledge of anything else problematic in the extreme.

The reading from Berkeley brings out the problems and advances a radical solution.

The next Reading gave Reid's response to the sceptical consequences Berkeley and Hume drew from Locke's premises. Reid argues that our fundamental beliefs are part of our natural constitution, not effects of reasoning. As such, a lack of good reasons for believing them, does not (as Hume assumed) make it unreasonable to believe them.

The other great eighteenth-century reaction to scepticism is exemplified in the Reading from Kant. Kant argues – responding to Hume's analysis of causal thinking (see Reading 1/3) – that belief in causality is valid as a necessary contribution from us to the intelligibility of experience.

Following these reactions against scepticism, the Reading from Hume provided a reminder of scepticism in action, directed on this occasion against religious belief.

The final two Readings of Area 4 took a broader view of the issues. For Russell, the search for certainty was the very core of philosophy. The six requirements (or 'prejudices') he sets out, perhaps help to explain why a satisfying theory of knowledge will not come easily.

The Reading from Cohen searches for a justification for the empiricism of Locke, Berkeley, Hume and Russell, and in its very last sentence offers a surprising new 'take' on Hume's problem of induction. Since the empiricist rejection of innate ideas, and the corresponding demand for a sensory basis for all knowledge, underlie so much of epistemology, Cohen's examination of empiricism itself is a fitting end to Area 4.

Empiricism holds that all our knowledge derives from sense experience. When the knowledge we claim goes beyond the experience we have, or even beyond any experience we could possibly have, empiricism turns sceptical. Empiricism becomes a radical programme of conceptual reform, however, through the claim that even our knowledge of the *meanings of words* must have a complete basis in sense experience (*SP*, pp. 41–3) . This implies that if a word tries to go beyond what we do or might experience (like 'cause' in its ordinary sense of *making happen*) then that word must really be meaningless.

In Area 5, we will see various attempts to get the relationship between word-meanings and sense-experiences right.

Language

The readings in this area set out to explain what makes human language possible.

36

John Locke (1632–1704) on language – from *Essay Concerning Human Understanding*, bk 3, ch. 2: 1748

The concept of language offered in the following extract is certainly not original to Locke – in fact, it's probably what common sense tells us about language, if we ask – but Locke puts it on the page in a particularly clear and explicit way.

'Man, though he has great variety of thoughts . . . from which others, as well as himself, might receive profit and delight; yet they are all within his own breast, invisible and hidden from others, nor can [they] of themselves be made to appear. The comfort and advantage of society not being to be had without communication of thoughts, it was necessary that man should find out some external sensible signs, [by means of which] those invisible ideas, which

his thoughts are made up of, might be made known to others. For this purpose nothing was so fit, either for plenty or quickness, as those articulate sounds, which with so much ease and variety he found himself able to make. Thus we may conceive how words which were by nature so well adapted to that purpose, came to be made use of by men, as the signs of their ideas; not by any natural connexion that there is between particular articulate sounds and certain ideas, for then there would be but one language amongst all men; but by a voluntary imposition, whereby . . . a [particular] word is made arbitrarily the mark of [a particular] idea. The use then of words is to be sensible marks of ideas; and the ideas they stand for are their proper and immediate signification.

The use men have [for] these marks being either to record their own thoughts for the assistance of their own memory, or as it were to bring out their ideas, and lay them before the view of others; words in their primary or immediate signification stand for nothing but the ideas in the mind of him that uses them, [no matter] how imperfectly . . . or carelessly those ideas are collected from the things which they are supposed to represent. When a man speaks to another, it is [in order] that he may be understood; and the end of speech is, that those sounds, as marks, may make known his ideas to the hearer . . . Nor can any one apply them as marks, immediately to any thing else, but the ideas that he himself [has in mind]. For this would be to make them signs of his own conceptions, and yet apply them to other ideas; which would be to make them signs, and not signs, of his ideas at the same time; and so in effect to have no signification at all.

Words being voluntary signs, they cannot be voluntary signs imposed by him on things he knows not. That would be to make them signs of nothing, sounds without signification. A man cannot make his words the signs either of qualities in things, or of conceptions in the mind of another, whereof he has none in his own. Till he has some ideas of his own, he cannot suppose them to correspond with the conceptions of another man; nor can he use any signs for them: For thus they would be the signs of he knows not what, which is in truth to be the signs of nothing. But when he represents to himself other men's ideas by some of his own, if he consent to give them the same names that other men do, it is still to his own ideas; to ideas that he has, and not to ideas that he has not [. . .]

But though words as they are used by men, can properly and immediately signify nothing but the ideas that are in the mind of the speaker; yet they in their thoughts give them a secret reference to two other things.

First, They suppose their words to be marks of the ideas in the minds also of other men, with whom they communicate: For else they should talk in vain, and could not be understood, if the sounds they applied to one idea were such as by the hearer were applied to another: Which is to speak two languages. But in this, men stand not usually to examine, whether the idea they and those they discourse with have in their minds, be the same; but think it enough that they use the word, as they imagine, in the common acceptation of that language; in which they suppose, that the idea they make it a sign of is precisely the same, to which the understanding men of that country apply that name.

Secondly, Because men would not be thought to talk barely of their own imagination, but of things as really they are; therefore they often suppose the words to stand also for the reality of things . . . Though give me leave here to say, that it is a perverting the use of words, and brings unavoidable obscurity and confusion into their signification, whenever we make them stand for any thing, but those ideas we have in our own minds [. . .]

Words by long and familiar use, as has been said, come to excite in men certain ideas so constantly and readily, that they are apt to suppose a natural connexion between them. But that they signify only men's peculiar ideas, and [do so] by a perfectly arbitrary imposition, is evident in that they often fail to excite in others (even that use the same language) the same ideas we take them to be signs of: And every man has so inviolable a liberty to make words stand for what ideas he pleases, that no one has the power to make others have the same ideas in their minds that he has, when they use the same words that he does . . . It is true, common use by a tacit consent appropriates certain sounds to certain ideas . . . which so far limits the signification of that sound, that unless a man applies it to the same idea, he does not speak properly: And let me add, that unless a man's words excite the same ideas in the hearer, which he makes them stand for in speaking, he does not speak intelligibly. But whatever be the consequence of any man's using of words differently . . . this is certain, their signification, in his use of them, is limited to his ideas, and they can be signs of nothing else.'

Comments and questions

Locke repeatedly insists that words stand for ideas in the mind, the relevant idea constituting the meaning of the corresponding word. He supposes too that when one person successfully communicates with another, what happens is that the ideas in the mind of the former are duplicated in the mind of the latter.

But if Locke is right to say that ideas are 'invisible and hidden' and cannot 'be made to appear', it will be impossible to check – in any direct way – that communication ever *is* successful. Is this really a consequence of Locke's account? Is it a damaging consequence?

....

....

Locke imagines that each person knows the meaning of what he or she hears or says, by remembering which ideas should be associated with which words.

Is there anything peculiar about the idea of a remembered connection which nobody else can possibly confirm for you, and which you yourself have no way of checking? (Wittgenstein's famous 'private language argument' – though I have not attempted to take extracts from it – urges that there is something so peculiar about this as to be unintelligible. The interested reader might enjoy Wittgenstein's *Philosophical Investigations* I. 243–308).

....

....

37

Gilbert Ryle (1900–76) on Mill's theory of names – from 'The Theory of Meaning', in *British Philosophy in the Mid-Century*: **Allen and Unwin, 1957 (ed. C. A. Mace)**

In this extract, Ryle gives a clear and accessible account of the beginnings of modern 'theory of meaning'.

'We can all use the notion of *meaning*. From the moment we begin to learn to translate English into French and French into English, we realize that one expression does or does not mean the same as another. But we use the notion of meaning even earlier than that. When we read or hear something in our own language which we do not understand, we wonder what it means and ask to have its meaning explained to us [. . .]

The shopkeeper, the customer, the banker and the merchant are ordinarily under no intellectual pressure to answer or even ask the abstract questions What is purchasing power? and What are exchange-values? They are interested in the prices of things, but not yet in the abstract question What is the real nature of that which is common to two articles of the same price? Similarly, the child who tries to follow a conversation on an unfamiliar topic, and the translator who tries to render Thucydides into English are interested in what certain expressions mean. But they are not necessarily interested in the abstract questions What is it for an expression to have a meaning? or What is the nature and status of that which an expression and its translation or paraphrase are both the vehicles of [...]

For our purposes it is near enough true to say that the first influential discussion of the notion of meaning given by a modern logician was that with which John Stuart Mill opens his *System of Logic* (1843). He acknowledges debts both to Hobbes and to the Schoolmen, but we need not trace these borrowings in detail.

... it is difficult to exaggerate the influence which he exercised, for good and for ill, upon British and Continental philosophers ... Mill's theory of meaning set the questions, and in large measure, determined their answers for thinkers as different as Brentano ... Meinong and Husserl ... Bradley, Jevons, Venn, Frege, James, Peirce, Moore and Russell. This extraordinary achievement was due chiefly to the fact that Mill was original in producing a doctrine of meaning at all. The doctrine that he produced was immediately influential, partly because a doctrine was needed and partly because its inconsistencies were transparent. Nearly all of the thinkers I have listed were in vehement opposition to certain parts of Mill's doctrine, and it was the other parts of it from which they often drew their most effective weapons.

... it seemed natural to suppose that the meanings of sentences are compounds of the components, which are the meanings of their ingredient words. Word-meanings are atoms, sentence-meanings are molecules. I say that it seemed natural, but I hope soon to satisfy you that it was a tragically false start. Next Mill, again following Hobbes's lead, takes it for granted that all words, or nearly all words, are names, and this, at first, sounds very tempting. We know what it is for 'Fido' to be the name of a particular dog,

and for 'London' to be the name of a particular town. There, in front of us, is the dog or the town which has the name, so here, one feels, there is no mystery ... The assimilation of all or most other single words to names gives us, accordingly, a cosy feeling. We fancy that we know where we are ... Meanings, at least word-meanings, are nothing abstruse or remote, they are, *prima facie*, ordinary things and happenings like dogs and towns and battles.

Mill goes further. Sometimes the grammatical subject of a sentence is not a single word but a many-worded phrase, like 'the present Prime Minister' ... Mill has no qualms in classifying complex expressions like these also as names, what he calls 'many-worded names' ... So descriptive phrases are coined by us to do duty for proper names. But they are still, according to Mill, names ... [though] when Mill calls a word or phrase a 'name', he is using 'name' not, or not always, quite in the ordinary way ... A name is an expression which can be the subject of a subject-predicate sentence ... 'name', for him, does not mean merely 'proper name'. He often resisted temptations to which he subjected his successors [...]

I am still not quite sure why it seems so natural to assume that all words are names, and even that every possible grammatical subject of a sentence, one-worded or many-worded, stands to something as the proper name 'Fido' stands to the dog Fido, and, what is a further point, that the thing it stands for is what the expression means ... people still find it natural to assimilate all words to names, and the meanings of words to the bearers of those alleged names. Yet the assumption is easy to demolish.

First, if every single word were a name,

then a sentence composed of five words, say, 'three is a prime number' would be a list of the five objects named by those words. But a list, like 'Plato, Aristotle, Aquinas, Locke, Berkeley' is not a sentence. It says nothing, true or false ...

More than this. I can use the two descriptive phrases 'the Morning Star' and 'the Evening Star', as different ways of referring to Venus. But it is quite clear that the two phrases are different in meaning ... Venus is one and the same, but what the two phrases signify are different. As we shall see in a moment Mill candidly acknowledges this point and makes an important allowance for it.

Moreover, it is easy to coin descriptive phrases to which nothing at all answers [for example, 'the fastest flying carpet in the world'] ...

[Furthermore], if Hillary was, *per impossibile*, identified with what is meant by the phrase 'the first man to stand on top of Mt. Everest', it would follow that the meaning of at least one phrase was born in New Zealand, has breathed through an oxygen mask and has been decorated by Her Majesty. But this is patent nonsense ...

Finally, we should notice that most words are not nouns ... How could 'ran' or 'often' or 'and' or 'pretty' be the name of anything? They could not even be the grammatical subject of a sentence ...

Mill himself allowed that some words like 'is', 'often', 'not', 'of', and 'the' are not names, even in his hospitable use of 'name'. They cannot by themselves function as the grammatical subjects of sentences ... Yet they certainly have meanings. 'And' and 'or' have different meanings, and 'or' and the Latin 'aut' have the same meaning ...

Even more to Mill's credit was the fact that he noticed and did partial justice to the point, which I made a little while back, that two different descriptive phrases may both fit the same thing or person ...

Mill, in effect, met this point with his famous theory of denotation and connotation. Most words and descriptive phrases, according to him, do two things at once. They *denote* the things or persons that they are, as he unhappily puts it, all the names of. But they also *connote* or signify the simple or complex attributes by possessing which the thing or person denoted is fitted by the description ...

... As a thing or person can be described in various ways, the various descriptions will differ in connotation while still being identical in denotation ... They carry different bits of information or misinformation about the same thing, person or event [...]

Mill got a further important point right about ... genuine proper names [like 'Fido' or 'Mill']. He said that while most words and descriptive phrases both denote and connote, proper names only denote and do not connote. A dog may be called 'Fido', but the word 'Fido' conveys no information or misinformation about the dog's qualities, career or whereabouts, etc. There is ... no question of the word 'Fido' being paraphrased, or correctly or incorrectly translated into French. Dictionaries do not tell us what proper names mean – for the simple reason that they do not mean anything ... Proper names are arbitrary bestowals, and convey nothing true and nothing false, for they convey nothing at all.

... Saying is not naming and naming is not saying.

This brings out a most important fact. Considering the meaning (or Mill's 'connotation') of an expression is considering what can be said with it, i.e. said truly or said falsely ... In this, which is the normal sense of 'meaning', the meaning of a sub-expression like a word or phrase, is a functional factor of a range of possible assertions, questions, commands and the rest. It is tributary to sayings. It is a distinguishable common locus of a range of possible tellings, askings, advisings, etc. This precisely inverts the natural assumption with which, as I said earlier, Mill and most of us start, the assumption namely that the meanings of words and phrases can be learned, discussed and classified before consideration begins of entire sayings, such as sentences. Word-meanings do not stand to sentence-meanings as atoms to molecules ... but more nearly as the tennis racket stands to the strokes which are or may be made with it. This point, which Mill's successors and predecessors half-recognised to hold for such little words as 'if', 'or', 'all', 'the' and 'not', holds good for all significant words alike. Their significances are their roles inside actual and possible sayings. Mill's two-way doctrine, that nearly all words and phrases both denote, or are names, and connote, i.e. have significance, was therefore, in effect, though unwittingly, a coalition between an atomistic and a functionalist view of words. By an irony of fate, it was his atomistic view which was, in most quarters, accepted as gospel truth for the next fifty or seventy years.'

Ryle goes on to discuss the effects of all this on Mill's successors, up to and including the later Wittgenstein, whose posthumous *Philosophical Investigations* had been published only four years before Ryle's article.

Comments and questions

Ryle endorses Mill's view that genuine proper names only denote: they have no meaning of their own. But then, *how* do they denote? Why does the word 'Napoleon' denote *this* man and 'Wellington' *that* one? Isn't it true that we know who is denoted by 'Napoleon' because we associate a body of information with the name 'Napoleon'? And isn't this associated information, more or less, a meaning?

....

....

Ryle makes a contrast between 'atomism' (the view that words have meaning one by one, and independently of each other), and 'functionalism' (in this context, the view that the meaning of a word is a function of all the utterances in which it occurs). Another name for 'functionalism' is 'holism' (because the meanings of whole utterances are supposed to come first). Though holism seems less appealing to common sense at first sight, it has important strengths (see *SP*, pp. 142–3).

Atomism has the nice atoms-molecules analogy: independently existing word-meanings combine together to form sentence-meanings as atoms combine to form molecules. Can you think of a better analogy for holism (or functionalism) than Ryle's tennis racket?

....

....

38

Ludwig Wittgenstein (1889–1951) on proper names – from
Philosophical Investigations: **1953**

According to Mill, a proper name such as 'Aristotle' refers, but does not have meaning: it has denotation but not connotation. Gottlob Frege (1848–1925) argued that proper names *must* have meaning, or something very like it, in the following ingenious way . . .

Sometimes the same person has two proper names. For example, 'Tully' and 'Cicero' both refer to the same Roman statesman. Now compare two statements, 'Tully = Cicero' and 'Tully = Tully'. Both are true, but the first gives us information – it could give someone new knowledge – while the second tells us nothing. This means that there must be *some* difference between the name 'Tully' and the name 'Cicero'. But what could this difference be? It's plainly not a difference in denotation (since the two names have the same denotation), so it must be a difference in connotation. So names do have connotation after all: they have sense as well as reference.

According to Frege, then, proper names have 'sense'. Unfortunately, this view is also open to counter-arguments, the most serious of which is this: whenever a word has a meaning, it's possible to create statements which are true simply in virtue of that meaning. For example, the word 'bachelor' means 'an unmarried man'. Now compare:

1. All bachelors are unmarried
and

2. All bachelors are untidy.

The first is true simply because of what the word 'bachelor' means – there is no need to check it against evidence from the real world. But in order to know that the second is true (supposing for a moment that it is), we need to take evidence from the real world. We need experience of the habits of real bachelors (see *SP*, pp. 190–4 for more on these two types of statement).

So if proper names have meanings, it must be possible to create statements which are true simply in virtue of that meaning. But when we look at proper names – such as 'Aristotle' or 'Marilyn Monroe' – it seems impossible to create statements of this kind. So proper names *don't* have meaning after all.

In short, Frege's view and Mill's view seem to exhaust the field – either proper names do have meanings or they don't – and yet both seem open to serious objections. A way out of this impasse was suggested by Ludwig Wittgenstein . . .

'79. Consider this example. If one says "Moses did not exist", this may mean various things. It may mean: the Israelites did not have a single leader when they withdrew from Egypt – or: their leader was not called Moses – or: there cannot have been anyone who accomplished all that the Bible relates of Moses – or: etc. etc. We may say, following Russell: the name "Moses" can be defined by means of various descriptions. For example, as "the man who led the Israelites through the wilderness", "the man who lived at that time and place and was then called 'Moses'", "the man who as a child was taken out of the Nile by

Pharaoh's daughter" and so on. And according as we assume one definition or another the proposition "Moses did not exist" acquires a different sense, and so does every other proposition about Moses. – And if we are told "N did not exist", we do ask: "What do you mean? Do you want to say . . . or . . . etc?"

But when I make a statement about Moses, – am I always ready to substitute some *one* of these descriptions for "Moses"? I shall perhaps say: By "Moses" I understand the man who did what the Bible relates of Moses, or at any rate a good deal of it. But how much? Have I decided how much must be proved false for me to give up my proposition as false? Has the name "Moses" got a fixed and unequivocal use for me in all possible cases? – Is it not the case that I have, so to speak, a whole series of props in readiness, and am ready to lean on one if another should be taken from under me and vice versa? – Consider another case. When I say "N is dead", then something like the following may hold for the meaning of the name "N": I believe that a human being has lived, whom I (1) have seen in such-and-such places, who (2) looked like this (pictures), (3) has done such-and-such things, and (4) bore the name "N" in social life. – Asked what I understand by "N", I should enumerate all or some of these points, and different ones on different occasions. So my definition of "N" would perhaps be "the man of whom all this is true". – But if some point now proves false? – Shall I be prepared to declare the proposition "N is dead" false – even if it is only something which strikes me as incidental that has turned out false? But where are the bounds of the incidental? – If I had given a definition of the name in

such a case, I should now be ready to alter it.

And this can be expressed like this: I use the name "N" without a *fixed* meaning. (But that detracts as little from its usefulness, as it detracts from that of a table that it stands on four legs instead of three and so sometimes wobbles.)

Should it be said that I am using a word whose meaning I don't know, and so am talking nonsense? – Say what you choose, so long as it does not prevent you from seeing the facts. (And when you see them there is a good deal that you will not say.)

(The fluctuation of scientific definitions: what to-day counts as an observed concomitant of a phenomenon will to-morrow be used to define it.)'

Comments and questions

Wittgenstein points out that we tend to associate a proper name (such as 'Moses') with a loose network of information – 'loose' in the sense that if one piece of this information proves false, we can rely on the rest to pick out the reference of the name. This hints at a solution to the main problem for the Fregean view: perhaps it's impossible to create statements which are true simply in virtue of the meaning of a proper name, because that meaning consists of a loose network of information, not a single fixed definition. John Searle took and developed this hint in a classic article called 'Proper Names' (1958).

Suppose a proper name, such as 'Aristotle', successfully refers. Then, according to Searle's so-called 'cluster theory', there must be a list – large but loose – of descriptions of Aristotle . . .

D1: teacher of Alexander
D2: student of Plato
D3: bald in middle age
D4: lived in Athens
D5: born in Stagira
D6: son of a doctor
D7: author of *De Anima*
D8: spoke with a lisp, and so on.

Some of these descriptions may turn out to be false. We might discover, for example, that Aristotle was brought to Stagira as an infant, but actually born somewhere else. Nevertheless, the cluster of descriptions as a whole is more true of one particular person than of anyone else. And that's why the name 'Aristotle' denotes that particular person. Searle wrote:

> We can now resolve our paradox: does a proper name have a sense? If this asks whether or not proper names are used to describe or specify characteristics of objects, the answer is 'no'. But if it asks whether or not proper names are logically connected with characteristics of the object to which they refer, the answer is 'yes, in a loose sort of way'.

In his 1958 article, Searle regarded the network of information associated with the name as primarily descriptive, while in his 1983 book *Intentionality*, he includes perceptual information. But in both cases, the reference of the name is fixed by the network of information: the name refers to whoever (or whatever) the information is most true of.

This is certainly an improvement on the claim that a proper name is associated with a single, specific description. But does a name really 'attach' to the thing it names

because the information associated with the name is more true of that thing than of anything else?

....

....

In the final parenthesis of *PI*, Reading 79, Wittgenstein connects the 'looseness' of proper names, with a kind of 'looseness' in the meaning of a scientific term. The term 'acid', for example, has been defined in many different ways, though chemists have mostly agreed about most of the denotation of the term. Lavoisier believed (mistakenly) that all acids contain oxygen – in fact he coined the name 'oxygen' from Greek roots meaning 'originator of sharpness/acidity' – but he would have agreed with earlier and later chemists that certain paradigmatic substances such as *aqua regia* were acids.

If the meaning of the term is fixed by its definition, then (it seems to follow) when the definition changes, the meaning changes too. But in that case, the meaning of the word 'acid' changes when the theory of acids changes. A Newtonian theory of acids (based on the sharp arrow-shaped formations of corpuscles) is radically different from Lavoisier's theory, which is radically different again from G. N. Lewis's idea that acids are proton donors. And it seems to follow from this, that if the meaning of the word 'acid' has changed, the new theory and the old don't disagree – they're inevitably talking at cross purposes, 'incommensurable'. This in turn suggests that theory change is not a neat, rational process, in which the new theory clearly outperforms the old. Scientific progress comes to seem more vulnerable to non-rational influences.

Is it better to say, then, that the meaning of a scientific term is fixed by its denotation, rather than the other way round? (We'll look at a view of this kind in Reading 5/40).

....

....

39

Saul Kripke (b. 1940) on naming – from 'Naming and Necessity', in *Semantics of Natural Language*: Harvard University Press, 1980 (eds D. Davidson and G. Harman)

In this selection, Kripke takes issue with Searle's view of naming. He puts forward in its place a striking new picture, in which the reference of a name is determined by an initial 'act of baptism'.

 'According to [Searle's] view ... the referent of a name is determined not by a single description but by some cluster or family. Whatever in some sense satisfies enough or most of the family is the referent of the name [...]

... Consider Richard Feynman, to whom many of us are able to refer. He is a leading contemporary physicist. Everyone *here* (I'm sure!) can state the contents of one of Feynman's theories so as to differentiate him from Gell-Mann. However, the man in the street, not possessing these abilities, may still use the name 'Feynman.' When asked he will say: well he's a physicist or something. He

may not think this picks anyone out uniquely. I still think he uses the name 'Feynman' as a name for Feynman [...]

... Let's suppose that someone says that Gödel is the man who proved the incompleteness of arithmetic, and this man is suitably well educated and even able to give an independent account of the incompleteness theorem ...

... Imagine the following blatantly fictional situation ... Suppose that Gödel was not in fact the author of this theorem. A man named 'Schmidt,' whose body was found in Vienna under mysterious circumstances many years ago, actually did the work in question. His friend Gödel somehow got hold of the manuscript and it was thereafter attributed to Gödel. On [Searle's] view, then, when our ordinary man uses the name 'Gödel' he really means to refer to Schmidt, because Schmidt is the unique person satisfying the description, 'the man who discovered the incompleteness of arithmetic' ...

... it does not seem that if most of the [descriptions] are satisfied by a unique object, then [that object] is the referent of the name. This seems simply to be false [...]

Someone, let's say a baby, is born; his parents call him by a certain name. They talk about him to their friends. Other people meet him. Through various sorts of talk the name is spread from link to link as if by a chain. A speaker who is on the far end of this chain, who has heard about, say, Richard Feynman, in the marketplace or elsewhere, may be referring to Richard Feynman even though he can't remember from whom he first heard of Feynman ... A certain passage of communication reaching ultimately to the man himself does reach the speaker. He is then referring to Feynman even though he can't identify him uniquely ... a chain of communication going back to Feynman himself has been established, by virtue of his membership in a community which passed the name from link to link, not by a ceremony that he makes in private in his study ...

... of course not every sort of causal chain reaching from me to a certain man will do for me to make a reference. There may be a causal chain from our use of the term 'Santa Claus' to a certain historical saint, but still the children, when they use this, by this time probably do not refer to that saint. So other conditions must be satisfied in order to make this into a really rigorous theory of reference. I don't know that I'm going to do this because ... rather than giving a set of necessary and sufficient conditions which will work for a term like reference, I want to present just a *better picture* than the picture presented by the received views.

... What I think the examples I've given show is not simply that there's some technical error here or some mistake there, but that the whole picture given by this theory of how reference is determined seems to be wrong from the fundamentals.

... what is true is that it's in virtue of our connection with other speakers in the community, going back to the referent himself, that we refer to a certain man.

There may be some cases where the description picture is true ... 'Jack the Ripper' was a possible example [because police and newspapers used the name 'Jack the Ripper' to mean 'whoever committed these murders'] ... But in general this picture fails. In general our reference depends not just on what we think ourselves, but on other people in the community, the history of how

the name reached one, and things like that.

... An initial 'baptism' takes place. Here the object may be named by ostension, or the reference of the name may be fixed by a description. When the name is 'passed from link to link', the receiver of the name must, I think, intend when he learns it to use it with the same reference as the man from whom he learned it ...

... [this] hardly eliminates the notion of reference; on the contrary, it takes the notion of intending to use the same reference as a given.

To repeat, I may not have presented a theory, but I do think that I have presented a better picture ...'

Comments and questions

When someone points at a tree and says, 'Look at that!', and we look, do we acquire *descriptions* of the tree? It seems more natural to say that we acquire observations or perceptions which we might – or might not – use as the basis of descriptions.

And when someone mentions to you a name you haven't heard before, and you intend to use the name (pending further information) to refer to whoever or whatever the other person uses it to refer to, is that intention a matter of acquiring the *description* '... refers to whoever or whatever the speaker uses it to refer to'? Again, it seems that the intention is something else, though we could of course go on to describe it if we choose.

It seems then, that neither the origin of the chain nor the passing on from link to link essentially involve descriptions. Is that a serious blow to Searle's 'cluster' theory (see *SP*, pp. 134–41)?

Kripke's Feynman and Gödel examples suggest that the reference of a proper name is mostly not fixed by associated descriptions. Is that true? Which picture of naming – Searle's or Kripke's – should we adopt?

40

Hilary Putnam (b. 1926) on language – from 'Meaning and Reference': *The Journal of Philosophy*, **70/19, 1973**

In this stimulating article, Putnam argues that two people might be physically identical, might have the same verbal dispositions, might utter the same words with the same ideas in mind – and yet might mean something different. Putnam argues that this is because real-world samples on the one hand, and the opinions of experts on the other, play a role in determining the meaning of what someone says. Meaning is, at least in part, *social*.

 'For the purpose of the following science-fiction examples, we shall suppose that somewhere there is a planet we shall call Twin Earth. Twin Earth is very much like Earth: in fact, people on Twin Earth even speak *English* [. . .]

One of the peculiarites of Twin Earth is that the liquid called 'water' is not H_2O but a different liquid whose chemical formula is very long and complicated. I shall abbreviate this chemical formula simply as XYZ. I shall suppose that XYZ is indistinguishable from water at normal temperatures and pressures. Also, I shall suppose that the oceans and lakes and seas of Twin Earth contain XYZ and not water, that it rains XYZ on Twin Earth and not water etc.

If a space ship from Earth ever visits Twin Earth, then the supposition at first will be that 'water' has the same meaning on Earth and Twin Earth. This supposition will be corrected when it is discovered that 'water' on Twin Earth is XYZ, and the Earthian space ship will report somewhat as follows.

'On Twin Earth the word "water" means XYZ.'

Symmetrically, if a space ship from Twin Earth ever visits Earth, then the supposition at first will be that the word 'water' has the same meaning on Twin Earth and on Earth. This supposition will be corrected when it is discovered that 'water' on Earth is H_2O [. . .]

Now let us roll the time back to about 1750. The typical Earthian speaker of English did not know that water consisted of hydrogen and oxygen, and the typical Twin Earthian speaker of English did not know that 'water' consisted of XYZ. Let $Oscar_1$ be such a typical Earthian English speaker, and let $Oscar_2$ be his counterpart on Twin Earth. You may suppose that there is no belief that $Oscar_1$ had about water that $Oscar_2$ did not have about 'water'. If you like, you may even suppose that $Oscar_1$ and $Oscar_2$ were exact duplicates in appearance, feelings, thoughts, interior monologue, etc. Yet the extension [thing or stuff referred to] of the term 'water' was just as much H_2O on Earth in 1750 as in 1950; and the extension of the term 'water' was just as much XYZ on Twin Earth in 1750 as in 1950. Oscar$_1$ and Oscar$_2$ understood the term 'water' differently in 1750 *although they were in the same psychological state*, and although, given the state of science at the time, it would have taken their scientific communities about fifty years to discover that they understood the term 'water' differently. Thus the extension of the term 'water' (and, in fact, its 'meaning' in the intuitive preanalytical usage of that term) is *not* a function of the psychological state of the speaker by itself.'

> Putnam's claim here is that the state of the speaker's mind does not by itself determine what he or she is talking about. Locke's identification of meaning with ideas in the mind is a mistake.

'... Suppose I point to a glass of water and say 'this liquid is called water.' My 'ostensive definition' of water [asserts] ... that the necessary and sufficient condition for being water is bearing the relation *same$_L$* to the stuff in the glass ...

The key point is that the relation *same$_L$* is a *theoretical* relation: whether something is or is not the same liquid as *this* may take an indeterminate amount of scientific investigation to determine [...]

Before discussing this example further, let me introduce a *non*-science-fiction example. Suppose you are like me and cannot tell an elm from a beech tree. We still say that the extension of 'elm' in my idiolect is the same as the extension of 'elm' in anyone else's, viz., the set of all elm trees ... Thus 'elm' in my idiolect has a different extension from 'beech'

in your idiolect (as it should). Is it really credible that this difference in extension is brought about by some difference in our *concepts*? My *concept* of an elm tree is exactly the same as my concept of a beech tree (I blush to confess) ... Cut the pie any way you like, 'meanings' just ain't in the *head*!

[This example depends] upon a fact about language that seems, surprisingly, never to have been pointed out: that there is *division of linguistic labour*. We could hardly use such words as 'elm' and 'aluminium' if no one possessed a way of recognizing elm trees and aluminium metal; but not everyone to whom the distinction is important has to be able to make the distinction.

... everyone to whom gold is important for any reason has to *acquire* the word 'gold'; but he does not have to acquire the *method of recognizing* whether something is or is not gold. He can rely on a special subclass of speakers [...]

...Words like 'now', 'this', 'here' have long been recognized to be *indexical,* or *token-reflexive* – i.e., to have an extension which varies from context to context or token to token. For these words, no one has ever suggested the traditional theory that 'intension determines extension' [what you have in mind determines what you refer to].

... Our theory can be summarized as saying that words like 'water' have an unnoticed indexical element: 'water' is stuff that bears a certain similarity relation to the water *around here*. Water at another time or in another place or even in another possible world has to bear the relation *same$_L$* to our 'water' *in order to be water* ...

The theory that natural kind words like 'water' are indexical leaves it open, however, whether to say that 'water' in the Twin

Earthian dialect of English has the same *meaning* as 'water' in the Earth dialect and a different extension – which is what we normally say about 'I' in different idiolects – thereby giving up the doctrine that 'meaning (intension) determines extension', or to say, as we have chosen to do, that difference in extension is *ipso facto* a difference in meaning for natural kind words, thereby giving up the doctrine that meanings are concepts, or indeed, mental entities of *any* kind.

It should be clear, however, that Kripke's doctrine that natural kind words are rigid designators and our doctrine that they are indexical are but two ways of making the same point.

We have now seen that the extension of a term is not fixed by a concept that the individual speaker has in his head, and this is true both because extension is, in general, determined *socially* – there is division of linguistic labour as much as of 'real' labour – and because extension is, in part, determined *indexically* . . . Traditional semantic theory leaves out two contributions to the determination of reference – the contribution of society and the contribution of the real world; a better semantic theory must encompass both.'

Comments and questions

Should we say that the meaning of the word 'water' is different for Oscar₁ and Oscar₂ (as Putnam suggests), or should we say that the word means the same but turns out to refer to two different chemicals? The meaning of the word 'now' doesn't change, even though it refers to lots of different times (depending on when it's said). If we decided to say that the meaning was the

same for Oscar₁ and Oscar₂, would that seriously damage Putnam's case?

....

....

One consequence of Putnam's 'indexicality' point is that the meanings of crucial terms can remain (more or less) unchanged across theory change in science. It's easy to suppose, for example, that when the way we test for acidity changes, or when the theory explaining acidity changes, the meaning of the term 'acid' changes. This seems to imply that the old theory and the new one are really talking about different things. But if the 'old' and 'new' experts agree on samples of acids, then, on Putnam's account, at least the core of the meaning of the term is agreed between them: 'old' and 'new' experts agree that an 'acid' is something the same as *this* or *this*, whatever the true theory of acids turns out to be. In this way, 'old' and 'new' theorists can genuinely discuss the differences between them (which seems a good thing).

A consequence of the 'division of labour' point is that a person can use a term (and this applies to proper names as well as natural kind terms like 'gold') without being able to determine what the term refers to – as long as he or she can turn to someone else who *does* know how to determine the reference.

Both of these consequences require us to accept that we very often talk, without really, or fully, knowing what we mean. Is this acceptable to common sense?

....

....

41

W. V. Quine (1908–2000) on language – from 'Mind and Verbal Dispositions', in *Mind and Language*: Oxford University Press, 1975 (ed. S. Guttenplan)

Quine here provides a very clear statement of his views on language and the mind.

'Descartes supposed that man is the only animal endowed with mind; the others are automata. It is held widely and on better evidence, that man is the only animal endowed with language. Now if man is unique in enjoying these two gifts, it is no coincidence. One may argue that no mindless creature could cope with so intricate a device as language. Or one may argue conversely that no appreciable mental activity is conceivable without linguistic aids.

Most thought simply *is* speech, according to the pioneer behaviourist John B. Watson: silent, repressed, incipient speech. Not all thought is that. A geometer or an engineer may think also by means of little incipient tugs of the muscles that are used in drawing curves or twirling cogwheels. Still, the muscles that play by far the major role, according to Watson's muscular theory of meditation, are the muscles used in making speeches.

Conversely, there is an age-old and persistent tendency to try to explain and analyse the physical phenomenon of speech by appealing to mind, mental activity, and mental entities: by appealing to thoughts, ideas, meanings. Language, we are told, serves to convey ideas. We learn language from our elders by learning to associate the words with the same ideas with which our elders have learned to associate them [cf. Reading 5/36 and *SP*, pp. 142–9] . . .

Such an account would of course be extravagantly perverse. Thus consider the case where we teach the infant a word by reinforcing his random babbling on some appropriate occasion. His chance utterance bears a chance resemblance to a word appropriate to the occasion, and we reward him . . . In so doing we encourage the child to repeat the word on future similar occasions. But are we causing him to associate the word with the same *idea* that we adults associate it with? Do we adults all associate it with the same idea ourselves, for that matter? And what would that mean?

The moral of this is that the fixed points are just the shared stimulus and the word; the ideas in between are as may be and may vary as they please, so long as the external stimulus in question stays paired up with the word in question for all concerned . . .

A theory of mind can gain clarity and substance, I think, from a better understanding of the workings of language, whereas little understanding of the workings of language is to be hoped for in mentalistic terms [. . .]

People persist in talking . . . of knowing the meaning, and of giving the meaning, and of sameness of meaning, where they could omit mention of meaning and merely talk of understanding an expression, or talk of the equivalence of expressions and the paraphrasing of expressions. They do so because the notion of meaning is felt somehow to *explain* the understanding and equivalence of expressions. We understand expressions by knowing or grasping their meanings; and one expression serves as a translation or paraphrase of another because they mean the same. It is of course spurious explanation, mentalistic explanation at its worst.

In all we may distinguish three levels of purported explanation, three degrees of depth: the mental, the behavioural, and the physiological. The mental is the most superficial of these, scarcely deserving the name of explanation. The physiological is the deepest and most ambitious, and it is the place for causal explanations. The behavioural level, in between, is what we must settle for in our descriptions of language . . . the understanding of an expression . . . the equivalence that holds between an expression and its translation or paraphrase . . . need to be explained, if at all, in behavioural terms: in terms of dispositions to overt gross behaviour [. . .]

In what behavioural disposition then does a man's knowledge of the truth conditions of the sentence 'This is red' consist? Not, certainly, in a disposition to affirm the sentence on every occasion of observing a red object, and to deny it on all other occasions; it is the disposition to assent or dissent when asked in the presence or absence of red. Query and assent, query and dissent – here is the solvent that reduces understanding to verbal dispositions. Without this device there would be no hope of handing language down the generations, nor any hope of breaking into newly discovered languages . . .

This approach applies primarily to terms, or occasion sentences, rather than to standing sentences . . . '

I 'Occasion sentences' are those – like 'It's

raining' – where assent changes depending on circumstances. 'Standing sentences' are those – like 'Rain is wet' – which people tend to assent to in all circumstances.

'Standing sentences can be queried too, but the stimulating situation at the time of querying them will usually have no bearing on the verdict . . . I do not know how, in general, in terms of behavioural dispositions, to approximate to the notion of understanding at all, when the sentences understood are standing sentences. Perhaps it cannot be done, taking standing sentences one by one . . .

[If it cannot be done, it is] because the sentences one by one simply do not have their own separable empirical implications. A multiplicity of standing sentences will interlock, rather, as a theory; and an observation in conflict with that theory may be accommodated by revoking one or other of the sentences – no one sentence in particular [. . .]

Moreover, in a behavioural account of equivalence, just as in a behavioural account of understanding, we encounter difficulty when we move to standing sentences. Since a man is apt to assent to a standing sentence, if asked, in all sorts of circumstances or in none, the coinciding of dispositions to assent to two standing sentences gives no basis for equating them.

I am persuaded, indeed, that a satisfactory equivalence concept is impossible for standing sentences. My view of this matter can be conveyed most clearly if we consider translation between two languages. I am persuaded that alternative manuals of translation can exist, incompatible with each other, and both of them conforming fully to the dispositions to behaviour on the part of the speakers of the two languages. The two manuals would agree on observation sentences but conflict in some of the standing sentences . . . neither manual is right to the exclusion of the other.

This indeterminacy of translation is unsuspected in mentalistic semantics, because of the facile talk of meaning . . .

Of course, translation must go on. Indeterminacy means that there is more than one way; we can still proceed to develop one of them, as good as any . . .

I have been inveighing against mentalistic semantics and urging in its place the study of dispositions to behaviour. This move could be represented alternatively and more picturesquely as a matter not so much of substitution as of identification: let us *construe* mind as a system of disposition to behaviour. This version somewhat recalls Gilbert Ryle and Wilfred Sellars, who have urged a generally dispositional philosophy of mind . . .

I spoke of three levels of purported explanation: the mental, the behavioural, and the physiological . . . Now the relation of [the behavioural] level to the third and deepest, the physiological, begins to be evident when we examine the notion of a *disposition* to behaviour and consider what we mean by a disposition.

. . . Take the classical example, solubility in water. This is a physical trait that can be specified, with various degrees of thoroughness, in various ways. It can be described quite fully, I gather, in terms of the relative positions of small particles . . . The dispositional way of specifying physical traits is as frequent and as useful as it is because we are so often not prepared, as we now

happen to be in the case of solubility, to specify the intended physical trait in other than the dispositional style.

. . . Hardness, for instance, is the disposition to resist if pressed, or to scratch. Redness, said of a body, is the disposition to blush in white light. Hardness and redness come finally, like solubility, to be explained in terms of minute structure, but our first access to these physical traits is dispositional . . .

. . . solubility is an objective physical arrangement of particles, but known first in dispositional terms.

Dispositions to behaviour, then, are physiological states or traits or mechanisms. In citing them dispositionally we are singling them out by behavioural symptoms, behavioural tests [. . .]

Our three levels thus are levels of reduction: mind consists in dispositions to behaviour, and these are physiological states . . . I would not identify mind quite wholly with verbal dispositions; with Ryle and Sellars I would identify it with behavioural dispositions, and *mostly* verbal. And then, having construed behavioural dispositions in turn as physiological states, I end up with the so-called identity theory of mind: mental states are states of the body.

However, a word of caution is in order regarding the so-called identity theory. How does it differ from a repudiation theory?

. . . instead of saying that mental states are identical with physiological ones, we could repudiate them; we could claim that they can be dispensed with, in all our theorizing, in favour of physiological states, these being specified usually not in actual physiological terms but in the idiom of behavioural dispositions . . . [The] advantage here is that it discourages a possible abuse of the identity theory. For, product though the identity theory is of hard-headed materialism, we must beware of its sedative use to relieve intellectual discomfort. We can imagine someone appealing to the identity theory to excuse his own free and uncritical recourse to mentalistic semantics. We can imagine him pleading that it is after all just a matter of physiology, even if no one knows quite how. This would be a sad irony indeed, and the repudiation theory has the virtue, over the identity theory, of precluding it.

Until we can aspire to actual physiological explanation of linguistic activity in physiological terms, the level at which to work is the middle one; that of dispositions to overt behaviour. Its virtue is not that it affords causal explanations but that it is less likely than the mentalistic level to engender an illusion of being more explanatory than it is. The easy familiarity of mentalistic talk is not to be trusted.'

Comments and questions

Quine seems to be saying that when we talk about ideas and meanings, that's really just an easier way of talking about dispositions to (mostly verbal) behaviour. Further, when we talk about dispositions to behaviour, that's really just an easier way of talking about physiological states and processes.

Suppose someone said, in reply, that nothing would distinguish those physiological states and processes from surrounding ones if it weren't for the fact that they explain the dispositions we're interested in. Nothing would distinguish *these* wavelengths of reflected light from others, for example, if they weren't the ones that make a thing look *red*. The electromagnetic spectrum is a continuum after all.

Could it be said, in the same way, that nothing would pick out the dispositions to behaviour which Quine puts so much stress on, if they weren't the ones which underlie meanings and ideas? Is it true, in other words, that without meanings and ideas, there would just be a sea of indistinguishable physics?

....

....

Quine seems content to accept indeterminacy of translation as a consequence of his behaviourism. How strong, and how reliable, is our common sense intuition that there *is* a single correct translation into another language of a standing sentence like 'Grass is green'? Strong and reliable enough to serve as a refutation of Quine's behaviourism?

....

....

Plato (c. 429–347 BC) on universals – from *Parmenides*, 130f.

Plato's *Parmenides* is a late dialogue (or conversation), centring on Parmenides, a distinguished visitor to Athens. In the extract which follows, Plato represents Socrates as holding a theory of forms, though troubled by some aspects of it: Parmenides, on the other hand, rejects the theory of forms, and tries to show Socrates that it is fatally flawed.

What is the theory of forms? One use of the theory is to explain classification. We classify, for example, various shapes as triangles. An equilateral triangle drawn in the sand is a triangle, and so is an imaginary scalene triangle joining three mountain tops. Now, how is it possible for us to classify both these things as triangles? Plato argued that if A and B deserve the same name, then A and B must have something in common. But what real property does the triangle in the sand have in common with the 'three peaks' triangle? Since there seems to be no real material property in common, there must – Plato thought – be a real *non-material* property or standard involved. Plato envisaged these abstract 'forms' as perfect examplars – of triangularity for example.

Let's take another example. We call a certain painting, a certain line of poetry, a certain piece of music beautiful. If they deserve the same adjective, they must have something in common. But painting, poetry and music, considered as material objects or events, seem to have nothing in common. So there must (according to the argument) be something *non-material* which they all share. They all have some share of the 'form' of the beautiful. And so on for other classifications, such as 'human', 'rational', 'good'.

The theory of forms did other work for Plato too. For example, Plato distinguished – as we still do – between knowledge and true belief. I might believe that X loves Y and it might be true as a matter of fact that X loves Y, and yet if you ask me if I *know* that X loves Y, I'd have to say no. But how

do we make this distinction between knowing and truly believing?

Plato thought that real knowledge was something unchanging: if you really know something, you don't change your mind. Real knowledge, therefore, should be understood as acquaintance with the unchanging world of the forms.

Moral knowledge too is derived, Plato thought, from acquaintance with the eternal forms of goodness and justice. The person best able to give us moral guidance, therefore, is the person who has trained and worked towards acquaintance with the eternal world of the forms.

All this naturally had consequences for other parts of Plato's world-view. For example, since classification and knowledge prove that we are acquainted with the eternal world of the forms, part of *us* must be eternal too – which provides evidence that the soul is immortal.

Late in his life, however, Plato began to acknowledge problems in the theory of forms, and in the following 'drama of ideas', he makes Socrates the defender of the theory and has Parmenides bring out some of the problems.

'When Socrates finished [commenting on Zeno's paradoxes], Parmenides said, 'Socrates, your enthusiasm for argument is wonderful. Now tell me, do you distinguish forms from the things which have a share of them? . . .

'Yes I do,' said Socrates.

'. . . For example, a form of justice, existing independently and by itself, and of beautiful and good, and so on?'

'Yes'.

'And is there a form of *man* separate from

living human beings, and *fire*, or *water?*'

'I have often been puzzled, Parmenides,' he said, 'about whether these forms exist in the same way as the others.'

'And what about . . . hair and mud . . . and other things which are worthless or trivial? Are you puzzled about whether to say there is an independently existing form for them too?'

'Not at all,' said Socrates. 'Those things are surely just what we see them to be . . .'

'You are still young, Socrates,' said Parmenides, 'and philosophy has not yet taken hold of you, as I think it will one day . . . Now, because of your youth, you still pay attention to what people think. Now tell me again: do you think that there are certain forms, and that the things around us get their names by having a share of these forms? As for example, things that have a share of likeness become like, and so on for largeness, beauty and justice?'

'Yes, certainly,' said Socrates.

'Do the things that get a share of the form, share the whole form or part of it? . . . Could the whole form be in each real thing?'

'What prevents it, Parmenides?'

'If the whole form were in many separate real things, then one and the same thing (the form) would at the same time be divided and multiple.'

'Not if it was like one and the same day, which is in many different places at once without being separated from itself . . .'

'Very clever, Socrates,' said Parmenides. 'You spread one and the same thing over many different places at once, like a sail over a number of men, and then claim that one thing is shared between them. Is that what you mean to say?'

'Perhaps,' he said.

'Well, in that case, would the whole sail be over each man, or part over each?'

'Part.'

'So according to you, Socrates, the forms can be divided into parts, and the things that share them have each a part of the form?'

'So it appears.'

'And is that what you want to say – that *one* form can be divided in this way?'

'No it isn't,' he replied.

'No,' said Parmenides. 'If we divide largeness, for example, then the things which share the resulting parts would be smaller, wouldn't they?'

'Which is impossible,' said Socrates . . .

'Then in what way, Socrates, can real things get a share of a form? . . . How do you deal with this problem?'

'It seems very difficult.'

'Here's another problem for you . . . Think about the form of *largeness* alongside real things which are large. Don't they all have something in common?'

'It seems so.'

'So you're going to need another form of *largeness* over and above real large things and the form of *largeness* we already have. And over and above all those, again, yet another form of *largeness*, by which they will all be large. So in all cases, one form will not be enough: you'll need a multitude.'

'But Parmenides,' said Socrates, 'Couldn't these forms be concepts, existing only in the mind? In that way, couldn't we escape the regress?'

'Well,' Parmenides replied, 'could it be a thought of nothing?'

'No, that's impossible . . .'

'So it must be a thought of something which we think as covering all real cases of a certain kind?'

'Yes'.

'A thought then of some characteristic – the same for all the real cases of that kind?'

'That seems inevitable.'

'Now if real things *must* share this thought – as you believe – then it seems that things themselves must be thoughts, because no one in fact might have thought or be thinking about them at all.'

> Translation alert: here I try to explain what I think the point is, rather than using a more literal translation (such as, 'in virtue of the necessity by which you say others have a share of forms, does it not seem to you either that each is composed of thoughts and all think, or that, though thoughts, they are unthought?').

'Still, Parmenides,' said Socrates, 'it's surely clear that the forms stand as definite paradigms in the nature of things, and that real things are likenesses of them. When I talk about sharing, what I really mean is this likeness.'

'Well,' said Parmenides, 'if something resembles a form, the form must be like the thing. Or is there any way A could be like B without B being like A?'

'There is not.'

'So if A is like B, A and B must have something in common?'

'True.'

'And isn't that 'something in common' the form itself?'

'Certainly.'

'But then if a form is like a real thing, another form will always appear alongside it . . . The generation of new forms will never stop . . .'

'You are right.'

'Then getting a share of a form is not a matter of likeness, is it? We must look for some other explanation.'

'So it seems.'

'You see, then, Socrates, how great the difficulties are, if someone says forms exist independently?'

'Yes indeed . . .'

'There are many other difficulties,' said Parmenides, 'but the greatest of all is this . . . There is no convincing reply to someone who says that we can never know the forms.'

'Why is that Parmenides?'

'If the forms exist independently, then they don't exist in us . . . But if we have knowledge of the forms, then it must be in virtue of a form of knowledge, must it not?'

'Yes'.

'Which is not in us, but independent of us?'

'Yes.'

'Then none of the forms is known by us, since we have no share of knowledge itself?'

'It seems not.'

'It follows that what is really beautiful, or good, is unknowable for us?'

'So it appears . . .'

'These difficulties and many more follow if we hold that the forms exist independently of us . . . If on the other hand, we refuse to say that things in the same class have something in common, we utterly destroy the power and significance of thought and language. I think you are well aware of that sort of consequence.'

'Yes,' Socrates replied.

'What will you do about philosophy then? Which way will you turn while these things are unknown?'

'For the moment, at least, I am not sure.'

'...Your impulse towards argument is noble, and indeed divine. But train yourself more thoroughly while you are young – work through these problems which the multitude regard as useless. Otherwise the truth will escape you.'

Comments and questions

In this conversation, Parmenides ties Socrates in the kind of knots which Socrates went on, with great distinction, to tie others in. Can you help Socrates untie himself? What *should* he have said?

....

....

43

John Searle (b. 1932) on computer 'understanding' – from 'Minds, Brains and Programs': *Behavioral and Brain Sciences*, **vol. 3, 1980**

In this controversial article, Searle tries to refute the claim (of what he calls 'strong' AI) that computers can literally be said to understand and have other cognitive states. This is the claim that when a chess player says of a program, for example, 'It knows I'm attacking the King', that kind of claim can, at least with some programs, be taken quite literally.

Searle begins with a program which seems to 'understand':

 'Very briefly, and leaving out the various details, one can describe Schank's program as follows: The aim of the program is to simulate the human ability to understand stories. It is characteristic of human beings' story-understanding capacity that they can answer questions about the story even though the information that they give was never explicitly stated in the story. Thus, for example, suppose you were given the following story: "A man went into a restaurant and ordered a hamburger. When the hamburger arrived it was burned to a crisp, and the man stormed out of the restaurant angrily, without paying for the hamburger or leaving a tip." Now, if you are asked "Did the man eat the hamburger?" you will presumably answer, "No, he did not"... Now Schank's machines can similarly answer questions about restaurants in this fashion. To do this, they have a 'representation' of the sort of information human beings have about restaurants, which enables them to answer as above, given these sorts of stories... Partisans of strong AI claim that in this question and answer sequence the machine is not only simulating a human ability but ... that the machine can literally be said to *understand* the story [...]

One way to test any theory of the mind is to ask oneself what it would be like if my mind actually worked on the principles that the theory says all minds work on. Let us apply this test to the Schank program with the following *Gedankenexperiment*. Suppose that I'm locked in a room and given a large batch of Chinese writing. Suppose furthermore (as is indeed the case) that I know no Chinese, either written or spoken ... To me, Chinese writing is just so many meaningless squiggles. Now suppose further that after this first batch of Chinese writing I am given a second batch of Chinese script together with a set of rules for correlating the second batch with the first batch. The rules are in English, and I understand these rules as well as any other native speaker of English. They enable me to correlate one set of formal symbols with another set of formal symbols, and all that 'formal' means here is that I can identify the symbols entirely by their shapes. Now suppose that I am also given a third batch of Chinese symbols, together with some instructions, again in English, that enable me to correlate elements of this third batch with the first two batches, and these rules instruct me how to give back certain Chinese symbols with certain sorts of shapes in response to certain sorts of shapes given me in the third batch. Unknown to me, the people who are giving me all these symbols call the first batch a 'script', they call the second batch a 'story', and they call the third batch 'questions'. Furthermore, they call the symbols I give them back in response to the third batch 'answers to the questions', and the set of rules in English that they gave me, they call the 'program' . . . after a while I get so good at following the instructions for manipulating the Chinese symbols and the programmers get so good at writing the programs that from the external point of view – that is, from the point of view of somebody outside the room in which I am locked – my answers to the questions are absolutely indistinguishable from those of native Chinese speakers. Nobody just looking at my answers can tell that I don't speak a word of Chinese. But . . . I produce the answers by manipulating uninterpreted formal symbols [. . .]

. . . it seems to me quite obvious in the example that I do not understand a word of the Chinese stories. I have inputs and outputs that are indistinguishable from those of the native Chinese speaker, and I can have any formal program you like, but I still understand nothing. For the same reasons, Schank's computer understands nothing of any stories, whether in Chinese, English, or whatever . . . the computer has nothing more than I have in the case where I understand nothing [. . .]'

Searle now considers various objections which have been raised against this thought experiment. One of these objections claims that the reason the computer/subject does not understand, is that it/he is cut off from interaction with the real world. Here's the objection, followed by Searle's reply:

'"Suppose we wrote a different kind of program from Schank's program. Suppose we put a computer inside a robot, and this computer would not just take in formal symbols as input and give out formal symbols as output, but rather would actually operate the robot in such a way that the robot does something very like perceiving, walking, moving about, hammering nails, eating, drinking – anything you like. The robot would, for example, have a television camera attached to it that enabled it to see, it would have arms and legs that enabled it to 'act', and all of this would be controlled by its computer 'brain'. Such a robot would, unlike Schank's computer, have genuine understanding and other mental states."

The first thing to notice about the robot reply is that it tacitly concedes that cognition is not solely a matter of formal symbol manipulation . . . But the answer to the robot reply is that the addition of such 'perceptual' and 'motor' capacities adds nothing by way of understanding . . . to Schank's original program. To see this, notice that the same thought experiment applies to the robot case. Suppose that instead of the computer inside the robot, you put me inside the room and, as in the original Chinese case, you give me more Chinese symbols with more instructions in English for matching Chinese symbols to Chinese symbols and feeding back Chinese symbols to the outside world. Suppose, unknown to me, some of the Chinese symbols that come to me come from a television camera attached to the robot and other Chinese symbols that I am giving out serve to make the motors inside the robot move the robot's legs or arms. It is important to emphasise that all I am doing is manipulating formal symbols: I know none of these other facts. I am receiving 'information' from the robot's 'perceptual' apparatus, and I am giving out 'instructions' to its motor apparatus without knowing either of these facts . . . I don't understand anything except the rules for symbol manipulation. Now in this case I want to say the robot has no intentional states at all; it is simply moving about as a result of its electrical wiring and its program . . . '

Comments and questions

The person in the Chinese room does three main things – sorting the input, checking the input against the rule book, and selecting the output. None of this seems to involve or require an understanding of Chinese. That understanding seems to lie, in a derivative way, in the rule book, and primarily, in the programmer who wrote the rule book.

So by distinguishing the human subject of the experiment from the rule book, Searle's argument strongly distinguishes the hardware from the software of the corresponding computer. The argument might well suggest that the mere hardware of a computer can't be said to understand a narrative or anything else. But when people say a computer 'understands', they usually mean the hardware in combination with the software – which corresponds to Searle's experimental subject plus the English-language rule book which he or she does understand.

So if someone says that the person in combination with the rule book, jointly and in a derivative way, display an understanding of Chinese, is that wrong? When people say computers understand, do they mean anything more than that?

....

....

Think about Searle's 'computer-inside-a-robot'. What might the difference be between you and a suitably programmed computer+robot, as a result of which you *can* – and the computer+robot *cannot* – genuinely understand, believe, perceive, act and so on?

....

....

Overview of Area 5

Locke's view of language embodies, in a particularly sharp form, the paradox which language presents to common sense. Language is for communication, and yet the content it communicates – an idea in the speaker's mind – is something essentially private. Locke, characteristically, just embraces both halves of the contradiction. But most modern writers feel that any theory of language which pictures us as communicating the incommunicable needs work.

The Reading from Quine presents a behaviouristic solution: we simply get rid of ideas. Searle's Chinese Room argument reminds us, however, that mere behavioural adequacy falls short of what we normally think of as understanding language.

Putnam's examples bring out the importance of public and external (rather than purely mental) elements in fixing meaning. The meaning of a term like 'water' is fixed partly by a real-world sample: 'water' is stuff like *that stuff there*. This implies that the meaning of the word 'water' is not fixed purely by an idea in a given speaker's head. The beech/elm example emphasises the social nature of meaning. An individual can properly use a term like 'beech', with only the vaguest idea in his or her head, because *other* people in the speaker's speech community know more exactly what a beech or elm tree is.

This problem (of the role of individual mental contents in giving meaning to language) is also a factor in our attempts to understand proper names. Kripke emphasises the role of the social act of baptism: proper names are typically made to stand for the things and people they name by some kind of public naming ceremony. Wittgenstein reminds us that even when we do associate identifying information with a name, that information is more like a loose and shifting cloud of facts, rather than a hard and fast definition. Searle insists that this cluster of information is nevertheless held in the minds of speakers and hearers. For him, the *point* of the naming ceremony is to ensure that different people have the same content in mind.

But whether meanings are ideas or something else, the question remains whether proper names have them or not. Ryle's account of Mill's theory provides a lucid introduction to this tricky problem.

The 'ideas or something else' question surfaces also in Plato's wonderful discussion of general names. The 'Parmenides' character in the dialogue argues persuasively not only against the theory of *abstract* forms (that the meanings of general terms depend on eternal prototypes), but also against the theory – which Socrates half-heartedly tries at one point – that the forms are human concepts.

Area 5, as a whole, focussed on questions about the *meaning* of language, and the part played by mental contents in creating meaning. These mental contents are derived mostly (or for empiricists, wholly) from perception. It's important, therefore, to understand just what happens in the mind when we see or hear. Area 6 takes up this vexed and ancient problem.

AREA 6
Objectivity

The readings in this area ask how we should understand the relationships between perception, thought and truth.

Roderick Chisholm (b. 1916) on perception – from 'The Evidence of the Senses', *Philosophical Perspectives*, vol. 2: Ridgeview, 1988 (ed. J. E. Tomberlin)

In this article, Chisholm discusses three ancient accounts of perception, and argues that one of them provides the basis of a coherent – in fact the only coherent – response to scepticism.

'The principal source of our philosophical problem lies in the fact that perception is inextricably bound up with *appearing* – with being appeared to in some way. The person who perceives that there is a tree before him *takes* there to be a tree. And when one takes there to be a tree (when one thinks that one perceives a tree), then one is appeared to in a certain way and one believes that *what* it is that is appearing in that way is a tree. In the case of the

person who is hallucinating, we may say that, although he is *appeared to* in a certain way, there is nothing that is *appearing* to him in that way [...]

If you perceive that there is a tree before you, then you believe that your perceptual experience is an experience of a tree – or, in our terminology, you think you are appeared to by a tree. It would be misleading to call the appearance the '*object*' of perception. But it would be accurate to say that, it is *by means of* what you know about the appearance, that you apprehend the object of appearance. The philosophical problem of perceptual evidence turns on this question: How is it possible for appearances to provide us with information about the things of which they *are* appearances?

The difficulty, as we know, has to do with what is sometimes called 'perceptual relativity'. The appearances that we sense are a function, not only of the nature of the things we perceive, but also of the conditions under which we perceive these things ...

Sextus Empiricus had cited these examples:

The same water which feels very hot when poured on inflamed spots seems lukewarm to us. And the same air seems chilly to the old but mild to those in their prime, and similarly the same sound seems to the former faint, but to the latter clearly audible. The same wine which seems sour to those who have previously eaten dates or figs seems sweet to those who have just consumed nuts or chickpeas; and the vestibule of the bathhouse which warms those entering from the outside chills those coming out.

... we find [three theories of perception]

in ancient Greek philosophy. These are: (1) the *dogmatic* theory; (2) the *inductive* theory; and (3) the *critical* theory. The first was 'the theory of the evident perception' set forth by the Stoic, Chrysippus (279–206 B.C.); the second was the so-called commemorative theory developed by Sextus Empiricus (c.150–250); and the third was the theory of the Academic skeptic, Carneades (c.213–129 B.C.). The first two theories have some initial plausibility, but it is the theory of Carneades, I think, that is closest to the truth.

(1) The Dogmatic Theory

According to 'the theory of the evident perception,' the appearance presents us with *two* things – the appearance itself and the external thing that appears: there is a way of appearing that present *itself* to the subject and also presents *another* thing to the subject – a thing that *appears* in a certain way to the subject. It was held that, whenever we have an evident perception, we can tell from the nature of the perceptual experience itself that the perception is veridical [truthful]. The experience was said to be irresistible. 'The perception, being plainly evident and striking, lays hold of us, almost by the very hair, as they say, and drags us off to assent, needing nothing else to help it' [. . .]

[This] seems to imply that the appearance that is yielded by a veridical perception could not be duplicated in an unveridical perception or in an hallucination. And this is contrary to what we know . . .

The theory is excessively dogmatic. We must go further if we are to have a satisfactory account of the evidence of the senses.

(2) The Inductive Theory

The theory of 'the commemorative perception' that was set forth by Sextus was an 'inductive' theory. Sextus agrees with Chrysippus that our perceptual experience provides us with a *sign* of the independently existing thing. But he rejects the dogmatism of Chrysippus; the nature of the appearance provides no logical guarantee of the nature of the object . . . Smoke signifies fire for us because we have made an induction that correlates smoke with fire: We have found in the past that smoke is generally accompanied by fire. This much is quite obvious. But now Sextus goes on to take a further step. Many have failed to see just how doubtful this further step is.

He says that the inductive correlation that we have made between smoke and fire gives us the clue to the relation between appearances and the external things that the appearances make known to us. He seems to suggest that we have made an inductive correlation between tree-appearances and external trees: We have found that tree-appearances are generally accompanied by an existence of external, physical trees. The nature of an appearance, then, may *make probable* some hypothesis about the nature of the external object [. . .]

To see that there is something wrong with this account of perception, we have only to ask: What was the nature of those *earlier* experiences wherein we found that a tree-like appearance was accompanied by the apprehension of an external, physical tree? How was it made known to us *then* that there was a tree there? We are given no clear answer to this question. I would say, therefore, that the 'inductive' theory does not provide us with what we are looking for.

(3) The Critical Theory

We have seen that, according to Sextus' inductive theory, the probability . . . is derived from an inductive correlation or frequency. But Carneades appeals to no such correlation . . . Carneades knows that we cannot make any inductive inferences about external things until have some *perceptual data* about such things. And it follows from this that, if we are to have any positive justification for what we believe about the external world, our experience must provide us with a probability which is not derived from an induction [. . .]

One of the things Carneades was saying seems to have been this:

Taking something to be F tends to make it probable that there is something one is taking to be F.

Here, then, we have the beginnings of an answer to our question about perceptual evidence: 'What aspect of our experience justifies what kind of belief about physical things?' The fact that the perceiver *takes* there to be a tree . . . tends to make it probable that there *is* in fact an external object upon which the taking is directed [. . .]

. . . This view was subsequently developed further by H. H. Price. He made the following suggestion in his book, *Perception* (1932):

[T]he fact that a material thing is perceptually presented to the mind is *prima facie evidence* of the thing's existence and of its really having that sort of surface which it ostensibly has; there is

some presumption in favour of this, not merely in the sense that we do as a matter of fact presume it (which of course we do) but in the sense that we are entitled to do so.

Price adds: 'Clearly the principle is *a priori*: it is not the sort of thing we could learn by empirical generalization based upon observation of the material world [. . .]'

This account of perceptual evidence requires further analysis and explication. We should try to describe more accurately the conditions under which our perceptual takings and the ways in which we are appeared to may inform us about the things around us. But the general view of perception that it represents seems to me to be the only coherent alternative to scepticism.

The view implies that the evidence about external things that is yielded by perception is *indirect* . . . What we know about such things is made evident to us . . . by certain psychological facts that present themselves to us directly.

This use of 'indirect' may give pause to some. For one may say: 'Ordinarily, we perceive such things as trees, ships and houses *directly*. If you were standing here before me, I would perceive you directly. I would perceive you *indirectly* if I were to see your shadow on the floor – in which case I would perceive the floor *directly*.' But these facts are consistent with saying that, when I *do* perceive you directly, I do so by becoming aware of *other* things that serve to make it evident for me that you are the object of my perception.'

Comments and questions

Chisholm says that it is 'accurate to say that

I see a tree by knowing about an appearance of the tree'.

Is it?

....

....

To see the weakness of the inductive theory, Chisholm says we need only ask how we discovered that past tree-like appearances were accompanied by real trees (this discovered correlation being supposed to justify us in trusting some present appearances over others).

Chisholm believes that the inductive theory has no answer to this question. He prefers the 'critical' theory, which holds that we have an *a priori* guarantee that past tree-like appearances were probably correlated with real trees.

Now, to say that this guarantee is *a priori* is to say that it is not derived from experience. Where, then, might this information (about the correlation between tree-appearances and real trees) come from? What entitles us to rely on it?

....

....

Chisholm says, in rejecting the dogmatic theory, that 'the nature of the appearance provides no logical guarantee of the nature of the object'. How, then, can he hold that it *does* provide a logical guarantee of the (probable) *existence* of the object?

....

....

45

A. J. Ayer (1910–89) on perception – from 'Phenomenalism': *Proceedings of the Aristotelian Society*, **XLVII, 1946**

In this extract, A. J. Ayer defends a modern version of Berkeley's Idealism (see Area 4/30). He first introduces the term 'sense-datum' as 'a means of referring to appearances without prejudging the questions what it is, if anything, that they are appearances *of*, and what it is, if anything, that they appear *to*.' He continues:

'Now if the word 'sense-datum' is understood in this way, then if it is ever true that a physical object is being perceived, it must also be true that some sense-datum is being sensed. If, for example, it is a fact that I am seeing a match-box, in the appropriate sense of the word 'see', then it *follows* that, in the appropriately different sense of the word 'see', I am seeing some sense-datum. But the converse does not hold . . . from the fact that I am sensing the sense-data that I am now sensing it does not *follow* that I am perceiving a match-box . . . Thus, when I say, truly as it happens, that I am now perceiving a match-box, part of what I am saying is that I am sensing sense-data of a certain kind; but only part. I am saying that and something more. But what more? that is our problem. And the phenomenalists' answer to it is that the more that I am saying is that further sense-data of the match-box would, in the appropriate conditions, be obtainable.

If this answer is correct, then it seems to follow that the statement that I am perceiving this match-box . . . [and] the statement that this match-box exists must . . . be equivalent to some set of statements about sense-data . . . [This] means simply that statements about physical objects are somehow reducible to statements about sense-data . . .

The first point to be made is that if we confine ourselves to actual sense-data, this claim can evidently not be upheld. For to revert to our example, this match-box is not continuously perceived by me or by anybody else. And yet at times when no one is perceiving it, that is, when there are no sense-data that are directly relevant to its existence, the match-box may still exist . . . what this means is that some at least of the statements about sense-data that are supposed to yield the equivalence of statements about physical objects will have to be hypothetical . . .'

That is, they will be statements like, 'If someone were to look in that direction, they would receive such-and-such sense-data.'

'Now it would seem that the best way for a phenomenalist to prove his case would be to set about giving us some examples. We should expect him to take a statement like 'there is a flower-pot on the window-sill,' and give us its equivalent in terms of sense-data. But this is something that no phenomenalist has ever yet done, or even, to my knowledge, seriously tried to do . . . One reason for this, of course, is the poverty of our sensory language. The vocabulary that we have for describing colours, shapes and the rest is not sufficient for our purpose: so that we are constantly reduced to saying things like 'the sort of sense-data that you get when you look at a match-box' . . . But I suppose that a suitable vocabulary could be invented, if some ingenious person thought that it was worth his trouble . . . But there are more serious difficulties.

One that is often brought forward is that no statement about a physical object can be conclusively verified on the ground that however much favourable evidence there may be for it, it is always conceivable that further evidence will show it to have been false all along. And from this premiss it is correctly deduced that no statement about a physical object can be equivalent to any finite set of statements about sense-data . . . I used to accept this argument but now I am inclined to reject it [because] . . .

. . . the occurrence of these visual sense-data, taken in conjunction with what I remember, fully justifies the statement that this is a match-box, and would justify it, I should now maintain, even if the 'match-box' were to vanish the next instant [. . .]

. . . but I do not think that it is ever possible to discover a finite set of statements about sense-data of which it can truly be said in a particular case that precisely these are necessary [to allow us to infer that a match-box is present] . . . there will always be an indefinite number of other sensory experiences that would have done just as well . . . And this is one reason why it is impossible to translate a statement about a physical object into any finite set of statements about sense-data. It is not, as has sometimes been suggested, that the physical object is eternally on probation . . . The reason is that all statements about physical objects are indefinite […]

… it turns out that for the reasons I have given, statements about physical objects cannot be translated into statements about sense-data. Consequently, the phenomenalist is obliged to give up his original position. But he need modify it only slightly. He cannot show you precisely what you are saying about sense-data when you make a given statement about a physical object, because you are not saying anything precise about sense-data. Nevertheless … what you are saying, though vague, still refers ultimately to sense-data and does not refer to anything other than sense-data …

… if we are not referring to sense-data, and exclusively to sense-data, when we talk about physical objects, it is difficult to see what we can be referring to … the only alternative … is the iron curtain theory of perception: that physical objects are there sure enough but we can never get at them […]

If this line of argument is correct, then the solution of the 'problem of perception' may be to treat our beliefs about physical objects as constituting a theory, the function of which is to explain the course of our sensory experiences … it may not be possible to rewrite [statements about physical objects] as statements about sense-data. Nevertheless, they will function only as means of grouping sense-data … '

Berkeley himself considered this idea but rejected it, in favour of the more radical view that all and any talk about 'physical objects' is incoherent.

Comments and questions

It seems that once we admit appearances as real things – or appearings as real events – then actual and possible appearances/appearings will constitute all the evidence we could ever have for physical objects, and so come to seem more real than them. If we want to avoid the conclusion that match-boxes, test tubes, the fingers on your hand, are all theoretical entities, where should we stop this slide?

....

....

46

Gilbert Ryle (1900–76) on perception – from *The Concept of Mind*: 1949

In this extract, Ryle attacks the sense-datum theory, the view that in perception, we directly perceive, not the external horse or tree, but a mental entity such as a colour patch, which we interpret as evidence of the external thing.

 'It may be said [in defence of the theory] that … it remains an unchallengeable fact that in seeing I am directly presented with patchworks of colours momentarily occupying my field of view, in hearing I am directly presented with noises, in smelling with smells, and so forth … Two-dimensional colour patches are what I see in the strictest sense of 'see'; and these are of horses and jockeys, but at best the looks, or visual appearances, of horses and jockeys. If there are not two candles, then the squinter does not really see two candles, but he certainly sees two bright somethings, and these can be nothing but two proprietary 'candle-looks' or sense-data . . .

Let us consider, then, the hackneyed instance of a person looking at a round plate tilted away from him, which he may therefore describe as looking elliptical; and let us see what, if anything, requires us to say that he is descrying a something which really is elliptical. It is agreed that the plate is not elliptical but round, and for the argument's sake we may concede that the spectator is veraciously reporting that it looks elliptical (though round plates, however steeply tilted, do not usually look elliptical). The question is whether the truth of his report that the plate looks elliptical implies that he really is espying, or scanning, an object of sense which is elliptical, something which, not being the plate itself, can claim to be entitled a 'look' or 'a visual appearance of the plate'. We may also grant that if we are bound to say that he has come across an object of sense which is really elliptical and is a visual appearance of the plate, then this elliptical object is a two-dimensional colour patch, momentary in existence and proprietary to one percipient, i.e. that it is a sense-datum and therefore that there are sense-data.

Now a person without a theory feels no qualms in saying that the round plate might look elliptical. Nor would he feel qualms in saying that the round plate looks as if it were elliptical. But he would feel qualms in following the recommendation to say that he is seeing an elliptical look of a round plate. Though he talks easily enough in some contexts of the looks of things, and easily

enough in other contexts of seeing things, he does not ordinarily talk of seeing or of scanning the looks of things, of gazing at views of races, of catching glimpses of glimpses of hawks, or of descrying the visual appearances of tree-tops. He would feel that, if he mixed his ingredients in these fashions, he would be talking the same sort of nonsense as he would if he moved from talking of eating biscuits and talking of taking nibbles of biscuits to talking of eating nibbles of biscuits. And he would be quite right. He cannot significantly talk of 'eating nibbles,' since 'nibble' is already a noun of eating, and he cannot talk of 'seeing looks', since 'look' is already a noun of seeing.

. . . In saying that the plate looks elliptical, he is not characterizing an extra object, namely 'a look', as being elliptical, he is likening how the tilted round plate does look to how untilted elliptical plates do or would look . . .

In other words, the grammatically unsophisticated sentence 'the plate has an elliptical look' . . . expresses a fairly complex proposition of which one part is both general and hypothetical. It is applying to the actual look of the plate a rule or recipe about the typical looks of untilted elliptical plates.'

Comments and questions

Ryle points out that 'the plate has an elliptical look' might naively be understood to mean:

1. there's a plate, and there's a look of the plate, and though the plate is round, the look is elliptical.

Ryle argues, however, that the correct

analysis of the sentence is more complex, something like:

2. the plate looks as an untilted elliptical plate would look, if seen straight on.

The first analysis commits us to the existence of 'looks'; the second commits us only to the existence of plates. And this makes it look as if we have no real need for 'ideas of perception' or 'sense-data'.

But suppose someone now says that Ryle's preferred analysis dodges the issue, because the whole problem is to understand what's involved in saying 'the plate looks to me shiny or elliptical (or whatever). On the sense-datum theory, I can say that the plate looks X to me because I have in consciousness something which licenses that adjective. It may be careless to say that I 'see' this something, for the reasons Ryle gives, but nevertheless, it's *because* this something is present to my consciousness that I can say 'the plate looks X to me'. Ryle's preferred analysis gives no account of what lies behind my ability to say this.

How would you respond to this objection on Ryle's behalf?

....

....

If my judgements about external things depend on the testimony of *internal* things (or events), and if the external things are never directly present to consciousness, how can I check that the testimony of the internal things – *whatever* they are – is reliable?

....

....

Thomas Reid (1710–96) on ideas – from *Essays on the Intellectual Powers of Man*, essay 4, ch. 2: 1785

In this extract, Reid tries to explain – without invoking Lockean ideas – how it is that people think and imagine.

'The philosopher says, I cannot conceive a centaur without having an idea of it in my mind. I am at a loss to understand what he means. He surely does not mean that I cannot conceive it without conceiving it. This would make me no wiser. What then is this idea? Is it an animal, half horse and half man? No. Then I am certain it is not the thing I conceive. Perhaps he will say, that the idea is an image of the animal, and is the immediate object of my conception, and that the animal is the mediate or remote object.

To this I answer – *First*, I am certain that there are not two objects of this conception, but one only; and that one is as immediate an object of my conception as any can be.

Secondly, This one object which I conceive, is not the image of an animal – it is an animal. I know what it is to conceive an image of an animal, and what it is to conceive an animal; and I can distinguish the one of these from the other without any danger of mistake. The thing I conceive is a body of a certain [shape] and colour, having life and spontaneous motion. The philosopher says, that the idea is an image of the animal; but that it has neither body, nor colour, nor life, nor spontaneous motion. This I am not able to comprehend.

Thirdly, I wish to know how this object

comes to be an object of my thought, when I cannot even conceive what it means; and, if I did conceive it, this would be no evidence of its existence, any more than my conception of a centaur is of its existence. Philosophers sometimes say that we perceive ideas, sometimes that we are conscious of them. I can have no doubt of the existence of anything which I either perceive or of which I am conscious; but I cannot find that I either perceive ideas or am conscious of them [. . .]

But may not a man who conceives a centaur say, that he has a distinct image of it in his mind? I think he may. And if he means by this way of speaking [what people ordinarily mean], who never heard of the philosophical theory of ideas, I find no fault with it. By a distinct image in the mind, [people] mean a distinct conception; and it is natural to call it so, on account of the analogy between an image of a thing and the conception of it. On account of this analogy, obvious to all mankind, this operation is called imagination, and an image in the mind is only a periphrasis for imagination. But to infer from this that there is really an image in the mind, distinct from the operation of conceiving the object, is to be misled by an analogical expression; as if, from the phrases of deliberating and balancing things in the mind, we should infer that there really is a balance existing in the mind for weighing motives and arguments.

The analogical words and phrases used in all languages to express conception, do, no doubt, facilitate their being taken in a literal sense. But, if we only attend carefully to what we are conscious of in this operation, we shall find no more reason to think that images really do exist in our minds, than that

balances and other mechanical engines do.

. . . if [ideas really do exist in the mind] their existence and their nature must be more evident than anything else, because we know nothing but by their means. I may add, that, if they [exist], we can know nothing besides them. For, from the existence of images, we can never, by any just reasoning, infer the existence of anything else, unless perhaps the existence of an intelligent Author of them. In this, Bishop Berkeley reasoned right . . . '

Comments and questions

At one point, Reid attacks the claim that there are mental representations, on the grounds that the representation cannot be an image of the thing represented, because 'it has neither body, nor colour, nor life, nor spontaneous motion'. Later, he says that it is natural to talk about images in the mind because there is an analogy – 'obvious to all mankind' – between an image and a conception. Is this inconsistent?

....

....

Hobbes says drily that when someone says he saw something in a dream, that only means he dreamed he saw it. If someone says he has a mental image of something, does that mean *nothing* more than that he is imagining it? How do we imagine something – if not by being conscious of a mental image of it?

....

....

48

J. B. Watson (1878–1958) on behaviourism – from *Behaviorism*: W. W. Norton, 1925

In this polemical extract, J. B. Watson, one of the founders of behaviourist psychology, explains why the behaviourist revolution was needed.

'Possibly the easiest way to bring out the contrast between the old psychology [the introspective psychology of Wundt, James etc] and the new is to say that all schools of psychology except that of behaviorism claim that *'consciousness' is the subject matter of psychology*. Behaviorism, on the contrary, holds that the subject matter of human psychology is the *behavior or activities of the human being*. Behaviorism claims that 'consciousness' is neither a definable nor a usable concept; that it is merely another word for the 'soul' of more ancient times . . .

This concept ['soul'] led to the philosophical platform called 'dualism'. All psychology except behaviorism is dualistic. That is to say we have both a mind (soul) and a body. This dogma has been present in human psychology from earliest antiquity. No one has ever touched a soul, or has seen one in a test tube, or has in any way come into relationship with it as he has with the other objects of his daily experience. Nevertheless, to doubt its existence is to become a heretic and once might possibly even have led to the loss of one's head . . .

. . . it was the boast of Wundt's students, in 1879, when the first psychological laboratory was established, that psychology had at last become a science without a soul. For fifty years we have kept this pseudo-science, exactly as Wundt laid it down. All that Wundt and his students really accomplished was to substitute for the word 'soul' the word 'consciousness'.

To show how unscientific is the concept [of consciousness], look for a moment at William James' definition of psychology. 'Psychology is the description and explanation of states of consciousness as such' . . . Consciousness – Oh, yes – everybody must know what this 'consciousness' is. When we have a sensation of red, a perception, a thought, when we *will* to do something, or when we *purpose* to do something, or when we desire to do something, we are being *conscious* . . . [I]ntrospectionists . . . do not tell us what consciousness is, but merely begin to put things into it by assumption; and then when they come to analyze consciousness, naturally they find in it just what they put into it . . . Literally hundreds of thousands of printed pages have been published on the minute analysis of this intangible something called 'consciousness' . . .

. . . we find as many analyses as there are individual psychologists. There is no way of experimentally attacking and solving psychological problems and standardizing methods. In 1912 the behaviorists reached the conclusion that they could no longer be content to work with intangibles and unapproachables . . .

In his first efforts to get uniformity in subject matter and in methods the behaviorist began his own formulation of the problem of psychology by sweeping aside all mediaeval conceptions. He dropped from his scientific vocabulary all subjective terms such as sensation, perception, image, desire, purpose, and even thinking and emotion as they were subjectively defined.

The behaviorist asks: Why don't we make what we can *observe* the real field of psychology? ... we can observe *behavior – what the organism does and says*. And let me make this fundamental point at once: that *saying* is doing – that is, *behaving*. Speaking overtly or to ourselves (thinking) is just as objective a type of behavior as baseball [...]

It is the business of behavioristic psychology to be able to predict and to control human activity. To do this it must gather scientific data by experimental methods.'

Comments and questions

Watson defines thinking as speaking to oneself. Suppose a child's doll was made which muttered things quietly from time to time, whether or not anyone was near. Would it be thinking? If not, what more is needed in order to make this a genuine case of 'speaking to oneself'?

....

....

Is 'consciousness' just another name for 'soul'?

....

....

Why, according to Watson, is introspection unscientific? Is he right?

....

....

Thomas Nagel (b. 1937) on qualia – from 'What is it Like to be a Bat?': *Philosophical Review* LXXXIII, 1974

Nagel's basic point in this well-known article is that consciousness remains a stumbling block for any scientific account, which pretends to be complete, of what a human being is. And in fact, since we confidently attribute consciousness to mammals other than ourselves, it's a stumbling block at least as far down the scale of creation as the 'fundamentally alien' bat.

'Conscious experience is a widespread phenomenon. It occurs at many levels of animal life, though we cannot be sure of its presence in the simpler organisms, and it is very difficult to say in general what provides evidence of it ... fundamentally, an organism has conscious mental states if and only if there is something that it is like to *be* that organism – something it is like *for* the organism.

We may call this the subjective character of experience. It is not captured by any of the familiar, recently devised reductive analyses of the mental, for all of them are logically compatible with its absence. It is not analysable in terms of ... functional states, or intentional states, since these could be ascribed to robots or automata that behaved like people though they experienced nothing ... [And] it is useless to base the defense of materialism on any analysis of mental phenomena that fails to deal explicitly with their subjective character. For there is no reason to suppose that a reduction which seems plausible when no attempt is made to account for consciousness can be extended to include consciousness ... If physicalism is to be defended, the phenomenological features [of experience] must themselves be given a physical account. But when we examine their subjective character it seems that such a result is impossible. The reason is that every subjective phenomenon is essentially connected with a single point of view, and it seems that an objective, physical theory will abandon that point of view.

... To illustrate the connexion between subjectivity and a point of view, and to make evident the importance of subjective features, it will help to explore the matter in relation to an example that brings out clearly the divergence between the two types of conception, subjective and objective.

I assume we all believe that bats have experience. After all, they are mammals, and there is no more doubt that they have experience than that mice or pigeons or whales have experience ...

I have said that the essence of the belief that bats have experience is that there is something that it is like to be a bat. Now we know that most bats (the microchiroptera, to be precise) perceive the external world primarily by sonar, or echolocation ... But bat sonar, though clearly a form of perception, is not similar in its operation to any sense that we possess, and there is no reason to suppose that it is subjectively like anything we can experience or imagine ...

... It will not help to try to imagine that one has webbing on one's arms, which enables one to fly around at dusk and dawn catching insects in one's mouth; that one has very poor vision ... ; that one spends the day hanging upside down by one's feet in an attic. Insofar as I can imagine this (which is not very far), it tells me only what it would be like for me to behave as a bat behaves. But that is not the question. I want to know what it is like for a *bat* to be a bat. Yet if I try to imagine this, I am restricted to the resources of my own mind, and those resources are inadequate to the task ...

... Reflection on what it is like to be a bat seems to lead us, therefore, to the conclusion that there are facts that do not consist in the truth of propositions expressible in human language. We can be compelled to recognise the existence of such facts without being able to state or comprehend them [...]

This bears directly on the mind-body problem. For if the facts of experience – facts about what it is like *for* the experiencing organism – are accessible only from one point of view, then it is a mystery how the true character of experiences could be revealed in the physical operation of that organism. The latter is a domain of objective facts *par excellence* – the kind that can be observed and understood from many points of view and by individuals with differing perceptual systems [...]

... It is difficult to understand what could be meant by the objective character of an experience, apart from the particular point of view from which its subject apprehends it ... But if experience does not have, in addition to its subjective character, an objective nature that can be apprehended from many different points of view, then how can it be supposed that a Martian investigating my brain might be observing physical processes which were my mental processes . . . ? [as Smart proposes in our next reading]

We appear to be faced with a general difficulty about psychophysical reduction. In other areas, the process of reduction is a move in the direction of greater objectivity, towards a more accurate view of the real nature of things [reducing temperature to molecular energy, for example, or lightning to electrical discharge, or sound to compression waves in air etc]. This is accomplished by reducing our dependence on individual or species-specific points of view . . .

Experience itself, however, does not seem to fit the pattern. The idea of moving from appearance to reality seems to make no sense here . . . If the subjective character of experience is fully comprehensible only from one point of view, then any shift to greater objectivity – that is, less attachment to a specific viewpoint – does not take us nearer to the real nature of the phenomenon: it takes us further away from it [. . .]

. . . It would be a mistake to conclude that physicalism must be false . . . it would be truer to say that physicalism is a position we cannot understand because we do not at present have any conception of how it might be true [. . .]

. . . Does it make sense . . . to ask what my experiences are *really* like, as opposed to how they appear to me? We cannot genuinely understand the hypothesis that their nature is captured in a physical description unless we understand the more fundamental idea that they *have an objective nature* . . .'

Comments and questions

One view (associated today with Paul and Patricia Churchland – see Reading 2/15, and Quine's remarks on the 'repudiation theory' in 5/41) is that if subjective experience cannot be captured by science, perhaps for the reasons Nagel sets out above, so much the worse for subjective experience. If our best science tells us it isn't there, we ought to accept that. In other words, we ought to regard subjective experience as a kind of illusion – we ought to 'eliminate' the subjective character of experience from our best list of what's real.

So, is your subjective character of experience *real*?

....

....

50

J. J. C. Smart (b. 1920) on mind/brain identity – from 'Sensations and Brain Processes': *Philosophical Review* **LXVIII, 1959**

Smart argues here that we should not regard mental events as *correlated with* brain events, because the two terms in a scientific correlation must be equally respectable, scientifically, and mental events are scientifically anomalous. Instead, we should adopt the hypothesis that mental events will, as a matter of fact, turn out to be nothing other than brain events.

 'Suppose that I report that I have at this moment a roundish, blurry-edged after-image which is yellowish towards its edge and is orange towards its centre. What is it that I am reporting?

... the suggestion I wish to resist is that I am reporting something irreducibly psychical.

Why do I wish to resist this suggestion? Mainly because of Occam's razor. It seems to me that science is increasingly giving us a viewpoint whereby organisms are able to be seen as physicochemical mechanisms; it seems that even the behaviour of man himself will one day be explicable in mechanistic terms. There does seem to be, so far as science is concerned, nothing in the world but increasingly complex arrangements of physical constituents. All except for one place: in consciousness. That is, for a full description of what is going on in a man you would have to mention not only the physical processes in his tissues, glands, nervous system, and so forth, but also his states of consciousness: his visual, auditory, and tactual sensations, his aches and pains. That these should be *correlated* with brain processes does not help, for to say that they are *correlated* is to say that they are something 'over and above'. You cannot correlate something with itself. You correlate footprints with burglars, but not Bill Sykes the burglar with Bill Sykes the burglar ... That everything should be explicable in terms of physics ... except the occurrence of sensations seems to me frankly unbelievable. Such sensations would be 'nomological danglers', to use Feigl's expression ...

... but it does seem to me as though, when a person says 'I have an after-image,' he *is* making a genuine report ... I am not so sure, however, that to admit this is to admit that there are nonphysical correlates of brain processes. Why should not sensations just be brain processes of a certain sort? [This is the thesis that] in so far as 'after-image' or 'ache' is a report of a process, it is a report of a process that *happens to be* a brain process. It follows that this thesis does not claim that sensation statements can be *translated* into statements about brain processes ... Nations are nothing 'over and above' citizens, but this does not prevent the logic of nation statements being very different from the logic of citizen statements, nor does it insure the translatability of nation statements into citizen statements.'

Comments and questions

Smart goes on to defend the mind/brain identity thesis against various standard objections. The objection which seems to give him most trouble is this: if science is to discover that sensations are in fact brain processes, it must be possible for scientists to identify sensations, to get them into a test tube, as it were, and work on them to discover their true nature. But if this were possible, sensations wouldn't be 'nomological danglers' in the first place.

Smart suggests that we can identify sensations sufficiently by reporting, for example, 'There is something going on in me which is like what goes on in me when I really see an orange.' This, Smart suggests, ties down the time and place of the 'something' sufficiently for scientists to get to work on it.

But would any scientist really begin work on a 'something' which only one person ever reported, a 'something' which nobody else could possibly observe? What do you think would happen to the grant application which proposed to study unconfirmable 'somethings'? Or is Smart's answer to the objection good enough?

....

....

51

Hilary Putnam (b. 1926) on functionalism – from 'Philosophy and our Mental Life', in *Mind, Language and Reality: Philosophical Papers*, **vol. 2: Cambridge University Press, 1975**

In this essay, Putnam argues (in essence) that the important thing for understanding a system's behaviour is its functional role, that is – roughly speaking – the correlations that exist between inputs to the system, internal states of the system, and outputs from the system (see *SP*, pp. 162–5). Putnam concedes that he is taking this notion for granted, and further that 'we have no detailed idea at present of what the normal form of description would look like [for] ourselves'. He says this lack of precision is 'sloppy' but not 'fatally sloppy' (though he later had more serious doubts about this).

His main aim is to show that, *if* functional role is crucial, then the following interesting consequences appear:

1. The physical implementation of the system is secondary – a computer using copper wire will be physically different from one using gold wire, but they might be functionally identical.
2. Mental states cannot, for this reason, be identical with brain states, because a creature with a different sort of brain – or none at all – might be functionally identical with us.
3. The debate over substance-dualism (see *SP*, pp. 36–8) is irrelevant. What

really explains us is not what we're made of (mind-stuff or matter) but our functional role.

'The question which troubles laymen, and which has long troubled philosophers . . . is this: are we made of matter or soul-stuff? To put it as bluntly as possible, are we just material beings, or are we 'something more'? . . .

People are worried that we may be debunked, that our behavior may be exposed as really explained by something mechanical. Not, to be sure, mechanical in the old sense of cogs and pulleys, but in the newer sense of electricity and magnetism and quantum chemistry and so forth. In this paper, part of what I want to argue is that this can't happen. Mentality is a real and autonomous feature of our world. But even more important . . . is the fact that this whole question has nothing to do with our substance . . . the question of the autonomy of our mental life does not hinge on and has nothing to do with that . . . question about matter or soul-stuff. We could be made of Swiss cheese and it wouldn't matter [. . .]

The concept which is key to unravelling the mysteries in the philosophy of mind, I think, is the concept of *functional isomorphism*. Two systems are functionally isomorphic if *there is a correspondence between the states of one and the states of the other that preserves functional relations* [. . .]

. . . For example, a computer made of electrical components can be isomorphic to one made of cogs and wheels. In other words, for each state in the first computer, there is a corresponding state in the other and . . . the sequential relations are the same – if state A is followed by state B in the case of the electronic computer, state A would be followed by state B in the case of the computer made of cogs and wheels, and it doesn't matter at all that the *physical realizations* of those states are totally different . . . a computer made of electrical components can be isomorphic to one made of cogs and wheels or to human clerks using paper and pencil . . .

Assume that one thesis of classical materialism is correct, and we are, as a whole, just material systems obeying physical laws. Then . . . our mental states, e.g. *thinking about next summer's vacation*, cannot be *identical* with any physical or chemical states. For it is clear from what we already know about computers etc., that whatever the program of the brain may be, it must be physically possible, though not necessarily feasible [in practice], to produce something with that same program but quite a different physical and chemical constitution . . . to identify the state in question with its physical or chemical realization would be quite absurd, given that the realization is in a sense quite accidental [the physical realisation, Putnam will argue, has no explanatory usefulness within psychology].

. . . Does it matter that the soul people [if people have souls] have, so to speak, immaterial brains, and that the brain people [if people have only bodies] have material souls? What matters is the common structure . . . of which we are, alas, in deep ignorance, and not the hardware, be it ever so ethereal [. . .]

So if I am right, and the question of matter or soul-stuff is really irrelevant to any question of philosophical or religious significance, why so much attention to it, why so much heat? The crux of the matter seems to be that both the Diderots of this world and the Descartes of this world have agreed that if we are matter, then there is a physical explanation for how we behave . . . I think the traditional dualist says, '*wouldn't it be terrible if we turned out to be just matter, for then there is a physical explanation for everything we do*.' And the traditional materialist says, '*if we are just matter, then there is a physical explanation for everything we do. Isn't that exciting!*' . . .

I think they are both wrong . . . in assuming that if we are matter, or our souls are material, then there is a physical explanation for our behavior [. . .]'

Putnam now imagines a simple wooden peg passing through a hole in a board, and compares two 'explanations' of the fact that it passes through. Explanation A describes the peg as a rigid lattice of atoms, and the board likewise, and tries to deduce from the laws of particle physics or quantum electrodynamics that there is at least one trajectory which enables the peg-lattice to pass through the board-lattice. Explanation B is the simple common sense explanation that both peg and board are rigid and the hole is bigger than the peg.

Putnam claims that B 'is a correct explanation whether the peg consists of molecules, or continuous rigid substance, or whatever'. He says that even if A really is an explanation, 'it is just a terrible explanation, and why look for terrible explanations when good ones are available?' He continues:

'The fact is that we are much more interested in generalizing to other structures which are rigid and have various geometrical relations, than we are in generalizing to *the next peg that has exactly this molecular structure*, for the very good reason that there is not going to *be* a next peg that has exactly this molecular structure [. . .]

We were only able to deduce a statement which is lawful at the *higher* level, that the peg goes through the hole which is larger than the cross-section of the peg . . .

The conclusion I want to draw from this is that we do have the kind of autonomy that we are looking for in the mental realm. Whatever our mental functioning may be, there seems to be no serious reason to believe that it is *explainable* by our physics and chemistry. And what we are interested in is not: given that we consist of such and such particles, could someone have predicted that we would have this mental functioning? because such a prediction is not *explanatory*, however great a feat it may be. What we are interested in is: can we say at this autonomous level that since we have this sort of [functional] structure, this sort of program, it follows that we will be able to learn this, we will tend to like that, and so on [. . .]

What is the importance of [computing] machines in the philosophy of mind? . . . Machines forced us to distinguish between an abstract structure and its concrete realization . . . in the case of computing machines, we could not avoid rubbing our noses against the fact that what we had to count as to all intents and purposes the same structure could be realized in a bewildering variety of different ways; that the important properties were not physico-chemical . . . machines made us catch on to the idea of functional organization as extremely important [. . .]

. . . what we are really interested in, as Aristotle saw, is form and not matter. *What is our intellectual form?* is the question, not what the matter is . . . My conclusion is that we have what we always wanted – an autonomous mental life. And we need no mysteries, no ghostly agents . . . to have it.'

Comments and questions

Imagine a large display made up of individual light bulbs. Each light bulb has a number. When you say, 'Oh, that's a smiley face!', the operator says 'That's a 26-35-39-43-54-69-65-77.' The operator also knows that any pattern of light bulbs obeying a certain numerical formula (let's call it S) will tend to make children smile, tend to make adults say, 'Look at the smiley face!' and so on. Suppose, finally, that a neuroscientist finds a similar numerical formula S* such that an activation of cells somewhere in the visual system of the brain, corresponding to the formula, triggers activation of motor cells which normally lead to smiling.

Here are four kinds of explanation of the fact that little Jimmy smiled:

1. He saw a smiley face (common sense).
2. He received an input from the display corresponding to formula S (functionalist).
3. Cells in the visual system corresponding to formula S* were simultaneously activated (neurological).
4. Cell c103 released transmitter t46 in the vicinity of cell c785, which etc. etc. etc. . . . (atomistic, or half-way to it).

Is only one of these really explanatory? Is one *better* than all the rest? If so, what makes it better?

....

....

Do the third and fourth kinds of explanation threaten the autonomy of our mental life?

....

....

52

F. H. Bradley (1846–1924) on truth – from *Appearance and Reality*, chs 2 and 15: 1893

In this rather visionary extract, Bradley first attacks the correspondence theory of truth (see *SP*, pp. 170–2). He then argues that the trajectory created by our attempts to find the truth can only end in 'thought's suicide', a kind of higher union with reality.

 '[Truth] exists, as such, in the world of ideas. And ideas, we have seen, are merely symbols. They are general and adjectival, not substantive and individual [like real things] . . . The idea is the fact with its existence disregarded, and its content mutilated . . . No idea can be real.

If judgement is the synthesis of two ideas, then truth consists in the junction of unreals . . .

. . . reality is not a connection of adjectives, nor can it be so represented. Its essence is

to be substantial and individual . . . the fact is not given *directly* in any truth whatever. It can never be stated categorically. And yet, because adjectives depend on substantives, the substantive is implied. Truth will then refer to fact *indirectly*.

6. More ordinary considerations might perhaps have led us to anticipate this result. The common-sense view of facts outside us passing over into the form of truth within us, or copying themselves in a faithful mirror, is shaken and perplexed by the simplest enquiries. What fact is asserted in negative judgements? Has every negation I choose to invent a real counterpart in the world of things? Does *any* logical negation, as such, correspond to fact? Consider again hypothetical judgements. *If* something is, *then* something else follows, but should neither exist, would the statement be false? It seems just as true without facts as with them, and, if so, what fact can it possibly assert? The disjunctive judgement will again perplex us. 'A is *b* or *c*' must be true or false, but how in the world can a *fact* exist as that strange ambiguity '*b* or *c*'? We shall hardly find the flesh and blood alternative which answers to our 'or'.

If we think these puzzles too technical or sought out, let us take more obvious ones. Have the past and future we talk of so freely any real existence? Or let us try a mere ordinary categorical affirmative judgement, 'Animals are mortal.' This seems at first to keep close to reality: the junction of facts seems quite as the junction of ideas. But . . . if ideas are adjectives, this cannot be the case . . . 'Animals' seems perhaps to answer to a fact, since all the animals who exist are real. But in 'Animals are mortal,' is it only animals now existing that we speak of? Do we not mean to say that the animals born hereafter will certainly die? . . . We *mean*, 'Whatever is an animal will die,' but that is the same as '*If* anything is an animal *then* it is mortal.' The assertion is really about mere hypothesis; it is not about fact.

. . . In universal judgements we never mean 'all'. What we mean is 'any', and 'whatever', and 'whenever'. But these involve 'if' [. . .]

7. This result [that 'no truth can state fact'] is however not easy to put up with. For, if the truth is such, then all truths, it would seem, are no better than false. We cannot so give up the categorical judgement, for, if that is lost, then everything fails . . . Universal judgements were merely hypothetical . . . But in singular judgments [it might seem] the case is otherwise. Where the subject, of which you affirm categorically, is one individual, or a set of individuals, your truth expresses fact [. . .]

8. But, if judgement is the union of two ideas, we have not [after all] escaped . . . Ideas are universal, and, no matter what it is that we try to say and dimly mean, what we really express and succeed in asserting, is nothing individual . . . in 'I have a toothache' both the I and the toothache are mere generalities. The *actual* toothache is not any other toothache, and the *actual* I is myself as having this very toothache. But the truth I assert has been and will be true of all other toothaches of my altering self . . . it is vain that we add to the original assertion 'this', 'here', and 'now', for they are all universals. They are symbols whose meaning extends to and covers innumerable instances.

Thus the judgement will be true of any case whatsoever of a certain sort; but, if so, it cannot be true of the reality; for that is unique, and is a fact, not a sort [. . .]

Truth is the object of thinking, and the aim of truth is to qualify existence [with ideas]. Its end, that is, is to give a character to reality in which it can rest. Truth is the predication of such content as, when predicated, is harmonious, and removes inconsistency and with it unrest. And because the given reality is never consistent . . . it is compelled to take the road of indefinite expansion. If thought were successful, it would have a predicate consistent with itself and agreeing entirely with the subject. But on the other hand, the predicate must always be ideal . . . and therefore, in and by itself, devoid of existence [. . .]

. . . Hence truth shows a dissection and never an actual life. Its predicate can never be equivalent to its subject. And if it became so, and if its adjectives could be at once self-consistent and re-welded to existence, it would not be truth any longer. It would have then passed into another and a higher reality [. . .]

. . . We have seen that in judgement we always find the distinction of fact and truth, of idea and reality. Truth and thought are not the thing itself, but are of it and about it [. . .]

Still a mere denial, I admit, is not quite satisfactory. Let us then suppose that the dualism inherent in thought has been transcended. Let us assume that existence is no longer different from truth, and let us see where this takes us. It takes us straight to thought's suicide . . . Thought is relational and discursive, and if it ceases to be this, it commits suicide; and yet, if it remains thus, how does it contain immediate presentation? Let us suppose the impossible accomplished; let us imagine a harmonious system of ideal contents united by relations, and reflecting itself in self-conscious harmony . . . Thought, in a word, must have been absorbed into a fuller experience . . . when thought begins to be more than relational, it ceases to be mere thinking . . . And the question is *not* whether the universe is in any sense intelligible. The question is whether, if you thought it and understood it, there would be no difference left between your thought and the thing . . .

. . . in this whole all divisions would be healed up. It would be experience entire, containing all elements in harmony . . . We cannot imagine, I admit, how in detail this can be. But if truth and fact are to be one, then in some such way thought must reach its consummation. But in that consummation thought has certainly been so transformed, that to go on calling it thought seems indefensible . . .'

Comments and questions

Let's see if we can capture, plainly and soberly, Bradley's main ideas.

First, he attacks the correspondence theory of truth, on the grounds that there are no plausible facts for many judgements to correspond to. There are no disjunctive facts, for example, for disjunctive judgements to correspond to.

One response to this is to analyse facts – and judgments too – into smaller units and suppose that correspondence works on this smaller scale. There may not be a {b or c} fact, but there may be a fact {b} and a fact {c}. Correspondingly, the judgement should be analysed, not as 'A is (b or c)' but as '(A is b) or (A is c)' – that is, as composed of two constituent judgements. And as long as one of the constituent judgements corresponds to the facts, it might be argued, the judgement is true.

If this saves a correspondence account of

disjunction, what about negation (Bradley's first example)? Well, we can say that 'Animals are not mortal' does not correspond to a {not-being-mortal} fact. We can analyse the judgement as 'It is not the case that animals are mortal.' The judgement then corresponds to exactly the same fact as 'Animals are mortal', but asserts (falsely) that the fact does not obtain. Wittgenstein's *Tractatus* pursues a sophisticated version of this general strategy.

So one question is: How powerful is Bradley's attack on the correspondence theory?

....

....

There's another idea in what Bradley says, however, which attacks truth, no matter which theory of it we espouse. Bradley says that language can only present reality to us indirectly: judgements can give us only a verbalised facsimile of the facts, never the facts themselves.

Now you might react impatiently to this, saying that that's exactly what language is *supposed* to do for us. I don't want real mosquitoes every time I say the word 'mosquito'. But Bradley's claim is that our search for better and more comprehensive truths points inevitably in the direction of this impossible, or mystical, union of judgement and reality. Is the natural end-point of language – paradoxically – a kind of knowledge which we cannot put into words? (The *Tractatus*, incidentally, put forward a view very like this.)

....

....

53

Michael Dummett (b. 1925) on anti-realism – from 'Realism' (1963), in *Truth and Other Enigmas*: Gerald Duckworth, 1978

In this important article, Dummett sets out various philosophical problems as problems of realism vs. anti-realism, reviving interest in the radical empiricist idea that the meaning of a statement can't go beyond the evidence we have or might get for it.

'. . . I shall take as my preferred characterisation of a dispute between realists and anti-realists one which represents it as relating . . . to a class of statements, which may be, e.g., statements about the physical world, statements about mental events, processes or states, mathematical statements, statements in the past tense, statements in the future tense, etc. This class I shall . . . term 'the disputed class'. Realism I characterise as the belief that statements of the disputed class possess an objective truth-value, independently of our means of knowing it: they are true or false in virtue of a reality existing independently of us. The anti-realist opposes to this the view that statements of the disputed class are to be understood only by reference to the sort of thing which we count as evidence for a statement of that class. That is, the realist holds that the meanings of statements of the disputed class are not directly tied to the kind of evidence for them that we can have, but consist in the manner of their determination as true or false by states of affairs whose existence is not dependent on our possession of evidence for them. The anti-realist insists, on the contrary, that the meanings of these statements are tied directly to what we count as evidence for them, in such a way that a statement of the disputed class, if true at all, can be true only in virtue of something which we could know and which we should count as evidence for its truth. The dispute thus concerns the notion of truth appropriate for statements of the disputed class; and this means that it is a dispute concerning the kind of *meaning* which these statements have [. . .]

. . . The realist and the anti-realist may agree that it is an objective matter whether, in the case of any given statement of the class, the criteria we use for judging such a statement to be true are satisfied: the difference between them lies in the fact that, for the anti-realist, the truth of the statement can only consist in the satisfaction of these criteria, whereas, for the realist, the statement can be true even though we have no means of recognising it as true [. . .]'

To give a recent example, Thomas Nagel, in Reading 6/49, suggested that there are facts (about the experience of a bat) which we cannot discover, or even state or comprehend in human language. In Dummett's terms, Nagel is a realist about the experience of other minds.

Dummett goes on to consider various classes of disputed statements, including statements about the past and future.

'. . . Since Aristotle, philosophers have disagreed as to whether it is proper to ascribe truth or falsity to statements about the future; and those who adopt the anti-realist position that it is not form to themselves a picture of the temporal process on which, although both past and present states of affairs are already in existence, future states of affairs are simply not yet *there* to render our statements about them true or false. A vivid description of such a picture is given in Broad's *Scientific Thought*. There are, however, two versions of this anti-realist view about the future. According to one, all future-tense statements must be interpreted as rendered true or false, if at all, only by present tendencies and present intentions . . . According to the other version of anti-realism about the future, we do have another use of future-tense statements, a use according to which they are not made definitively true or false by anything in the present, but will be rendered true or false at the time to which they refer: nevertheless, since they are not *yet* true or false, the law of the excluded middle [that every well-formed statement is either true or not true] does not hold for them.

Most philosophers would adopt a realist view of statements about the past; an exception is provided by Ayer in *Language, Truth and Logic*, where he argues that a statement about the past can be true only if there is something in the present (or future) which we count as (conclusive) evidence for it. Yet the justification of the realist view has occasioned much dispute. It seems natural to say that we can never have, now or in the future, direct evidence for the truth of a statement about what is now past, since all our evidence at any time must consist in what is the case at that time: it therefore appears to follow, as Russell concluded, that a Cartesian doubt about the past is unanswerable. Now the usual way of

philosophers with a Cartesian doubt is to declare it senseless: but this would apparently involve us in holding an anti-realist view of statements about the past, the view, namely, that a statement about the past, if true, can be true only in virtue of what is or will be the case, and that therefore there may be statements about the past which are neither true nor false [. . .]'

A 'reductionist' says that statements of one kind can be *reduced* to statements of another kind – that everything which can be said using the first kind of statement can be rephrased in terms of the second. In effect, this means that the first kind of statement could be excluded from language without any real loss. If we go on using statements of the first kind, that's only because they're more familiar or convenient.

Russell in Reading 2/9 proposes that statements about material objects can be reduced to statements about sensibilia, and this is a reductionist phenomenalism of the kind Dummett goes on to discuss:

'In many [cases], anti-realism takes the form of a species of reductionism' [. . .]

Ayer held that statements about the past relate only to present memories and records, while others have held that a meaningful statement about the future can relate only to present tendencies and intentions . . .

. . . It is not always insisted [by anti-realists] that we must *know* the truth of some reductive statement giving the evidence for the truth of a statement of the disputed class: only that there must be some true statement of the reductive [type] whose truth, if we knew it, we should count as evidence. Nor is there necessarily claimed to be a *translation* of statements of the disputed class into statements of the reductive [type] [. . .]

. . . anti-realism need not take the form of reductionism . . . there is no reductive class [of statements] . . . about the future or the past: for neither a memory nor an intention can be characterised independently of what it is a memory *of* or an intention to *do*.

. . . phenomenalism [a modern version of Berkeley's Idealism] is a reductive version of anti-realism, and all the arguments against it centre on this feature of it: the arguments against sense-data fail if it not assumed that a sense-datum language is in principle intelligible prior to, and independently of, the material-object language.' [See for example, Reading 6/45].

Dummett goes on to defend a non-reductive form of phenomenalism, concluding that realism about the external world 'scored too easy a victory because anti-realists chose to be reductionists when they need not, and should not, have been'.

Comments and questions

Where would a realist and an anti-realist disagree about the statement 'It's a sin to tell a lie'?

....

....

Can you think of any general arguments in favour of realism or anti-realism – or must we decide on a case by case basis?

....

....

Are you a realist about

1. the past
2. the future?

....

....

Overview of Area 6

Area 6 deals principally with perception, our main (and for empiricists, only) source of objective knowledge. There is a problem, canvassed in Area 4, about the extent to which perception can be taken at face value. But Area 6 focusses on the extent to which perception involves mental representations. The more deeply mental components are involved, the less objective is any knowledge which the senses give.

Chisholm's chief concern in our first Reading is with the reliability of perception, but he nevertheless finds it necessary to hold – like Locke – that we become aware of trees and clouds only indirectly, by becoming aware directly of other, psychological, things.

Ayer advances a similar view, holding that any theory of perception must invoke sense-data. He argues that a statement about trees or clouds will not be *translatable* into any number of statements about sense-data: rather, trees and clouds are to be seen as theoretical entities useful for predicting the course of our sense-data. Both views clearly threaten our claims to know about an objective, mind-independent world.

But both tend to treat appearances as *things*, and this tendency is resisted in different ways by Ryle and Reid. Ryle argues that to talk of seeing sense-data is as nonsensical as it would be to talk of eating nibbles. There are no sense-data involved in perception. Unfortunately, this leaves us waiting for an account of what *is* involved when someone becomes aware of a round plate looking elliptical (or for that matter, round).

Reid also denies that any kind of mental entity is involved. When I imagine a centaur, there is no literal image, just a process of imagining. This too seems to reject one natural theory (that imagining occurs through an image being present to consciousness) without providing a real alternative, or explaining why no alternative is needed.

The Reading from Watson presents an even more radical rejection of anything inner. Watson argues that 'consciousness' is an inherently unscientific concept – a modern equivalent of 'soul'. And in a way, Nagel, in the following extract, agrees. He points out that the contents of consciousness are subjective through and through. No distinction can be applied to them, between how the thing seems to a particular observer and how it really is. Nagel is unwilling, however, to dispense with consciousness. For him, consciousness is unquestionably real, even though it cannot be brought within any kind of science which aims for increasing objectivity.

Nagel points out that the unscientific nature of consciousness prevents it from being a candidate for any kind of scientific reduction, either to brain states and processes (as in the Smart reading which follows Nagel), or to functional states. Putnam's functionalism, in fairness, is not so much an attempt to reduce consciousness to something scientifically respectable, as to put forward a better way of explaining system behaviour.

These Readings are of course relevant to Area 2 and the question of the reality of the mind. They are also directly relevant, as already mentioned, to Area 4. Truth, knowledge and reality are obviously interlocking concepts and all three engage closely with the nature of the mind and its thoughts.

The Bradley Reading represents another attempt to relate truth to the immediacies of experience. According to Bradley, truth cannot be understood as correspondence with reality: instead, truth (which involves a subject and predicate, even if only in thought) essentially aims to *present* reality. Truth aims at immediacy, but if a true judgement could present the fact, subject-predicate thought would disappear, replaced by thought's immediate union with reality. In this way, Bradley argues, combining symbols or ideas to form judgements is an inherently unstable act – it cannot achieve the state of cognitive equilibrium it aims at, and if it could, it would thereby destroy itself.

The final Reading of Area 6 returns again to the question of perception (defending a non-reductive version of the view that what we really *know* in perception is sense-data)

but from a very general perspective. Dummett leans towards the radical empiricist view that we cannot mean by a statement anything more than the evidence we can in principle amass for it. There can be no evidence-transcendent meaning. For example, when we say 'There is a tree in the quad', we can only mean 'I have, and in other circumstances *would* have, such-and-such sense-data', because these sense-data exhaust the possible evidence for making the statement. In short, anti-realism holds that truth which tries to go beyond the limits of possible knowledge becomes meaningless – to claim *that* degree of objectivity is gibberish.

A number of closely related themes have become knotted together in Area 6 – truth, knowledge, reality, mind, and now meaning too – and we may well begin to feel overwhelmed. One way forward is to find a single issue where these themes can be, to some degree, disentangled. In Area 7, we look at debates about the truth, and the meaning, of religious claims about God.

AREA 7

God

The Readings in this area deal with the nature and justification of religious belief.

54

Norman Malcolm (1911–90) on the ontological argument – from 'Anselm's Ontological Arguments': *The Philosophical Review,* **1960**

In this interesting article, Malcolm distinguishes two versions of the ontological argument. One is the familiar version (see *SP*, pp.188–9) in which Anselm argues that since God is the greatest conceivable being, and since we could conceive a greater being than God if He did not exist (namely, the same being but really existing too), God must exist. In this familiar version of the argument, Anselm regards existence as a perfection (that is, regards a thing as 'greater' if it exists than if it doesn't).

Against this version, Malcolm agrees with Kant that existence is not like wisdom or benevolence, a quality which improves its possessor – it is not, as Anselm's first version of the argument requires, a perfection.

However, Malcolm finds another version of the argument in Anselm:

 "'...it is possible to conceive of a being which cannot be conceived not to exist: and this is greater than one which can be conceived not to exist. Hence, if that, than which nothing greater can be conceived, can be conceived not to exist, it is not that than which nothing greater can be conceived. But this is a contradiction. So truly, therefore, is there something than which nothing greater can be conceived, that it cannot even be conceived not to exist. And this being art thou, O Lord, our God.'"

. . . Previously I rejected *existence* as a perfection. Anselm is maintaining in the remarks last quoted, not that existence is a perfection, but that *the logical impossibility of non-existence is a perfection.* In other words, *necessary existence* is a perfection . . .

Some remarks about the notion of *dependence* may help to make this latter principle intelligible. Many things depend for their existence on other things and events . . . If we reflect on the common meaning of the word 'God' (no matter how vague and confused this is), we realize that it is incompatible with this meaning that God's existence should *depend* on anything . . . To conceive of anything as dependent upon something else for its existence is to conceive of it as a lesser being than God [. . .]

. . . Anselm adds the following acute point: if you can conceive of a certain thing and this thing does not exist then if it *were* to exist its nonexistence would be *possible.* It follows, I believe, that if the thing were to exist it would depend on other things both for coming into and continuing in existence . . .

What Anselm has proved is that the notion of contingent existence or of contingent nonexistence cannot have application to God. His existence must either be logically necessary or logically impossible. The only intelligible way of rejecting Anselm's claim . . . is to maintain that the concept of God, as a being a greater than which cannot be conceived, is self-contradictory or nonsensical [. . .]'

> Malcolm goes on to discuss whether the concept of God might be self-contradictory or nonsensical, defending the concept as one which 'has a place in the thinking and the lives of human beings'. He argues that those philosophers who have regarded the concept of a necessary being as arbitrary or absurd have ignored its real human setting. He concludes:

'At a deeper level, I suspect that the argument can be thoroughly understood only by one who has a view of that human 'form of life' that gives rise to the idea of an infinitely great being, who views it from the *inside* not just from the outside and who has, therefore, at least some inclination to *partake* in that religious form of life.'

Comments and questions

Is it true that Anselm's argument can only be understood by someone who already is, or already is inclined to be, a believer?

....

....

Can the mere idea of complete independence from other things, along with the definition of God as a being than which no greater being can be conceived, prove that a completely independent being really exists?

....

....

Thomas Aquinas (c. 1225–74) on the existence of God – from *Summa Theologiae*, part I, qu.2, art.3

In this famous passage, Aquinas sets out five arguments to prove that God exists.

'. . . the first and most obvious [proof] is based on change. For it is obvious to the senses that some things change. But whatever is changed is changed by something else . . . Now only some actual being can alter something else. For to change something is merely to bring it from a state of potentiality to one of actuality. But only something that is actual can bring another thing to actuality. For example, something actually hot like fire can transform something potentially hot like wood into something actually hot, and in this way, the fire changes the wood . . . it is quite impossible, however, that the same thing should have some property both actually and potentially: it cannot, therefore, be both agent and recipient of the change. In other words, it cannot change itself. Anything in the process of change, therefore, must be changed by something else, and this agent by yet another. An infinite regress here is out of the question, for in that case there would be nothing to initiate the change and so nothing would be changing now . . . We necessarily arrive, then, at some first mover which is not moved or changed by any other thing, and this is what all understand by God.

The second way is based on the idea of an efficient cause. In the perceptible world we discover an order among efficient causes. It is impossible that anything should be its own efficient cause, since it would then be prior to itself, which is impossible. An infinite regress is impossible because [in any chain of causes] if we eliminate a cause we eliminate its effects. So if no cause was first, there would be no intermediate or present causes, which is obviously false. It is necessary, therefore, to postulate some first efficient cause, which all call God.

A third way, based on possibility and necessity, goes like this. We discover that it is possible for some things to exist or not exist . . . But it is impossible that everything should be like this, because what *might* not exist is at some time non-existent. So if everything was merely possible, and nothing existed necessarily, then at some time nothing would exist. But in this case, nothing would exist at present, because things come into existence only by means of things which already exist . . . This is clearly false. Hence . . . there must be something which exists necessarily . . . But an infinite regress of necessary existents is impossible, just as an infinite regress of efficient causes is impossible, as has been explained. Therefore we must postulate something which exists necessarily but not through the agency of anything else . . . And this everyone calls God.

The fourth way is based on degrees in things: we find some things to be more good, or more true, or more noble etc, other things to be less so. But 'more' or 'less' express degrees of approximation to some superlative. For example, a thing is 'hotter' the more closely it approaches what is hottest of all . . . So whatever is the maximum of any kind is presupposed by all the things which belong to that kind, just as fire, which is hottest of all, is presupposed by whatever is hot . . . '

Translation alert: Aquinas uses here the Aristotelian term 'cause' which I've changed into 'presupposed by': he says that the greatest thing in a given class is the cause of all the things which are in that class, citing Book 2 of Aristotle's Metaphysics. I think this use of 'cause' is likely to mislead – but to tell the truth, 'presupposed by' may not be much better.

'. . . Therefore existence and goodness and all other perfections presuppose a maximum of the same kind, and this we call God.

The fifth way is based on the fact that things are guided. We see various things which lack knowledge, such as physical bodies, acting for some end. This is apparent from the fact that they always or generally act in the same fashion so as to achieve the best result. It is clear, therefore, that they do this not by chance but by design. Now things which lack knowledge act for an end only because they are directed by someone with knowledge, just as an arrow is aimed by an archer. There must, therefore, be someone who directs all natural things to their end. This we call God.'

Comments and questions

Aquinas sets out the arguments with great clarity and economy, and there has been a huge amount of discussion and commentary. One recurring question is this: even if we grant all the arguments, is the resulting 'God of the philosophers' also the God of belief? Would a superlative, necessary, designer, who set the chain of present events in motion, inspire *worship*?

....

....

56

Anthony Kenny (b. 1931) on teleology and design – from *Reason and Religion*, ch. 5: Blackwell, 1987

In this extract, Kenny discusses teleological explanation and its role in the argument from design to the existence of God.

 'G H von Wright, in his book *Explanation and Understanding*, drew a distinction between two traditions of scientific inquiry. One (which he called Aristotelian) could be regarded as teleological or finalistic; the other (which he called Galilean) could be regarded as causal or mechanistic . . .

I think von Wright's insight here is correct and profound . . . Clearly, teleological explanation applies not only to the science of man: it is omnipresent, *prima facie* at least, in biology. The Nobel-prize-winning biologist Jacques Monod, in his *Chance and Necessity*,

speaks of a 'fundamental characteristic common to all living beings without exception: that of being objects endowed with a purpose or project'. Do these two modes of intelligibility apply . . . at the most fundamental level of cosmic intelligibility? The argument from design seeks to show that they do: indeed that [teleological explanation] underlies [mechanistic].

Socrates, in Plato's *Phaedo*, describes his gradual disillusionment with the mechanistic explanations of natural science . . . For Socrates, teleological explanation was deeper, more profound, than mechanistic explanation.

At the opposite extreme from Socrates stood Descartes. 'I consider the usual inquiries about final causes to be wholly useless in physics; it could not but be rash for me to investigate the aims of God' . . .

Descartes, it is well known, rejected explanation of gravity in terms of the attraction between bodies, on the grounds that this was a teleological explanation which postulated in inert bodies knowledge of a goal or terminus. But the essence of teleological explanation is not the fact that the explanation is given [after the event], or by reference to the [end-point to which the process tends]. It is rather the part played in the explanation by the notion of purpose: the pursuit of good and the avoidance of evil . . . All teleological explanation is in terms of the benefit of agents . . .

The nature of teleological explanation is often misstated both by its critics and its defenders. Critics allege that to accept a teleological explanation is to accept backwards causation: the production of a cause by its effect. Whether or not backwards causation is the nonsense it is usually taken to be, teleological explanation does not involve any acceptance of it, as Charles Taylor showed. All that is necessary is that the law covering the behaviour of a teleological agent should be of the form 'A will do whatever behaviour B is required in circumstances C to achieve its goal G' . . .

At the other extreme, defenders of teleological explanation have been known to claim that all causal explanation is somehow teleological. Causal laws, it is argued, if they are not to be subject to constant falsification in the real world, must be stated in terms of the tendency of causal agents to produce certain effects. But are not laws stated in terms of tendencies teleological laws, since tendencies are defined in terms of their upshot? . . . But an act may be defined by its result, and a tendency be specified as a tendency to perform such an act, without this 'end' in the sense of final state being an 'end' in the sense of a goal. Not every result of an action is a goal of that action.

In truth, teleological agency is neither universal (as Aquinas maintained) nor mythological (as some modern sceptics have argued) [. . .]

. . . Let us call entities for which there can be good and bad *beneficiaries*. Not only living beings are beneficiaries: so are their parts, artefacts, environments; for them too things can be good or bad . . . Numbers, classes, rocks, dust, mud are not beneficiaries: things are not good or bad for them.

Only beneficiaries can have purposes, though not all beneficiaries have purposes. All trees are beneficiaries, like other living things; but an individual tree, in the wild, does not have a purpose . . .

There are two ways in which things may have purpose: they may exist to serve a purpose, and they may act for a purpose . . . Thus the organs of animals operate to serve a particular purpose which is their function . . . The circulation of the blood is the function which not only defines the heart, but gives the reason for its existence . . .

. . . however, animals have purposes, but not functions. That is to say, their existence does not in the normal case serve a purpose, but they perform many actions with a purpose: spiders weave webs, birds build nests, dogs dig up buried bones [. . .]

Common to both proponents and critics of the argument from design – nowadays at least – is the premise that explanation in terms of purpose . . . cannot be a rock-bottom, basic-level explanation: it must be reducible either to an explanation in terms of design (intelligent purpose) or to an explanation in mechanistic terms [. . .]

What, then, shall we say of the argument from design [Aquinas' fifth way]? The argument in its simplest form goes as follows:

1. Wherever there is purpose there is a designer.
2. There is purpose which has no designer in the natural world.
3. Therefore, there is a designer outside the natural world.

The second premise is undeniably true. The first premise is not a tautology, given the definitions I have offered of purpose and design: purpose is identified quite differently from design, purpose by identifying the regular goal-directed behaviour, design by locating the conception of the good from which it arises. But is it true [. . .]

The strongest reason for thinking it false is that it seems clear that there can be purpose without a designer if the purpose can be given a mechanistic explanation [...]

It is sometimes said that the argument from design leads to a 'God of the gaps': a God invoked merely to fill the gaps left by scientific explanation at any given point in history. If the argument from design is to succeed, the God it points to must be a God of necessary gaps, that is to say, gaps in explanation which can be demonstrated not to be capable of being filled by a particular type of explanation ... the God of contingent gaps would have only a precarious hold on worship.'

Comments and questions

Suppose we grant for a moment that living beings are 'endowed with a purpose or project', and allow that this means that explaining teleologically why living beings do the things they do can be satisfactory in itself. What if someone now points out that there is no sharp distinction between animate and inanimate things, no clear definition of what it is to be alive? Does it follow that teleological and mechanistic types of explanations are two extremes of a continuous spectrum? Must we either say that all teleological explanations contain within them the seeds of a mechanistic explanation, or vice versa? And if we must, which?

....

....

57

Anthony Flew (b. 1919) on religious belief – from 'Theology and Falsification': *University*, 1950

In this well-known article, Flew argues that since genuinely empirical claims must be falsifiable and since nothing would in reality falsify the claim that God exists, that claim has no real factual content. He begins with a parable:

'... Once upon a time two explorers came upon a clearing in the jungle. In the clearing were growing many flowers and many weeds. One explorer says, 'Some gardener must tend this plot.' The other disagrees, 'There is no gardener.' So they pitch their tents and set a watch. No gardener is ever seen. 'But perhaps he is an invisible gardener.' So they set up a barbed-wire fence. They electrify it. They patrol with bloodhounds ... But no shrieks ever suggest that some intruder has received a shock. No movements of the wire ever betray an invisible climber. The bloodhounds never give cry. Yet still the Believer is not convinced. 'But there is a gardener, invisible, intangible, insensible to electric shocks, a gardener who has no scent and makes no sound, a gardener who comes secretly to look after the garden which he loves.' At last the Sceptic despairs, 'But what remains of your original assertion? Just how does what you call an invisible, intangible, eternally elusive gardener differ from an imaginary gardener or even from no gardener at all?'

In this parable we can see how what starts as an assertion, that something exists

... may be reduced step by step to an altogether different status, to an expression perhaps of a 'picture preference' ... A fine brash hypothesis may thus be killed by inches, the death by a thousand qualifications.

And in this, it seems to me, lies the peculiar danger, the endemic evil, of theological utterance. Take such utterances as 'God has a plan,' 'God created the world,' 'God loves us as a father loves his children.' They look at first sight very much like assertions, vast cosmological assertions ...

Now to assert that such and such is the case is necessarily equivalent to denying that such and such is not the case ... And if there is nothing which a putative assertion denies then there is nothing which it asserts either: and so it is not really an assertion ...

Now it often seems to people who are not religious as if there was no conceivable event or series of events the occurrence of which would be admitted by sophisticated religious people to be a sufficient reason for conceding 'There wasn't a God after all' or 'God does not really love us then.' Someone tells us that God loves us as a father loves his children. We are reassured. But then we see a child dying of inoperable cancer of the throat. His earthly father is driven frantic in his efforts to help, but his Heavenly Father reveals no obvious sign of concern. Some qualification is made – God's love is 'not a merely human love' or it is 'an inscrutable love' perhaps ... We are reassured again. But then perhaps we ask: what is this assurance of God's (appropriately qualified) love worth, what is this apparent guarantee really a guarantee against?'

Comments and questions

Is there any sequence of events which a committed believer would accept as falsifying belief in God? No matter how bad things seem, wouldn't they be interpreted (as in the story of Job) as a 'test of faith'?

....

....

Is there any sequence of events which would persuade you that all your experience was a dream? Wouldn't you interpret anything which seemed to show this as a kind of mad hallucination?

....

....

What might a 'picture preference' amount to, if it doesn't involve any real difference about the facts?

....

....

Ludwig Wittgenstein (1889–1951) on religious belief – from *Lectures and Conversations on Aesthetics, Psychology and Religious Belief*: **Blackwell, 1970 (ed. C. Barrett)**

The following remarks come from notes taken by students at three lectures Wittgenstein gave in 1938. Like so many of

Wittgenstein's ideas, they seem important and full of insight, and yet intensely particular, resistant to generalisation.

'Suppose that someone believed in the Last Judgment, and I don't, does that mean that I believe the opposite to him, just that there won't be such a thing? I would say: 'Not at all, or not always [. . .]'

If someone said: 'Wittgenstein, do you believe in this?' I'd say: 'No.' 'Do you contradict the man?' I'd say: 'No [. . .]'

Would you say: 'I believe the opposite,' or 'There is no reason to suppose such a thing'? I'd say neither.

Suppose someone were a believer and said: 'I believe in a Last Judgment,' and I said: 'Well, I'm not so sure. Possibly.' You would say that there is an enormous gulf between us. If he said: 'There is a German aeroplane overhead,' and I said: 'Possibly. I'm not so sure,' you'd say we were fairly near.

It isn't a question of my being anywhere near him, but on an entirely different plane, which you could express by saying: 'You mean something altogether different, Wittgenstein [. . .]'

. . . he has what you might call an unshakeable belief. It will show, not by reasoning or by appeal to ordinary grounds for belief, but rather by regulating for all in his life.

This is a very much stronger fact – foregoing pleasures – always appealing to this picture [. . .]

. . . He will treat this belief as extremely well-established, and in another way as not well-established at all [. . .]

Suppose you had two people, and one of them, when he had to decide which course to take, thought of retribution, and the other did not. One person might, for instance, be inclined to take everything that happened to him as a reward or punishment, and another person doesn't think of this at all.

These people think entirely differently. Yet, so far, you can't say they believe different things.

. . . you can call it believing the opposite, but it is entirely different from what we would normally call believing the opposite.

I think differently . . . I have different pictures [. . .]

In one sense, I understand all he says – the English words 'God, 'separate', etc. I understand. I could say: 'I don't believe in this,' and this would be true, meaning that I haven't got these thoughts or anything that hangs together with them. But not that I could contradict the thing.

You might say: 'Well, if you can't contradict him, that means you don't understand him. If you did understand him, then you might.' That again is Greek to me. My normal technique of language leaves me. I don't know whether to say they understand each other or not.

These controversies look quite different from any normal controversies. Reasons look entirely different from normal reasons [. . .]

The point is that if there were evidence, this would in fact destroy the whole business [. . .]

A man would fight for his life not to be dragged into the fire. No induction. Terror. That is, as it were, part of the substance of the belief.

That is partly why you don't get in religious controversies, the form of controversy where one person is *sure* of the thing, and the other says: 'Well, possibly [. . .]'

. . . suppose we said that a certain picture might play the role of constantly admonishing me, or I always think of it. Here, an enormous difference would be between those people for whom the picture is constantly in the foreground, and the others who just didn't use it at all [. . .]

In a religious discourse we use such expressions as: 'I believe that so and so will happen,' and use them differently to the way in which we use them in science [. . .]

It has been said a thousand times by intelligent people that indubitability is not enough in this case. Even if there is as much evidence as for Napoleon. Because the indubitability wouldn't be enough to make me change my whole life.

[Christianity] doesn't rest on a historical basis in the sense that the ordinary belief in historic facts could serve as a foundation.

. . . they are not treated as historical, empirical, propositions.

Those people who had faith didn't apply the doubt which would ordinarily apply to *any* historical propositions. Especially propositions of a long time past, etc [. . .]

Here we have people who treat this evidence in a different way. They base things on evidence which taken in one way would seem exceedingly flimsy. They base enormous things on this evidence. Am I to say they are unreasonable? I wouldn't call them unreasonable.

I would say, they are certainly not *reasonable*, that's obvious.

'Unreasonable' implies, with everyone, rebuke.

I want to say: they don't treat this as a matter of reasonability [. . .]

If [someone] is religious and says he believes in Judgment Day, I won't even know whether to say I understand him or not. I've read the same things as he's read. In a most

important sense, I know what he means.

. . . Not clear what the criterion of meaning the same is. They might describe the same things. You might say, this already shows that they mean the same [. . .]

Whether a thing is a blunder or not – it is a blunder in a particular system. Just as something is a blunder in a particular game and not in another [. . .]

. . . Suppose someone dreamt of the Last Judgment, and said he now knew what it would be like. Suppose someone said: 'This is poor evidence . . .'

If you compare it with anything in Science which we call evidence, you can't credit that anyone could soberly argue: 'Well, I had this dream . . . therefore . . . Last Judgment'. You might say: 'For a blunder, that's too big.' If you suddenly wrote down numbers on the blackboard, and then said: 'Now, I'm going to add,' and then said: '2 and 21 is 13,' etc. I'd say: 'This is no blunder.'

There are cases where I'd say he's mad, or he's making fun. Then there might be cases where I look for an entirely different explanation altogether . . .

I mean, if a man said to me after a dream that he believed in the Last Judgment, I'd try to find out what sort of impression it gave him . . . I can't treat the words as I normally treat 'I believe so and so [. . .]'

What is the criterion for meaning something different? Not only what he takes as evidence for it, but also how he reacts, that he is in terror, etc [. . .]

Take 'God created man'. Pictures of Michelangelo showing the creation of the world. In general, there is nothing which explains the meanings of words as well as a picture, and I take it that Michelangelo was as good as anyone can be and did his best, and here is the picture of the Deity creating Adam.

If we ever saw this, we certainly wouldn't think this the Deity. The picture has to be used in an entirely different way if we are to call the old man in that queer blanket 'God', and so on.

... [Michelangelo] wouldn't have said that God or Adam looked as they look in this picture [...]

Suppose someone said: 'What do you believe, Wittgenstein? Are you a sceptic? Do you know whether you will survive death?' I would really, this is a fact, say: 'I can't say. I don't know,' because I haven't any clear idea what I'm saying when I'm saying: 'I don't cease to exist,' etc [...]

The whole *weight* may be in the picture.'

Comments and questions

Some people see relativism in these (and other) remarks by Wittgenstein. Is he saying that a non-believer cannot understand or evaluate religious belief?

....

....

Wittgenstein says that the disagreement between believer and non-believer is unlike the disagreement between two aircraft-observers. How *important* is this unlikeness?

....

....

Wittgenstein says religious belief is unshakeable, not *based* on historical beliefs or other evidence, a matter of taking certain pictures very seriously. Is this a fair and accurate account of the ordinary believer's belief in God?

....

....

59

Søren Kierkegaard (1813–55) on the 'absurdity' of belief – from *Concluding Unscientific Postscript*: **1846**

In this short extract, Kierkegaard contrasts the probable beliefs of everyday life with the intensity of faith – an idea which goes back to Tertullian's 'I believe *because* it is impossible.'

'The *absurd* is precisely by its objective repulsion the measure of the intensity of faith in its inwardness. Imagine a man who wishes to acquire faith: let the comedy begin. He wishes to have faith, but he wishes also to safeguard himself by means of an objective inquiry and its approximation-process. With the help of the approximation-process, the absurd becomes something different; it becomes probable; it becomes increasingly probable; it becomes extremely and emphatically probable. Now he is ready to believe, and he ventures to claim for himself that he does not believe in the way that shoemakers and tailors and simple folk believe, but only after long deliberation. At last he is ready to believe – and look! at this exact moment it has become impossible to believe. Anything that is almost probable, or probable, or extremely and emphatically probable, is something he can almost know, or as good as know, or extremely and emphatically almost know – but it is impossible to *believe*. For the absurd is the object of faith, and the only object that can be believed.'

Comments and questions

When a believer sings 'I know that my Redeemer liveth', is that, strictly speaking, a mistake? Would it be more correct to sing 'I have faith that my Redeemer liveth'? What's the difference between 'knowing' and 'having faith'?

....

....

    Both Wittgenstein and Kierkegaard say that religious belief cannot be likened to beliefs which we try to support with evidence. Is that true?

....

....

60

W. H. Newton-Smith (b. 1943) on metaphysics in cosmology – from 'The Origin of the Universe', in *Time in Contemporary Intellectual Thought*: Elsevier Science, 2000 reprint (ed. P. J. N. Baert)

In this wide-ranging and attractive paper, Newton-Smith attacks some recent speculations in cosmology as unscientific. This last reading revisits some of the questions about science raised in Area 1,

shows how some forms of religious belief might be described as 'metaphysics', and asks what the proper role of philosophy should be, among these great disputes.

 'Define metaphysics as unconstrained speculation which goes beyond the empirical data in the hope of providing fundamental explanations. The empirical data is what we might observe with our senses, perhaps with a little help from our instruments. Unconstrained speculation is speculation that goes so far beyond this data that there is no realistic hope that the data will decide between rival speculations. By fundamental explanations I mean explanations which purport to account for the ultimate constitution of the physical world and/or the ultimate origin of the universe.

    Much of the history of philosophy consisted of metaphysics under this definition. It is a case of "consisted" and not "consists", for at least in the English-speaking world in the Twentieth Century, there has been a concerted attempt to eradicate metaphysics. The attack on metaphysics started modestly enough in the early years of this century. It began with philosophers of science who sought to remove metaphysics from physics. Pierre Duhem, noting the irresolvable character of metaphysical disputes, proposed constituting the goal of physics so as to make it an "autonomous" subject. As long as metaphysical speculation was part of physics, the physicist would depend on the metaphysician. And the sins of the latter would be visited on the former. Referring to the metaphysicians of the nineteenth century, Duhem said that "the noise of their battles and the fracas of their collapse have wearied physicists". To avoid metaphysical contamination, he advocated "instrumentalism". The goal of science was not to be explanatory truth but empirical success. Theories were to be judged exclusively in terms of their abilities to make correct predictions. Duhem was fond of the image of the scientist as a do-it-yourselfer. This scientist had a utility cabinet with partitions grouping tools for different purposes. He took out a tool, a theory, and, as for the handy-man, the only question of interest was the usefulness of that theory in dealing with the empirical world, the world of things we can observe [. . .]

Anti-metaphysics was not exactly news in philosophical circles. Hume, after all, had condemned all "ideas not derived from impressions". In more modern terminology, we would say that for Hume no word had a meaning unless it stood for a type of experience or could be defined in terms of words which did stand for a type of experience. Among the ideas condemned on Hume's edict were Newton's conceptions of absolute space and absolute time. For absolute space, space considered apart from its contents, was not something which could be experienced or even defined in terms of things which could be experienced. While the anti-metaphysical perspective was not new, what was new was the take-up of this idea in scientific circles. Einstein himself played an important role in the conversion of the scientific community. For in sweeping away the Newtonian conceptions of space and time, Einstein gave Hume credit for his insights. It is in fact rather doubtful that reading Hume had anything to do with his generation of the Special Theory of

Relativity. But the fact that he said this had considerable impact.

Contemporary cosmologists take themselves to be working without metaphysics. Barrow and Silk claim it to be one of the great achievements of modern cosmological theory that "it has transformed the study of the universe from metaphysics into physics" (Barrow and Silk 1983, p. 226).

The Vienna Circle, the Logical Positivists of the twenties and thirties, never tired of citing this as an example of what could be achieved in science once metaphysics was banished. Reichenbach roundly condemned the greatest scientist of all time, Newton, for being a dogmatic metaphysician. The Positivists argued that science had made great strides through being anti-metaphysical. And they sought to legitimate their anti-metaphysical philosophy of science on the grounds that it described what it was about science that made science the great success it has been this century. Science, they said, was controlled by the empirical data. Science had progressed by banishing what was not so controlled, such as the Newtonian conceptions of space and time.

If science could achieve this by being anti-metaphysical, there was hope for philosophy if only it would emulate science. And so there was to be a new, scientific philosophy, which would be ruthlessly anti-metaphysical. This meant that there was little left of traditional philosophy. Any sentence was condemned as meaningless if there was no way of testing that sentence in experience. The only role left for philosophy in future was the analysis of the language of science. The glorious future was not long-lived. Someone was ungracious enough to point out that the fundamental principle of positivism – "untestable sentences are meaningless" – was itself an untestable sentence.

If positivism as such was in turn to be rejected, it left a legacy: a collective nervousness in the philosophical community about departing from the realm of the empirical. Some philosophers took the data to be ordinary language and the task of philosophy that of determining how words for notions which traditionally interested philosophers such as truth, causality or knowledge functioned in the vernacular. For another philosopher, the later Wittgenstein, the very asking of the traditional questions stemmed from an objectionable impulse to seek general, speculative explanatory theories. His therapeutic philosophy sought to remove those misunderstandings of ordinary language which had promoted this impulse to theorize illegitimately [. . .]

. . . [But] the impulse to speculate in a metaphysical vein goes deep in our culture. It has not gone away just because philosophers are hesitant to get involved . . . it is, in fact, alive and well; and it is being nurtured within cosmology . . . Cosmologists are indulging in the sort of metaphysical speculation that would prevent a young philosopher from getting tenure. And the reception of this, as evidenced by the position of Stephen Hawking's book on the best seller lists . . . shows that interest in metaphysics is as strong as ever within our culture [. . .]

Reference was made above to the impact of the Einsteinian revolution in science . . .

One can overdo this use of the image of revolution. In a political revolution, the agreed procedures for making political choices are replaced, if only temporarily, by force. This image suggested to some that in scientific revolutions everything is swept aside. Kuhn has been misinterpreted as saying that the normal procedures for scientific theory choice are suspended in favour of rhetoric, propaganda and the influence of personalities. Kuhn did appear to say at one stage that the concepts changed so radically that the theories of Einstein and Newton were incommensurable; that is, expressed in such different languages that no translation between them was possible. But that is absurd. Much is preserved in a revolution including a commitment to the basic procedures for making scientific decisions. What is also preserved is the empirical successes of the old theory. Einstein did not deny that the Newtonian theory worked well for most cases. Problems arose in cases involving great distance or rapid motion. In fact, part of the success of the Einsteinian theory derives from the fact that Einstein's theory explains just why Newton's theory worked when and where it did work. Newton's laws need a correcting factor, a factor which drops out for low velocities. It is this correcting factor which is responsible for the great transformations in our thinking about space and time. And what we should learn from this "revolution" is that it is highly likely that in due course some correction will be required in, say, Einstein's general theory of relativity. A slight correction, a correction that does not matter most of the time, can well lead to quite radical transformations in the general picture of things, the world view, provided by the theory. This is the cautionary tale. Be minded that the metaphysical speculations supported by a currently fashionable theory are highly likely to be swept away in due course. The next theory will preserve the empirical successes of

Einstein but may well not preserve the associated world-views […]'

> Newton-Smith goes on to show how the change from a Steady State model of the universe to a singularity model encourages some scientists to think they have found the ultimate beginning of everything. This is partly because a singularity is microscopic, and so for quantum reasons possibly uncaused, and partly because at a singularity various values become infinite and the laws of nature break down. He continues:

'The very positing of the BBS [Big Bang singularity] was metaphysical. The BBS involved various parameters taking on infinite values. Just what it is for an actual physical quantity to take on an infinite value is quite obscure. Once upon a time it was held to be a serious defect in a theory if it permitted this. The charge of metaphysics derives from the fact that there could be no direct empirical evidence that a physical parameter took on an infinite value rather than some enormously large finite value, as large as you like. It is no answer to say that an infinite value is to be preferred to a very large finite value on the grounds that a nice model involves that value. For what is at issue is the viability of that particular model. Mach and Duhem, who set physics on its anti-metaphysical course, would have firmly resisted any theory giving infinite values to parameters […]

The reasonable, if unexciting thing to say, given that one was even prepared to countenance the existence of singularities, was that we could say nothing about what went before or did not go before the BBS.

This plea for a candid acknowledgement of ignorance did not find favour. It was said that it failed to attend to the defining characteristic of a singularity. A singularity is a boundary beyond which the spacetime manifold cannot be extended. Certainly it is a property of singularities that they are points where the manifold is infinitely curved and matter is infinity dense. But their most important property is that of being a terminus to the further temporal extrapolation backwards of the spacetime. That being so, it is said that the singularity theorems show the time of the singularity to be the first time. Consequently, there was a first event.

[However], the General Theory of Relativity [on which Penrose and Hawking's singularity theory depended] does not have the vast body of observational successes of a theory like Quantum Mechanics, nor has it generated impressive technological spin-offs. Given, in particular, that the singularity theorems said that the General Theory broke down at the BBS, the empirical data did not favour holding the BBS to be an absolute beginning over holding the BBS to be a limit to our abilities to know […]

To treat the BBS as really existing was to introduce metaphysics into physics. To treat it as the beginning of the universe was *metaphysics squared*. For some cosmologists, the metaphysics did not stop even there. Being used to seeking explanations, they asked what could explain the occurrence of the BBS. *Ex hypothesi*, it was the first physical event or state, so no possibility existed of providing a causal explanation of its occurrence in terms of prior states of the universe. In what sense could it be explained? To some the only possible answer was a theological one. If there was an omnipotent, omniscient creator the occurrence of the BBS could be explained by reference to his or her actions. As it is standard scientific practice to infer the existence of something if that something provides the best possible explanation of some phenomenon (in this case the BBS), to posit the existence of such a creator was scientifically respectable [...]

Would it be methodologically reasonable from a scientific point of view to invoke [a creator god] X as the explanation of the BBS? The answer is quite clearly "no" for at least three reasons. First, it is a principle of scientific methodology that all things being equal, the weakest of the hypotheses which will explain the data is to be preferred. Clearly there are weaker hypotheses available. One could invoke, for instance, the existence of Y who is really powerful without being omnipotent (powerful enough to bring this world into existence but not powerful enough to bring certain other universes into existence) and really quite knowledgeable without being omniscient (Y could not quite see how things would work out in detail). All things being equal, Y is to be preferred to X. Indeed, if we imagine also that Y is not perfect, Y is much to be preferred. For even a cursory glance around the universe makes it highly unlikely its creator, if any, was perfect. For that case, one would expect British trains to run more to schedule. And one would have expected humans to be slightly more disposed to exercise their freewill in ways beneficial to their fellows if the creator had been all good.

A second methodological failure of the hypothesis of X (and Y for that matter) is that it does not generate novel predictions capable of falsification. Some methodologists, most notably Popper and his disciples, hold that no hypothesis counts as scientific unless it generates testable predictions. Even those methodologists who do not take such a strong line would hold that a hypothesis not generating novel falsifiable predictions was for that very reason suspect and not capable of playing an explanatory role.

[Thirdly], it is methodologically undesirable to introduce what might be called "terminal hypotheses" in science. A terminal hypothesis is one which precludes the possibility of seeking further explanations. If one were to ask in turn what explains the existence of X, one is likely to be told either that X is self-explanatory or that the request for a further explanation is inappropriate. To see how methodologically suspect such a response is, imagine someone in the early days of the atomic hypothesis, offering a version of that hypothesis which said either that atoms were self-explanatory or that a request for the explanation of the behaviour of atoms was inappropriate. This would not have had any credibility in comparison with an atomic theory which invited further explanatory investigations into the structure of atoms. On the basis of this and of the other two methodological considerations cited above, one has to conclude that X is methodologically suspect. It is not at all scientifically respectable to argue from the hypothetical BBS to the existence of a creator. Those scientists so inclined move from "metaphysics squared" to "metaphysics cubed".

... we tend to give great credibility to claims which are represented as being scientifically respectable. It should be clear by now that when those claims are baroque metaphysical constructions built on

— 183 —

speculative theories, our caution should be great. And if the theories are drawn from an area of science which is itself in great turbulence, caution should give way to complete agnosticism. That is the situation in contemporary cosmology [. . .]'

> Newton-Smith goes on to discuss recent versions of the singularity idea, various 'anthropic' principles, and metaphysics in quantum mechanics, and concludes:

'All of this makes one want to bring back Cardinal Bellarmine. Bellarmine persecuted Galileo on behalf of the Church, apparently with some reluctance. One of Bellarmine's tasks was the calculation of the date of Easter, something which he found it easier to do using a Copernican system rather than a Ptolemaic system. And consequently Bellarmine attempted to persuade Galileo to become an instrumentalist. If Galileo offered his version of the Copernican system as a mere tool, as a calculating device generating correct predictions, there would be no clash with the Scriptures. The Church in the person of Cardinal Bellarmine could use Galileo's device and Galileo could be encouraged to work on it further. This is not a very good reason for being an instrumentalist and Galileo declined to follow Bellarmine. Galileo claimed his theory to be true. Remarking that the Scriptures were also true and that the truth cannot conflict, he recommended that Bellarmine find an interpretation of the Scriptures which would render them consistent with his theory – a remark which did Galileo no good at all.

There had been good reasons, however, for being an instrumentalist with regard to the theory of Copernicus. For at the time the theories of Ptolemy and Copernicus fitted the data equally well. Either could be used to get the same, correct, predictions (even if Bellarmine found Copernicus computationally simpler). In the end, observations came to light which rendered Copernicus a better bet than Ptolemy. The situation in cosmology at present is somewhat similar. There is a range of theories that go so far beyond the available empirical data, that there is no reason to select one rather than the other with any degree of confidence. In this situation, the reasonable thing to do is to regard these theories as devices, one of which may some day warrant treatment as something more than a mere device, a mere model. Agnosticism should be the order of the day.

To take these models as true representations of the universe is bad science. To offer to the public these models as being the truth ("I believe we now know the cause of the Big Bang . . ."), is entirely irresponsible. It is to play on the credulity of the public with regard to what is represented to them as being scientifically respectable. Having taken the models as literally true descriptions of the universe and then to seek and derive grand metaphysical conclusions is to indulge in the Abstruse Philosophy that Hume wished to see ended . . . Once the nonsense being offered is exposed, it is likely to bring cosmology into disrepute.

Philosophy has lost sight of what ought to be one of its predominant goals: the dissemination of its reflections to the general public. The general public may not have adopted Hume's anti-metaphysics but at least it had the opportunity to follow his arguments. Hume put his reflections on the science of his day to the public in a lucid, lively and accessible fashion. That is what is particularly needed now. Unless philosophy as an institution provides this, the case of its survival as a discipline is questionable.'

Comments and questions

Newton-Smith distinguishes metaphysics from science as going beyond 'what we might observe with our senses, perhaps with a little help from our instruments'. Well, what's *wrong* with metaphysics, so defined (see Reading 4/35)? Is it fair to attack metaphysics – for example, the introduction of a creator god – with arguments from the methodology of science?

....

....

Newton-Smith criticises some cosmologists for putting forward unconfirmed theories as if they were true. He says 'Agnosticism should be the order of the day.'

Suppose someone responded like this: 'For an individual taken alone, agnosticism would be correct. But for the scientific community as a whole, it's best if various ideas are put forward and developed with all possible vigour. That way, we get a clearer picture of the range of possible theories, and new data have plenty of existing theories to bite on. This does involve individuals in saying things they can't really justify. But it's best for the rationality of the whole community, if some individuals give up (some of) their rationality as a sacrifice for the greater good.'

Would this be an acceptable response to Newton-Smith's view of scientific responsibility?

....

....

Newton-Smith believes that philosophy has lost direction after the rejection of logical positivism, and in particular, that it has become inaccessible to non-philosophers. Based on what you have read, do you think philosophy is too technical to be understood by non-philosophers?

....

....

Overview of Area 7

Area 7 deals, not only with the question whether God exists, but with the prior question of how best to *understand* religious claims such as 'God exists'.

The reading by Malcolm attempts first of all to get clear what Anselm's famous ontological argument really says, but it moves on to suggest that the argument may be fully intelligible only to someone who is already committed, or disposed to become committed, to belief in God. Anselm himself seems to have thought of his argument, not simply as providing a reason to believe in God, but as explaining what it *means* to believe in God.

Our second reading was a classical statement by Aquinas of 'five ways' to prove that God exists. One of these – the fifth of Aquinas' ways, aka the argument from design – was then discussed in the Reading by Kenny. Kenny also considered the possibility of a teleological approach to understanding the world, (according to *SP*, the rejection of teleology has been *the* defining event of modern philosophy).

The reading by Flew sharpens the contrast between a religious and scientific perception of the world. If Popper is right, the distinctive feature of scientific thinking is its openness to falsification. But, Flew asks, would a religious believer really allow anything to falsify his or her belief in God? If not, belief in God cannot really be a factual belief.

Wittgenstein also perceives a difference between religious belief and ordinary everyday belief, though he is less willing to characterise it in hard and fast terms. For Wittgenstein, disagreement about a religious belief brings with it interesting difficulties in mutual understanding, and interesting differences in attitudes to evidence. The difference between believer and non-believer is not simply a matter of 'picture preference': there are, if Wittgenstein is right, deep and subtle differences which call for very careful handling.

The Kierkegaard reading pursues the question of evidence for religious belief, arguing that the element of personal commitment in religious faith is incompatible with the cool weighing of evidence. We don't fall in love by listing reasons for believing that the person in question is lovable. And yet it would be silly to criticise falling in love as unscientific – wouldn't it?

Our final reading takes a broad view, ranging over many of these issues. Newton-Smith explains why 'metaphysics' has fallen out of fashion among philosophers, and criticises cosmologists who argue in the manner of Aquinas' first or second ways, from the Big Bang to a creator God. According to Newton-Smith, they, like Aquinas, are indulging in metaphysics.

Not that philosophers are above criticism, of course. Newton-Smith fears that philosophers have retreated from a critical role accessible to society at large, into technicalities of their own. This raises anew the question of the proper function of the philosopher vis-à-vis science (see *SP*, ch. 26).

Area 7 introduces *some* of the questions which make up the philosophy of religion. There are well-known problems which we haven't touched on, such as the problem of evil. But here as elsewhere in this book, the aim has been to present some of the best work from the Western tradition – to show by (a few) examples how people have grappled with deep and difficult issues, rather than to treat these issues in anything like full detail.

Further Reading

This anthology has been designed as a 'first toe in the water', and one aspect of that has been unusually stringent editing. Many of the articles we've looked at have been edited down to about 20 per cent of their original length, and the missing 80 per cent – even if it is not *essential* to the main argument – obviously deserves to be read. It would really be enough, therefore, to point the reader towards the original texts for further reading. In the course of exploring these originals, the reader will discover further references, and begin to shape an individual reading-trajectory, following his or her own nose. Which is (of course) exactly as it should be.

Having said that, however, a few additional ideas for Further Reading may be useful.

Science

A Historical Introduction to the Philosophy of Science by John Losee: Oxford University Press, 1972, 2001

The Rationality of Science by W. H. Newton-Smith: Routledge, 1981

Mind

Consciousness Reconsidered by Owen Flanagan: MIT Press, 1992

Modern Philosophy of Mind, ed. W. Lyons: Everyman, 1995

The Mystery of Consciousness by John R. Searle, NYREV, 1997

Freedom

Utilitarianism: For and Against by Bernard Williams and J. J. C. Smart: Cambridge University Press, 1973

Ethics: Inventing Right and Wrong by J. L. Mackie: Penguin, 1977

How Free Are You? by Ted Honderich: Oxford University Press, 2002

Knowledge

The Problem of Knowledge by A. J. Ayer: Penguin, 1956

Philosophy and the Mirror of Nature by Richard Rorty: Princeton, 1980

Contemporary Epistemology by Jonathan Dancy: Blackwell, 1985

Language

The Blue and Brown Books by Ludwig Wittgenstein: Blackwell, 1975

The Philosophy of Language, ed. A. P. Martinich: Oxford University Press, 1985

Objectivity

Objective Knowledge by Karl R. Popper: Clarendon, 1972

Representing and Intervening by Ian Hacking: Cambridge University Press, 1983

God

The Miracle of Theism by J. L. Mackie:

Oxford University Press, 1982

Reason and Religious Belief by Peterson,
Hasker, Reichenbach and Basinger: Oxford
University Press, 1991

Glossary

anti-realism: see 'empiricism'

behaviourism: the basic idea of behaviourism is that we should explain and predict what people do, not by mental processes and states (things like decisions and beliefs, unless these can be interpreted in behaviouristic terms), but by referring to publicly observable features of the situation, and a training history. Radical behaviourism holds that there are no mental processes or states; methodological behaviourism holds that whether mental states and processes exist or not, they aren't suitable subject matter for science. A classic example of behaviourism (mentioned in the Russell Reading, 4/34) was the work of the Russian psychologist Pavlov, but behaviourism was also the dominant theory in American psychology for the fifty years up to 1957 or so. The emphasis on overt behaviour was a reaction against what was seen as the sterility of German introspectionist psychology.

Like 'behaviourism', 'functionalism' indicates more of a tendency than a single well-defined position, but it differs from behaviourism in two main ways. First, it moves up from concrete behavioural routines to inputs and outputs more abstractly described, and second, it allows more explicitly for the system's internal processing. Its basic aim is not so much to predict and control behaviour, as to explain what we mean when we ascribe mental states and processes to a system.

For more on behaviourism see Readings 2/7, 2/10, 5/41, 6/48, or *SP*, pp. 159–60. For more on functionalism, see Reading 6/51, or *SP*, pp. 162–5.

causality: on any account, this is one of the fundamental concepts we use to make sense of the world. The question is: what sense should we make of the *concept*?

According to Aristotle, to describe A as the cause of B can properly mean several things. He argues, however, that the most important causal idea for scientific understanding is 'teleological', as when we say that B happens *in order that* A. Why does a giraffe have a long neck? To enable it to eat vegetation other animals can't reach, and so on. Aristotle called causes of this kind 'final causes'.

Around 1600, this teleological concept of causality began to give way to a mechanistic concept, according to which 'A caused B' means that A transmitted motion to B. Descartes was one writer who tried to show that this mechanistic kind of causality is enough to explain much of what we see around us.

But about a hundred years later, the mechanistic concept in turn came under attack from a less restrictive concept. Cartesian causality requires physical contact between causes and effects, but the successes of Newtonian gravity made this seem implausible. A concept of causality as mere correlation between events was powerfully advanced by Hume, as being truer to what we actually observe.

This tectonic shift from a very intuitive

and 'explanatory' concept of causality to a more purely descriptive, 'unsatisfying' one has had large effects on other important concepts (and tracing some of these effects was the central project of *Simply Philosophy*).

For more on causality see Readings 1/3, 4/32, 7/56 or *SP*, pp. 10–17, 30–2.

deduction: when we reason from existing knowledge to new knowledge, there seem to be basically two kinds of thinking we use.

Deductive thinking only makes explicit what is already present – implicitly – in existing knowledge. Inductive thinking goes beyond what is strictly present in existing knowledge, extending a pattern seen there to a new case or cases. Here's an example.

Suppose I draw half a dozen triangles of different shapes and sizes on a piece of paper, and measure the internal angles with a protractor. They add up to 180 degrees in all the triangles I've drawn, and I think to myself that there's a pattern here which allows me to say with confidence that the next triangle I draw will also have internal angles which sum to 180 degrees. This is an inductive process.

Now suppose instead that I realise that any triangle is exactly half of a parallelogram, and that any parallelogram has internal angles which sum to 360 degrees. Then I can deduce that any triangle *must* have internal angles which sum to 180 degrees.

Notice that the inductive process gives me only probability. It allows me to be fairly confident about the conclusion – and the more triangles I check, the more confident I can reasonably be. Inductive reasoning only

makes the new knowledge probable (though perhaps *extremely* probable). Deductive thinking allows me to conclude that such-and-such *must* be the case.

Inductive thinking is obviously essential for most of our dealings with the real world – we only know that the sun will rise tomorrow by induction from past cases – but it has tended to suffer by comparison with deduction. There are many different forms of inductive thinking, the rules which govern them are less well understood, and the conclusions they lead to are less certain. Attempts continue to explain how induction works and what makes it reasonable.

determinism: the view that every event has a cause or causes. This leads naturally to the view that any event could have been predicted (given sufficient knowledge of its cause or causes) – though chaos theory would object that in many cases, it is impossible to have sufficient knowledge for the purposes of prediction. Determinism also leads naturally to the view that whatever happens is made or compelled to happen by its cause or causes. Against this idea, Hume would object that causes don't compel (see entry on causality).

The problem of determinism is that a belief in causes seems essential to our efforts to make sense of the world, and yet the same belief seems to threaten – in one way or another – our conviction that we act freely. If our actions are not free, are we not puppets, without rationality or moral status?

For more on determinism, see Readings 3/16–20 or *SP*, chs 7–8.

dualism: any view which sets up an explanatory framework consisting of two main categories. Famous dualisms from past philosophy have been Plato's dualism of Being and Becoming, Descartes' dualism of mind and body, or Kant's dualism of noumena and phenomena (see entry on Idealism). But Aristotle's distinction between potentiality and actuality could equally well be called a dualism, as could Hume's distinction between Reason and Imagination.

There is often a tendency to react against dualisms, on the grounds that one side of the distinction is more fundamental or more important than the other. A behaviourist (see entry) thinks it's wrong to give mind and body equal importance, as Descartes does. An Idealist (see entry) also rejects the dualism of mind and body, but favours mind over body. Both the behaviourist and Idealist are 'monists' – they believe that *one* category is basically sufficient (though they disagree about which category is fundamental). Monists may try, in one way or another, to 'reduce' (see entry) their less favoured category to their more favoured one - or they may simply reject the less favoured category outright.

For more on dualism, see Readings 2/7, 2/9, 2/14–15, 3/20, 5/42, 6/49–51, or *SP*, pp. 36–9, 166–8.

empiricism: the basic idea of empiricism is that all human knowledge comes from experience. In Aristotle, this was a reaction against Plato's claim that much of our knowledge is recollected from a previous existence: in Locke, it was a reaction against Descartes' dependence on knowledge planted in the soul by God.

It may seem just common sense to claim that everything we know comes from our own experience (which includes our experience of others telling us things, and our experience of the workings of our own minds). But the claim has a radical edge. If our knowledge of the meanings of the words we use also comes exclusively from experience, then we cannot know the meaning of any word which is not solidly grounded in our experience. This is perhaps why people sometimes say that a blind person cannot really understand the meaning of colour words, and so on.

This idea can be carried further. None of us has any experience of the future. None of us has any experience of the contents of another person's mind. None of us has or could have experience of anything infinite. Radical empiricism therefore urges that we reinterpret what we say about the future, for example, in terms of what we *can* experience (present trends and evidence). In the same way, radical empiricism would have us limit what we say about others' states of mind to what we *can* experience – their overt behaviour. Radical empiricism in maths rejects the use of completed infinities.

This radical empiricism is sometimes called 'positivism' – it holds that language needs a positive basis in experience if it is to be meaningful. And one version of positivism was 'verificationism', which held that the real meaning of a statement can best be understood by asking how we would go about checking whether the statement was true. (A development of this, which thought it more realistic to ask how we would show that the statement was false, was called – yes – 'falsificationism'.)

In the last thirty years, these issues have resurfaced with new and allegedly more revealing names. The view that a statement can be meaningful even if we cannot possibly get evidence to determine whether it is true or false is called 'realism' (because the claim is that the asserted state of affairs might really exist, even if we can't possibly find out about it). The radical empiricist view, that we can't make sense of a statement which no experience of ours can check, is called 'anti-realism'. For example, a realist about other people's mental states says, 'Even if I can't look into X's mind and check that he feels persecuted, he either does or he doesn't.' The anti-realist (typically) says, 'I can't understand 'X feels persecuted' if it's interpreted as being about something I can't experience. So it has to be interpreted as being about something I *can* experience, namely X's behaviour, and dispositions thereto.'

It's worth mentioning that both relativity theory and the standard interpretation of quantum theory are strongly influenced by radical empiricism, and to the extent that they are successful, lend it considerable prestige.

For more on empiricism, see Readings 1/1–3, 2/7–9, 4/29, 4/34–5, 5/42, 6/53, 7/60 or *SP*, pp. 41–3.

epistemology: investigations into the source, extent and justification of human knowledge. Where does our knowledge come from? How much do we really know? How can we prove that we do know the things we think we know? These three questions are often pursued under threat from 'scepticism' (see entry) of one sort or another. They naturally lead us to ask what we really mean by the word 'knowledge', and this question is another major concern of epistemology.

Epistemology is one of the two core areas of philosophy, the other being 'metaphysics' (see entry).

For more on epistemology, see Readings 1/1–2, 1/6, 2/9, 4/26–35, 6/44–7, 6/52–3, 7/57–60 or *SP*, chs 11–15.

functionalism: see 'behaviourism'

Idealism: capitalised to distinguish it from the pursuit of high ideals, Idealism is the view that mind more truly or fundamentally exists than matter. An Idealist might hold, for example, simply that matter does not exist, that we have no good reason to believe that matter exists, that the existence of matter depends in some way on the existence of mind, or that the things we say about matter should be reinterpreted in such a way that they are seen to be really about mind. Any of these views could be called 'Idealist'.

The entry on 'empiricism' explained how radical empiricism can create pressure to reinterpret statements about the future, or other people's mental states, or infinity. In the same way, a radical empiricist like Berkeley argues that we never really experience matter: all our experience in perception is directly of ideas in our own minds (which, it's often supposed, *represent* external material things). But according to radical empiricism, we cannot meaningfully speak about something we cannot possibly experience. So whenever we speak about a material thing, that should really be reinterpreted in terms of actual or possible sequences of sense-impressions. If I say, 'There's a tomato on the windowsill,' that can only make sense (Berkeley thinks) if it really means, 'I'll have small, round, red sense-impressions if I look in the direction which provides large, rectangular, bright sense-impressions' and so on.

A technical term which went with attempts to say more clearly what these 'sense-impressions' are, was 'sense-data'. Another technical term, which generally means much the same as Idealism, is 'phenomenalism'. If this term draws on a Kantian distinction between 'noumena' (things as they are in themselves), and 'phenomena' (things as they seem to us – holding this distinct from *appearances* of things), it could attempt to sidestep the dualism of matter and mind, and in that way go beyond Idealism.

For more on Idealism, see Readings 2/9, 4/28, 4/30, 6/45–6 or *SP*, ch. 12.

induction: see deduction

materialism: the view that only matter exists, generally intended as a denial that there are mental states or processes, entities or properties distinct from material ones.

A problem with this is that our grasp on the concept of matter itself is less secure than it once seemed. Not only is matter now supposed to be interchangeable with energy, it is also supposed to be made up of sub-atomic particles with *very* unfamiliar characteristics, such as existence in a superposition of incompatible states. Unwilling to get entangled in these issues, some materialists prefer to be called 'physicalists', holding that only the entities

and properties of physics exist, whatever those turn out to be.

But there is a problem with this view too, since it seems to commit the holder to the claim that all the sciences will eventually be reducible (see entry) to physics. Even if this is true, it is an entanglement the physicalist (who usually only wants to deny the existence of things mental) would prefer to avoid.

An alternative term, which tries to avoid these problems, is 'naturalism'. The idea here is that only what exists in nature really exists: the world contains nothing supernatural. The problem with this is that a dualist about mind and body is likely to hold that both kinds of substance or property are perfectly natural. To describe mind as 'ghostly' or supernatural already begs the question against it.

For more on materialism, see Readings 2/7, 2/10–15, 3/20, 5/40–1, 6/48–51 or *SP*, ch. 5.

metaphysics: the (sprawling) branch of philosophy which deals with what exists and how it's organised. Does God exist? Do numbers exist? Does matter exist? Does time exist? Do minds exist? These existence questions, and other more abstract ones, are all parts of metaphysics.

But metaphysics also deals with attempts to find the most general kinds of relations which hold between things which exist. Does everything which exists have properties, and if so, how are we to understand the relation between a property and its possessor? Is the possessor a kind of substance in which properties inhere? Is there no real possessor over and above the properties? Are relations (like 'being to the right of') properties? Do they exist in the same way that properties exist – assuming properties do exist?

The property/possessor relation is one very general relation which holds among existents. Another is causality (see entry), and the problem of causality is generally regarded as being a central problem of metaphysics. Does everything which exists enter into causal relations? How are these causal relations to be understood?

Other central topics in metaphysics are change, and possibility. A topic which has migrated out of metaphysics, over the last millennium or so, is classification.

'Metaphysical' is sometimes used as a term of abuse by radical empiricists (see entry). In their attempts to answer the above questions, metaphysicians have often put forward ideas which no possible experience could confirm or disconfirm. For radical empiricists, claims which cannot be decided by some possible experience are meaningless, and there has accordingly been a strong tradition within empiricism, from Berkeley to the present day, of suspicion and hostility towards speculative metaphysics.

For more on metaphysics, see Readings 1/3, 2/9–15, 5/42, 6/49–52, 7/54–6, 7/60 or *SP*, chs 4, 16, 21–5.

monism: see dualism

naturalism: see materialism

phenomenalism: see Idealism

physicalism: see materialism

positivism: see empiricism

realism: see empiricism

reductionism: any attempt to show that an allegedly less fundamental kind of entity or property (E) can be cashed out in terms of an allegedly more fundamental kind (E_f). A number of scientific examples are commonly invoked: the reduction of lightning to electrical discharge, of gas temperature to average molecular kinetic energy, of sound to compression waves, and so on.

Reductionism is often expressed in terms of translatability between two ways of talking. Reductionists might claim, for example, that everything we presently say about E could be rephrased without loss, mentioning only E_f. Thus, anything factual we want to say about lightning could be said in terms of electrical discharges. In the same way, a reductionist version of Idealism (see entry) might claim that everything factual we currently say using the terminology of physical objects, could be said – less conveniently perhaps but without loss of content – in terms of sense-data. The consensus at the moment is that this particular claim is impossibly ambitious.

Alternatively, a reductionist might hold that everything we can *legitimately* say in the language of E, can be said in the language of E_f. This concedes that the reduction to the language of E_f would feel like a loss, but argues that it's not so much a loss as a saving. A modern Humean about causality (see entry) might say, for example, that our ordinary, untutored talk about causes includes an element (the idea of *making* happen) which is not legitimate. If we limit ourselves to talk about constant conjunctions, something *is* lost, but it's something we had no right to in the first place.

Finally, reductionism might be advanced as a thesis, not about translatability, but about what exists. Someone who says, for example, that nations are reducible to the individuals who constitute them, might not wish to be committed to either of the above translatability claims. He or she might think it quite legitimate to talk about the destiny of nations as something distinct from the destinies of any individual(s), for example, and yet want to maintain that a nation is nothing over and above the individuals who compose it.

Reductionists usually make some (greater or lesser) attempt to account for the present usefulness of E. A more sweeping alternative is just to give up E as a thoroughly bad lot. Eliminative materialism holds that our present talk about mental states and processes is just thoroughly confused and misleading. It will eventually be *replaced by* – not reduced to – talk about physical states and processes.

For more on reductionism, see Readings 1/3, 2/7–9, 2/15, 3/20, 3/23, 5/41, 5/43, 6/49–51, 6/53 or *SP*, chs 2, 13, 21.

relativism: like most of the other entries in this Glossary, 'relativism' is an umbrella term, gathering together several distinguishable positions united by a shared tendency or theme. In the case of 'relativism', this common tendency or basic idea is that our ability to judge is limited by our point of view.

Different kinds of relativism are, therefore, most easily distinguished by the *kind* and *topic* of the judgement they consider limited. The main *kinds* of judgement which relativists find problematic concern truth, rationality, meaning and value, and among the *topics* usually found problematic are morals and aesthetics, the human sciences and the 'hard' sciences, the experiences and the beliefs of others. So for example, a relativist might claim that the truth of a statement within a scientific theory cannot be judged by someone who does not adhere to that theory. Or that the rationality of a religious belief cannot be judged by someone who adheres to a different religion or to none. Or that the meaning of 'I'm depressed' or 'I'm in love' cannot be understood by someone who has never had those experiences. Or that the value of filial obedience or Cubism cannot be judged by someone who is not a Confucian or a painter.

Further subdivisions are possible (and probably useful), but I suppose it is already clear that one cannot really declare oneself for or against 'relativism' *tout court*. It's perfectly possible to be in favour of one kind of relativism and against another.

For more on relativism, see Readings 1/6, 2/8, 3/21–3, 4/26, 5/36, 7/58–9 or *SP*, pp. 180–1.

scepticism: basically, scepticism involves doubting or questioning received belief. Sceptics have questioned many different beliefs, for many different reasons, and with many different objectives in mind, but the common thread is that received belief should – at least occasionally – be made to justify itself.

As with relativism (see entry), different forms of scepticism can be distinguished, in a preliminary way at least, according to the kind and topic of the belief they question.

We all believe, for example, that other people have a mental life like our own – but a form of scepticism called 'solipsism' denies this, holding that there is no mind but my own. Without going this far, a sceptic might ask what reasons we can provide for believing that other people have minds. If we find it difficult to provide good reasons (for this or other beliefs), the sceptic may begin to challenge, not necessarily the truth of the belief, but perhaps the rationality of holding it.

To give another example, many people believe that talk about God, Heaven and the soul is referential in the ordinary way. God is a being, Heaven is a place and the soul is an entity: it just so happens that they're all invisible or out of immediate reach. Scepticism about the meaning of religious language challenges this widespread belief, suggesting (for example) that religious language might be emotive or expressive, and not referential at all.

Again, we all believe that certain actions are good or bad, just or unjust. Scepticism about value challenges this kind of belief, either with some surprising alternative view, or at least with a request for justification.

Scepticism, from ancient times to the present, has been probably the main stimulus to work in epistemology (see entry). The simplest reaction to scepticism – blunt reassertion of the challenged belief – is called 'dogmatism'.

For more on scepticism, see Readings 1/3–5, 2/9–13, 4/26–8, 4/30–3, 6/44–7, 6/52, 7/57–8 or *SP*, chs 11–15.

sense-data: see Idealism

solipsism: see scepticism

teleology: see causality

utilitarianism: the theory that the moral value of an action is to be decided by referring to its effect on the general happiness. According to utilitarianism, it is morally right, in any situation, to perform that action which will do most to increase the general happiness.

A number of questions arise more or less immediately. What about the individual's right to pursue his or her own happiness? Aren't there some actions which are just *wrong*, even if in a given situation they might be the best thing we could do for the general happiness? What is meant by the word 'happiness' here? Whose happiness is at issue – human beings only? all human beings? Is it as bad to let suffering happen as to cause it, assuming that the same amount of suffering results?

Different versions of utilitarianism arise in response to these questions. If 'happiness' means pleasure, for example, we arrive at a hedonistic form of utilitarianism, and since animals are capable of pleasure, it seems to follow that the 'general happiness' should include non-human as well as human animals. If we accept that it's mostly impossible in practice to calculate into the distant future which action will do most for the general happiness, then perhaps we have to consider a proposed action, not as a one-off event, but as belonging to a certain *type*. And if we judge actions as belonging to types liable to increase or decrease happiness, it's easier to see how we might come to think that some types of actions are just wrong, regardless of their consequences in a particular case.

In European thought, the rise of utilitarianism over the last 250 years, has coincided with the declining influence of religion. Utilitarianism offers a non-religious yet unifying, and in many ways appealing, theory of morality.

For more on utilitarianism, see Readings 3/23–5 or *SP*, ch. 10.

verificationism: see empiricism

Copyright Acknowledgements

Grateful acknowledgement is made to the following sources for permission to reproduce material previously published elsewhere. Every effort has been made to trace the copyright holders, but if any has been inadvertently overlooked, the publisher will be pleased to make the necessary arrangements at the first opportunity.

Science

1/1 Aristotle, from 'Analytica Posteriora', in *Logic*, vol. I, 1928, trans. G. R. G. Mure, and from 'Physica' in *Philosophy of Nature*, vol. II, ed. W. R. Ross, 1930, trans. R. P. Hardie and R. K. Gaye. Reprinted by permission of Oxford University Press.

1/2 Francis Bacon, from *Selected Aphorisms*, eds Spedding, Ellis and Heath, 1905, Routledge.

1/3 David Hume, from *An Inquiry Concerning Human Understanding* (1748), section VII, ed. C. W. Hendel, 1955, Liberal Arts Press.

1/4 Karl Popper, from *The Logic of Scientific Discovery*, 1959, Hutchinson. © Karl Popper 1959, © The Estate of Sir Karl Popper 2003. Reprinted by permission of the Estate of Sir Karl Popper.

1/5 Hilary Putnam, from 'The "Corroboration" of Theories', in *The Philosophy of Karl Popper*, ed. P. A. Schilpp, pp. 221–40. © Open Court 1974. Reprinted by permission of Open Court Publishing Company, a division of Carus Publishing, Peru, IL, USA.

1/6 Paul Feyerabend, from 'How to Defend Society against Science'. This article first appeared in *Radical Philosophy* 2, Summer 1975, and is reprinted here with permission.

Mind

2/7 B. F. Skinner, from *Science and Human Behaviour*, 1953, Macmillan.

2/8 C. S. Peirce, from 'How to Make our Ideas Clear', in *Popular Science Monthly* 12, 1878.

2/9 Bertrand Russell, from 'The Relation of Sense-data to Physics', in *Mysticism and Logic*, 1918, Longmans. Reprinted by permission of Taylor & Francis Books and the Bertrand Russell Peace Foundation.

2/10 Rudolf Carnap, from 'Psychology in the Language of Physics, in *Erkenntnis*, vol. 2, 1931, Felix Meiner Verlag, Leipzig. Reprinted by permission of Felix Meiner Verlag.

2/11 A. J. Ayer, from 'One's Knowledge of Other Minds', in *Philosophical Essays*, 1954, St. Martin's Press/Macmillan.

2/12 Norman Malcolm, from 'Knowledge of Other Minds', in *The Journal of Philosophy* LV, 1958.

2/13 Colin McGinn, from 'Consciousness and Space'. First published in *Journal of Consciousness Studies*, vol. 2, no. 3, 1995. © Imprint Academic, Exeter, UK. Reprinted by permission of Imprint Academic.

2/14 William James, from 'Does "Consciousness" Exist?', in *Journal of Philosophy, Psychology and Scientific Methods*, vol. 1, 1904.

2/15 Paul Churchland, from *Matter and Consciousness: A Contemporary Introduction to the Philosophy of Mind*, 1988, MIT Press. Reprinted by permission of The MIT Press.

Freedom

3/16 Peter Strawson, from 'Freedom and Resentment'. © The British Academy 1963. Reproduced by permission from *Proceedings of the British Academy*, vol. XLVIII, 1962.

3/17 Norman Malcolm, from 'The Conceivability of Mechanism', in *The Philosophical Review*, vol. LXXVII, 1968.

3/18 Daniel Dennett, from 'Mechanism and

Responsibility', in *Essays on Freedom of Action*, ed. T. Honderich, 1973, Routledge and Kegan Paul. Reprinted by permission of Routledge.

3/19 Max Black, from 'Making Something Happen', in *Determinism and Freedom*, ed. Sidney Hook, 1958, New York University Press. Reprinted with the approval of Ernest B. Hook.

3/20 Frederick Dretske, from 'Does Meaning Matter?', in *Information, Semantics and Epistemology*, ed. E. Villaneuva, 1990, Blackwell. Reprinted by permission of Enrique Villaneuva.

3/21 Thomas Hobbes, from *Leviathan* (1651), ed. C. B. MacPherson, chs 11, 13, 17, 1968, Penguin.

3/22 Immanuel Kant, from *Groundwork of the Metaphysic of Morals*, trans. H. J. Paton, 1953, Hutchinson.

3/23 Jeremy Bentham, from *An Introduction to the Principles of Morals and Legislation* (1789), ed. J. H. Burns and H. L. A. Hart, 1970, Athlone Press. Reprinted by permission of the Bentham Project, University College London.

3/24 Thomas Nagel, from 'War and Massacre', in *Mortal Questions*, 1979, pp. 53–74, Cambridge University Press. Reprinted by permission of Cambridge University Press and the author.

3/25 G. E. M. Anscombe, from 'Modern Moral Philosophy', in *Philosophy* XXXIII, 1958.

Knowledge

4/26 Galileo Galilei, from *The Assayer* (1623), in *Discoveries and Opinions of Galileo*, trans. Stillman Drake. © Stillman Drake 1957. Reprinted by permission of Doubleday, a division of Random House, Inc.

4/27 René Descartes, from 'Discourse on Method', in *Discourse on Method and the Meditations*, trans. F. E. Sutcliff, 1968, Penguin Classics. © F. E. Sutcliffe 1968. Reproduced by permission of Penguin Books Ltd.

4/28 John Locke, from *An Essay Concerning Human Understanding*, ed. J. W. Yolton, bk 4, ch. X, 1976, Dent. Reprinted by permission of Everyman's Library Plc.

4/29 Hilary Putnam and Noam Chomsky, from 'Linguistics and Philosophy', in *Language and Philosophy*, ed. Sidney Hook, pp. 60–94, 1969, New York University Press. Reprinted with the approval of Ernest B. Hook.

4/30 George Berkeley, from *A Treatise Concerning the Principles of Human Knowledge: Three Dialogues Between Hylas and Philonous*, ed. G. J. Warnock, 1986, Open Court Publishing. Reprinted by permission of Open Court Publishing.

4/31 Thomas Reid, from *Thomas Reid's Inquiry and Essays*, ed. R. E. Beanblossom and K. Lehrer, p. 56f, 1983, Hackett Publishing Company.

4/32 Immanuel Kant, from *Prolegomena to Any Future Metaphysics*, ed. P. G. Lucas, 1953, Manchester University Press. Reprinted by permission of P. G. Lucas.

4/33 David Hume, from *An Inquiry Concerning Human Understanding* (1748), ed. C. W. Hendel, section X, 1955, Liberal Arts Press.

4/34 Bertrand Russell, from *My Philosophical Development*, ch. 11, 1993, Routledge. Reprinted by permission of Routledge and The Bertrand Russell Peace Foundation.

4/35 L. Jonathan Cohen, from 'Why Should the Science of Nature be Empirical?', in *Impressions of Empiricism*, ed. G. Vesey, 1976, Macmillan.

Language

5/36 John Locke, from *Essay Concerning Human Understanding*, ed. J. W. Yolton, bk 3, ch. X, 1976, Dent. Reprinted by permission of Everyman's Library Plc.

5/37 Gilbert Ryle, from 'The Theory of Meaning', in *British Philosophy in the Mid-Century*, ed. C. A. Mace. © C. A. Mace 1957. Reprinted by permission of HarperCollins Publishers Ltd.

7/59   Søren Kierkegaard, from *Concluding Unscientific Postscript* (1846), trans. by D. F. Swenson and W. Lowrie, 1945, Oxford University Press.

7/60   W. H. Newton-Smith, from 'The Origin of the Universe', in *Time in Contemporary Intellectual Thought*, ed. P. J. N. Baert, ch. 4, pp. 53–76, © Elsevier Science 1999. Reprinted with permission from Elsevier Science.

Index

correspondence theory, Russell's views, 109

Darwin, Charles, 26
deduction, 191
deductive thinking, Popper's use in scientific methodology, 12
Dennett, Daniel, 61
  determinism and its compatibility with moral responsibility, 55–8, 79
denotation, 121, 122
Descartes, René, 90, 99, 131, 190, 192
  doubt as the test of knowledge, 82–4, 114
  and teleology, 172
determinism, 191
  and causality: Black's views, 58–60, 79
  compatibility with moral responsibility: Dennett's views, 55–8, 79
  and mechanism: Malcolm's views, 52–5, 79
  and morality: Strawson's views, 49–52, 79
dispositions to behaviour, 132, 133, 134
dogmatism, 197
doubt, as the test of knowledge: Descartes' views, 82–4, 114
Dretske, Frederick, meanings and causality, 60–3, 79
dualism, 192
Duhem, Pierre, metaphysics and science, 179–80, 182
Dummett, Michael, realism and anti-realism, 163–5, 167

Einstein, Albert, 14, 180, 181, 182
eliminative materialism, 45, 133–4
empiricism, 192–3
  Cohen's views, 110–13, 114–15
  and rationalism, 89–90
epistemology, 193
evolution, Aristotle's rejection, 4, 5
existence, quality, 169–70
experience
  Hume's views, 8
  James's views, 44
  Russell's views, 109
experiments, importance for development of scientific knowledge: Bacon's views, 7, 22

explanations, levels, 132, 133

falsifiability
  Feyerabend's views, 20
  Popper's views, 13, 14–15
  Putnam's views, 17, 18
falsification
  Kuhn's views, 18
  Popper's views, 15, 16
falsificationism, 192–3
Feyerabend, Paul, scientific methodology, 20–1, 22
fiction and reality, Peirce's views, 27
Flew, Anthony, religious belief lacking in factual content, 174–5, 186
folk psychology, Churchland's views, 45–6
forms, theory, 134–8, 141
freedom and moral goodness, 49–80
Frege, Gottlob, proper names, 123, 124
functionalism, 122, 190
  Putnam's views, 157–60, 166

Galileo Galilei, 184
  views on perception, 81–2, 114
General Theory of Relativity, 182
God
  existence: Descartes' views, 83; ontological argument, 169–70, 186; teleological arguments, Kenny's views, 172–4, 186; Thomas Aquinas' arguments for, 170–2, 173, 186
  knowledge about: Hume's views, 107

Hampshire, Stuart, the argument from analogy, 35, 36
Hawking, Stephen, 181, 182
Hobbes, Thomas
  human nature, 63–6, 80
  theory of meaning followed by J. S. Mill, 120
holism see functionalism
human nature
  Hobbes's mechanistic views, 63–6, 80
  Hume's views, 66
  rational nature: Kant's views, 68
human relationships
  intentional stances towards: Dennett's views, 56–8